Dedication

"I dedicate this book to my wife, Kirste, and my daughter, Aliyah. Kirste, you have provided me with love, support, encouragement, and advice throughout this project. Aliyah, you enable me to keep everything in perspective and to focus on what is truly important. I love you both with all my heart." Lee A. Freeman

"Dedicated to Liz, Lauren, and Douglas, who probably sacrificed as much as anyone to see this work published. Thanks for all of your support and encouragement!" A. Graham Peace

Information Ethics: Privacy and Intellectual Property

Table of Contents

Information Ethics: Privacy and Intellectual Property

Lee A. Freeman
University of Michigan - Dearborn, USA

A. Graham Peace
West Virginia University, USA

 Information Science Publishing

Hershey • London • Melbourne • Singapore

Acquisition Editor:	Mehdi Khosrow-Pour
Senior Managing Editor:	Jan Travers
Managing Editor:	Amanda Appicello
Development Editor:	Michele Rossi
Copy Editor:	Jane Conley
Typesetter:	Jennifer Wetzel
Cover Design:	Lisa Tosheff
Printed at:	Yurchak Printing Inc.

Published in the United States of America by
       Information Science Publishing (an imprint of Idea Group Inc.)
       701 E. Chocolate Avenue, Suite 200
       Hershey PA 17033
       Tel: 717-533-8845
       Fax: 717-533-8661
       E-mail: cust@idea-group.com
       Web site: http://www.idea-group.com

and in the United Kingdom by
       Information Science Publishing (an imprint of Idea Group Inc.)
       3 Henrietta Street
       Covent Garden
       London WC2E 8LU
       Tel: 44 20 7240 0856
       Fax: 44 20 7379 3313
       Web site: http://www.eurospan.co.uk

Library of Congress Cataloging-in-Publication Data

Information ethics : privacy and intellectual property / Lee Freeman, A. Graham
Peace, editors.
     p. cm.
  Includes bibliographical references and index.
  ISBN 1-59140-491-6 (hbk.) -- ISBN 1-59140-492-4 (pbk.) -- ISBN 1-59140-493-2
(eisbn)
 1. Information technology. 2. Information technology--Social aspects. 3.
Information technology--Moral and ethical aspects. 4. Intellectual property. 5.
Privacy, Right of. I. Freeman, Lee, 1971- II. Peace, A. Graham.
  T58.5.I5248 2005
  303.48'33--dc22
                         2004016390

British Cataloguing in Publication Data
A Cataloguing in Publication record for this book is available from the British Library.

All work contributed to this book is new, previously-unpublished material. The views expressed in
this book are those of the authors, but not necessarily of the publisher.

SECTION III: TECHNOLOGY'S IMPACT ON ETHICS

Preface

With the ever-increasing pace of technological change, it is often the case that ethical issues are overlooked in the rush to implement the latest information systems. Technology allows us to gather, process, and disseminate huge quantities of data with ease, and the information produced has increased greatly in value as the global marketplace becomes more competitive. While technology can help to increase profit margins, protect the world from terrorism, and spread knowledge to millions, it may be that fundamental rights and duties are being unconsciously neglected. Once eroded, many of these rights and duties may be gone forever.

Overall Objective

The overall objective and mission of this book is to report on the latest issues and dilemmas regarding information ethics in today's society, with a focus on intellectual property rights and privacy issues. The book brings together some of the leading authors in the field of information systems and information ethics in order to document and discuss the ethical issues of the information age, especially in the wake of the rising threat of terrorism. Such a compilation serves as a starting point for future research on these and related issues. The goal is not to solve the dilemmas presented — that would require more pages and discussion than possible in a single text — but to present the reader with a range of viewpoints regarding the issues seen to be important by those who study them on a daily basis.

Target Audience

This book is aimed at researchers, educators, and students interested in information systems, information science, and information ethics. However, business executives, government agencies, and interested citizens will find value in reading and thinking about the issues discussed.

The Chapters

The chapters are grouped together into six distinct sections. Each of these is introduced below.

Section I. Information Technology and Ethics/Theory

The book's editors begin Chapter I with a review of perhaps the most famous paper in the information ethics field. Eighteen years ago, ethicist Richard Mason presented what he saw to be the four most important ethical issues of the information age: privacy, accuracy, property, and accessibility. This framework has guided the field of information ethics for almost two decades, but the pace of technological growth has changed the landscape, reducing the relevance of some issues and raising the profile of others. For example, with the rise of the threat of terrorism, rights to privacy have come into question as countries attempt to ensure the safety of their citizens. Similarly, intellectual property rights have been severely undermined by the ease of sharing files that the Internet provides. Chapter I uses Mason's framework to place the other chapters in an overall context, while also updating Mason's work and introducing some ethical issues that could not have been anticipated in 1986. In particular, justified hacking — the concept of using hacking in an ethical manner — is discussed. The chapter lays the groundwork for the more specific chapters that follow.

Chapter II uses the Four Component Model of moral behavior, developed in the discipline of moral psychology, to explore the ethics of electronic communications and digital property. Crowell, Narvaez, and Gomberg argue that technology can impact the psychological components of sensitivity, judgment, motivation, and action. For example, technology can create a "psychological distance" between those who use technology as a communication device, thus negatively impacting the four factors listed above. This, in turn, can lead to a greater chance of unethical behavior; it is easier to behave unethically in a virtual communication setting than in a face-to-face meeting. A better understanding of the impact of technology on these factors can aid in developing educational techniques that strengthen moral sensitivity, judgment, motivation, and action in a world in which more and more daily activity is moving into a digital, virtual environment. The use of psychological constructs to study the ethics of technology usage provides a new and unique perspective on these issues.

Completing Section I, Mathieson presents a proposal to use technology to aid individuals in the ethical decision-making process. In Chapter III, he coins the term "Moral Dilemma Support System" (MDSS) to describe his proposed technology. While most of the chapters in this book focus on the ethical or unethical usage of technology, this chapter takes a different view, arguing that technology can be used to aid people in making more ethical decisions, but only if individuals want to do so. Mathieson does not describe the technical specifications of the system, instead choosing to focus on the system's proposed functionality. He ends with the thought that the system would have to be tailored to the environment in which it was to be used. At a time when many people raise the concern that technology may be leading to a more unethical world, this chapter provides some hope that technology can, in fact, be used to further humanity and aid in the individual's efforts to "do the right thing."

Section II. Intellectual Property Rights

The second section of the book delves into the realm of intellectual property rights. Who actually owns the digital information that is being created everyday, and what rights should the creators maintain? Chapter IV begins the discussion with a focus on ethical theory. Kimppa utilizes Locke's liberalism, classic utilitarianism, and Kant's deontology to study the current state of intellectual property rights, focusing on digitally distributable media such as software and music. The current trend of copyright and trademark law is leading to greater limitations on the sharing of information. After a thorough and interesting application of each theory to the specific situation of rights of ownership for immaterial property, the author concludes that three paths exist: one that continues the trend of developing stronger copyright protection to fend off piracy; a compromise path that lessens the control of intellectual property creators but seeks to provide some limited protection; or a path that completely abolishes all intellectual property rights, as seen to a great extent in the open source movement. While it may cause short-term hardship, Kimppa argues that the elimination of restrictions may be the most beneficial for society in the long run.

Chapter V takes a different approach to the intellectual property rights issue as de Vuyst and Fairchild focus on whether current copyright and trademark laws are an incentive for individuals and organizations to misallocate funds to the detriment of society due to excessive rent-seeking. Perhaps the typical intellectual property rights debate is focusing on the wrong thing when the question of "who owns intellectual property?" is discussed. Instead, the focus should be on whether the current state of legislation leads to unethical behavior. Would society not be better off if investments were made in more worthwhile things than commercial music or entertainment software? The chapter also provides an interesting history of the development of intellectual property rights beginning with their Roman origins.

Chapter VI focuses on the specific issue of software piracy, taking the more traditional Western view that piracy is an act that should be prevented, if possible, under the current legal climate. After a brief overview of the ethical principles involved, including an application of both utilitarian and deontological perspectives, and a review of recent research into the piracy phenomenon, El-Sheikh, Rashed, and Peace present the results of a study of piracy in Jordan. The data show that piracy is rampant, despite the fact that individuals overwhelmingly believe that it is fair for creators of software to receive payment for their work. Using the survey results and the latest predictive model of piracy behavior, the authors review the effectiveness of the efforts of the software industry in combating piracy and argue that the cost of the software is an overlooked factor. The impact of cultural relativism is also discussed — intellectual property rights are clearly a Western idea, making it unsurprising that non-Western cultures lead the world in piracy activity. Chapter VI concludes with the view that both software cost and cultural differences need to be studied further if software piracy is to be eliminated.

Section III. Technology's Impact on Ethics

The third section of the book focuses on the impact of technology on some traditional privacy issues and the ethical impacts of a completely new technology. Chapter VII studies the issue of publicly available information. Information in the public realm has always been available to those who wish to gather it. However, people's privacy was protected by the time and effort required to gather data from different sources. With the development of database technology and the Internet, it is now a simple matter to gather information on an individual from multiple publicly available datastores and to combine that information to create a detailed view. While each individual database poses little threat to an individual's privacy, the ubiquitous nature of information technology and the ability to combine data from these various sources may prove to be a different matter. Clearly, technology provides the opportunity to more cheaply and efficiently store information in public and governmental organizations, but the side effects may be more damaging. Miller, Urbaczewski, and Salisbury provide several suggestions to combat this threat, including the delayed availability of information, fees charged to the requester of the information, and opt-out capabilities. Above all, individuals need to be more aware of what information is available about them.

In Chapter VIII, Cassidy, Chae, and Courtney study the issue of consumer information, arguing that privacy regulations are not focusing on the underlying problem of "information externality." Using economic theory in combination with ethics, the authors argue that information gathered on consumers can lead to both benefits and costs. Consumers receive advertising that is more tailored to their specific needs, but spam clogs our email inboxes. An externality exists when a member of society either fails to pay the costs of information usage or fails to receive the benefits. Property rights are one method commonly used to combat externalities, but this chapter proposes the use of Ronald Coase's Theorem to the problem. Correcting the externality should lead to all parties behaving in a more efficient manner. A detailed ethical discussion follows, after which the principles developed are applied to the specific case of Doubleclick, a large Internet advertising agency.

In Chapter IX, Barger and Crowell discuss the fascinating concept of "parasitic computing," where a parasite computer takes a complex problem, breaks it up into smaller pieces, and distributes those pieces to hosts for processing without the knowledge of the owners and operators of those other computers. In effect, the parasite computer is stealing resources from other systems via readily available Internet protocols and technologies. Given the "shared" nature of the Internet, the authors argue that the determining ethical factor should be whether or not the host system is harmed by the parasite. A previously reported proof-of-concept demonstration is used as an example of the issues involved. As technology evolves and becomes more connected and ubiquitous, unforeseen ethical issues such as these will arise. Parasitic computing is a threat to both privacy and property, but also holds the promise of more efficient use of technology to solve complex problems.

Section IV. Privacy vs. Security

With the events of 9/11 and the increased focus on terrorism throughout the world, security has become a major issue. A trade-off exists between security and privacy — the more that is known about individuals and their actions, the easier it is to prevent criminal acts. However, this presents a conflict that is addressed in Chapters X and XI.

Chapter X specifically examines the state of the techniques being used to gather information before and after the 9/11 terrorist attacks. New technologies, such as biometrics and monitoring devices, increase the security of the population but also pose threats to individual privacy. Freeman details some of the technologies that have been developed and studies them in relation to the privacy issue. After a review of the ethics of privacy, three broad types of technologies are identified: communications surveillance, information surveillance, and identity surveillance. The chapter provides a framework by which it can be determined how technologies can affect privacy and whether or not they *should* be used. Oversight and common sense solutions can be identified to ameliorate the risks.

In Chapter XI, the USA PATRIOT Act becomes the focus of the debate. Created in the post-9/11 world, the PATRIOT Act is designed to use information to provide greater security for the United States. However, some believe that the increased violation of privacy rights is unjustified. Hartzel and Deegan argue that different justice perspectives can be used to reach different positions on the fairness of the PATRIOT Act. The U.S. Department of Justice uses procedural justice perspectives to defend the Act, while groups such as the ACLU utilize outcome-based justice to criticize it. The case of each is presented and analyzed. The authors argue that the potential outcomes of legislation such as the PATRIOT Act must be presented realistically in order to allow fair-minded individuals to reach a rational conclusion as to the pros and cons. Given the fear of further terrorist acts and the strong belief of privacy rights among many individuals, further debate on the proper trade-off of privacy rights vs. security is inevitable. These two chapters provide an excellent starting point.

Section V. The Healthcare Industry

Perhaps in no other area of society is information so necessary and privacy so expected than in the healthcare industry. This section presents two chapters that focus on issues in this area.

In Chapter XII, Joseph and Cook look at the balance of information in the doctor-patient relationship. In the past, an information asymmetry, or an imbalance in the distribution of information, has existed between doctors and patients, with the doctors in the position of power. This imbalance has created a unique set of ethical principles that have guided the healthcare industry for decades, if not centuries. However, technology, and specifically the Internet, has changed the balance dramatically. This chapter studies the ethical, technical, and social issues involved as the change has taken place. It is commonly believed that a reduction in information asymmetry is a good thing, as it appears to make the relationship more even and balanced. However, the authors argue that new ethical quandaries are created by the reduction of information asymmetry in the medical arena. The chapter is not meant to solve these new problems, but instead intends to make the reader aware of this somewhat counter-intuitive viewpoint.

Chapter XIII, on the other hand, focuses on the U.S. HIPAA legislation, which aims to protect patients' privacy. New technologies make it easier to transmit patient information between doctors and medical facilities, which has obvious beneficial aspects for patients. However, the increased availability of information and technology also leads to security concerns. After reviewing the HIPAA regulations, Deshmukh and Croasdell provide some insight into the ethical rationale behind the guidelines. Patient trust can only be ensured if patient information is protected.

Section VI. Codes of Ethics

Our book concludes with a discussion of diversity in codes of ethics. Codes of conduct are commonly discussed as a useful tool in encouraging ethical conduct in organizations and professions, and several of the chapters in this book mention such codes. Therefore, it seems appropriate to end this work with a chapter on this topic. In Chapter XIV, Brabston and Dahl examine three frameworks that could be used to create codes of ethics. Five examples of existing codes are used to demonstrate the frameworks. The authors recommend the creation of a unified code of information ethics by an independent organization, as opposed to disparate codes developed by diverse organizations.

The chapters in this book represent a wide range of authors and viewpoints. Sometimes the viewpoints agree, and other times they do not. Such is the nature of ethics. As technology becomes more and more an integral part of our everyday lives, questions regarding privacy rights and the ownership of intellectual property will only increase in complexity and frequency. It is imperative that a healthy discussion of these issues is ongoing for the sake of all involved.

Acknowledgments

This book would not have been possible without the cooperation of many people: the authors, the reviewers, our colleagues, the staff at Idea Group Inc. (IGI), and our families. To the authors who have each spent numerous hours writing, editing, and rewriting their chapters over the last year, without you there would be no book. To the reviewers, many of whom were also authors and therefore did double duty, your critical eye and constructive feedback has made each and every chapter the best it can be. We appreciate the time you spent reading and discerning the chapters.

To our numerous colleagues not directly involved with the writing or reviewing of chapters, without your ideas, discussions, and support, this book would have remained just an idea. To all of the staff at IGI, in particular Mehdi Khosrow-Pour, Jan Travers, and Michele Rossi, we thank you for your continued support, advice, and assistance with all aspects of the project from its initial proposal up through the final publication approvals.

And finally, to our families, without your love and support, there would be no book.

Lee A. Freeman, University of Michigan – Dearborn, USA
A. Graham Peace, West Virginia University, USA

SECTION I:

INFORMATION TECHNOLOGY AND ETHICS/THEORY

Chapter I

Revisiting Mason:
The Last 18 Years and Onward

Lee A. Freeman
University of Michigan - Dearborn, USA

A. Graham Peace
West Virginia University, USA

Abstract

Richard Mason's seminal paper describing the four ethical issues of the information age has guided the field of Information Ethics for almost 20 years. However, much has changed with regard to information technology since 1986, and perhaps Mason's four ethical issues — Privacy, Accuracy, Property, and Accessibility — have become dated. To set the stage for the following chapters, and to provide the reader with some context, this chapter takes a retrospective look at Mason's issues and discusses how they remain salient in today's information-rich and technology-driven society. Additional issues that have emerged since Mason's publication are also discussed, with a discussion of "justified" hacking as a focused and critical analysis of Mason's four issues. While no firm conclusions are reached regarding the ethics of specific actions, the chapter reinforces the continued use of the four ethical issues in future research, and it prepares the reader for the more detailed discussions that follow in the remaining chapters.

Introduction

Ethicist Richard Mason's 1986 paper, "Four Ethical Issues of the Information Age," was a landmark in the development of ethics research in the Management Information Systems (MIS) field, and has served as a guide for both researchers and practitioners for almost 20 years. However, much has changed since Mason's seminal work was first published. Computing power has increased at the speed predicted by Moore's Law (Moore, 1965), the Soviet Union has been replaced by terrorists as the main perceived threat to the Western world, and the dot.com boom has come and gone. The Internet has transformed the way people communicate, and wireless technologies promise constant connection from almost any point on Earth. Illegal file sharing clogs computer networks, viruses and worms pose a constant threat to PCs everywhere, and terrorism has raised questions regarding the balance of privacy versus security. Perhaps the only constant in the technology arena of the past twenty years is the virtual monopoly dominance by Microsoft of the PC operating system market.

The rapid pace of technology's advancement presents great challenges to those interested in its ethical use. There is little time to discuss the impact of a new technology prior to its implementation, and once a new system is in place, there is little chance of its use being limited. As the saying goes, if someone *can* do something, he probably will. Therefore, it is critical that both the public as a whole and those in the technology field do not become complacent when it comes to discussing the ethical consequences of technology's use. While computers can improve our lives greatly, there is the possibility of unintended harm if they are not used in a manner consistent with society's norms.

As an introduction to the more detailed works presented in this book, this chapter uses Mason's framework to provide the reader with an overview of the increasingly important field of Information Ethics, focusing specifically on the areas of privacy and property rights, which are the main subjects of this book. Issues that Mason could not have foreseen are then discussed, with the concept of "justified" hacking receiving some detailed analysis in light of Mason's four ethical issues. Despite the technological advancements of the past 20 years,

Mason's framework still proves to be a useful tool in organizing ethical discussion, and the issues he raised are as relevant today as in 1986.

Mason's Four Ethical Issues

Mason identified four ethical issues of the information age: privacy, accuracy, property, and accessibility. The following paragraphs summarize Mason's discussion and provide an update as to how the issues have developed over the past 18 years.

Privacy

Privacy is an issue that has been debated by philosophers for centuries. However, information technology changes the dynamic, as it allows for information to be gathered and shared on a scale never before seen. Mason foresaw two threats to privacy: the growth of information technology and the increased value of information in decision making. Given the remarkable increases in information technology performance and communication technology's ability to quickly transport information anywhere, anytime, the first threat is clearly greater than ever. Even Mason could not have predicted the remarkable growth in the ability to gather, store, combine, and disseminate data and information. Spybots and cookies monitor Internet users' actions, and Customer Relationship Management software allows companies to track the detailed behavior of consumers. Even technologies that users may believe are private are often not. For example, Google's recent announcement that it will begin to offer free e-mail accounts to users has come under fire as initial plans call for all e-mails to be scanned for keywords in order to better target the users for advertising purposes (World Privacy Forum, 2004). While privacy policies are often placed on Web sites, many users do not take the time to study them properly. The Internet itself has made information freely available to millions, when this information would have been difficult to obtain in the past. In Chapter VII, Miller, Urbaczewski, and Salisbury discuss issues surrounding the availability of public documents online.

Mason's second threat has also increased in importance and visibility. Information is power, as the saying goes. On a corporate level, increases in global competition (also partially caused by the use of information technology to eliminate geographic and political trade barriers) have led to an emphasis on better decision making. As Simon (1960) posited, an increase in information reduces uncertainty, which leads to more structured and, hopefully, better decisions. The pressures of global competitiveness have put an emphasis on excellent decision-making. Therefore, information is increasing in value.

Governments have also used these new technologies to create and maintain huge databases. The Echelon system, run by the United States and its allies, captures and monitors almost every electronic transmission on Earth from mammoth spy bases in places such as West Virginia, England, and Canada. The threat of terrorism certainly requires the monitoring of potential suspects, but what level of privacy are individuals willing to give up? The controversy surrounding the implementation of the United States' PATRIOT Act indicates that people are not willing to have all personal information made available, even if it leads to a world free of terrorist acts. This book provides two chapters on the issue of privacy and security. Chapter X, by Freeman, gives an excellent overview of information technology's impact on privacy in light of recent world events, while in Chapter XI, Hartzel and Deegan discuss the trade-off between privacy and security using the perspective of social justice.

In the specific case of medical information systems, there has been much discussion of the use of technology to ensure that medical personnel have the best information available when treating a patient. This includes the storage and communication of up-to-date patient information that can be very sensitive. In response to potential privacy violations, the United States' government has enacted national standards to protect the privacy of health information with the Health Insurance Portability and Accountability Act (HIPAA) of 1996 leading the way. In Chapter XIII, Deshmukh and Croasdell explore the issue of privacy in the healthcare industry and the specific impact of HIPAA, while Joseph and Cook, in Chapter XII, discuss the role of information imbalance in the patient-doctor relationship.

Finally, Cassidy, Chae, and Courtney (Chapter VIII) apply ethical, legal, and economic theories to the issue of consumer information. Through the chapters discussed in this section, the reader is exposed to a broad range of research and discussion that is currently ongoing in the privacy field. It is clear that the relevance of the privacy issue is as strong today as when first posited in Mason's framework.

Accuracy

When discussing accuracy, Mason focused on the innocent use of incorrect or missing data. When designing information systems, Mason argued, it is the designer's responsibility to be "vigilant in the pursuit of accuracy in information." He envisioned situations in which people were unintentionally harmed by inaccurate data, and this is certainly a concern. However, it is remarkable how organizations have implemented measures to guard against such problems. While inaccurate information is inevitable, given the quantity of data gathered and stored each day, accidental inaccuracies have proven to be more of an annoyance than an ethical issue on the level of piracy and property. This may be due to the fact that inaccurate information will almost certainly lead to poor decisions, and in today's increasingly competitive global marketplace, corporations must make the best decisions possible. Harm has undoubtedly been caused by inaccurate data, especially with regard to credit reports and other financial data, but it has not been a major issue in the past eighteen years in the manner that Mason alleged.

However, where accuracy *has* become an issue is the intentional falsification of information, as opposed to accidental errors. In particular, identity theft is becoming more of a concern as more and more business is undertaken in a virtual world, as opposed to face-to-face transactions between individuals who know each other. Business on the Internet requires only a credit card, an address, and a few other bits and pieces of personal information, each of which can be stolen by a competent thief. Stories of the horrors of identity theft abound, and credit card companies now use advertisements that stress their efforts to reduce the possibility of a criminal using the customer's account for unauthorized purchases. While Mason could not have foreseen this particular aspect of the accuracy issue, it is apparent that accuracy problems are still with us today, albeit of a different nature than first described by Mason.

Property

Mason viewed intellectual property rights as "one of the most complex issues we face as a society." We still are "protected" by the same "imperfect institutions" that Mason described: copyrights, patents, oaths of confidentiality, and loyalty. However, while Mason focused on expert systems and artificial intelligence as potential threats, the real threat in today's world is one Mason addressed nearer to the end of the section: bandwidth. Mason referred to this as a "scarce and limited" resource, which was certainly true in 1986. However, in 2004, bandwidth has expanded to capacities impossible to predict just two decades ago. It is this bandwidth, and the ubiquitous nature of the technology needed to use it, that has led to the most discussed current threat to intellectual property rights—illegal downloading of software, music, and videos. With the widespread introduction of Napster in the late 1990s, followed by such technologies as WinMX, Kazaa, and bittorrenting, the sharing of digitized products and information is easy enough for almost anyone to accomplish. A brief search of the Internet yields many opportunities to download illegally "cracked" (i.e., copyright protection removed) versions of almost any major software package. Similarly, music files, often in lossless compression formats such as flac, are freely available, and the increased capacity of bandwidth and disk space has given rise to the sharing of video and movie files over the Web.

The RIAA and other industry trade groups have fought back with some effect, filing hundreds of lawsuits in an effort to dissuade potential pirates. It is interesting to note that individuals who would rarely consider breaking the law cannot seem to stop themselves when it comes to committing the illegal act of downloading a copyright protected song or movie. The numbers are staggering. Not including music downloaded via the Internet, it is estimated that 1.8 billion CDs were pirated in 2002 alone, resulting in US$4.6 billion in lost sales for the recording industry (IFPI, 2003).

In Chapter VI, El-Sheikh, Rashed, and Peace focus on the issue of software piracy, providing a review of the literature to date, a more detailed analysis of the problem, and a study of piracy behavior in the country of Jordan. The Middle East is often listed as one area of the world where piracy is prevalent. The authors provide some interesting views on the future of piracy and give suggestions on potential remedies. De Vuyst and Fairchild provide a more comprehensive discussion of intellectual property rights in Chapter V, including a comparison of intellectual property rights with more traditional material property rights, while Kimppa, in Chapter IV, focuses on the specific situation of intellectual property rights and digital media. The issue of intellectual property rights, and the issues proposed by Mason, are perhaps more relevant today than at anytime in history.

Accessibility

Mason raised the limited bandwidth issue while transitioning to his section on Accessibility. He continued the discussion by stating that literacy is humankind's main access to information. In today's world, computer literacy is, therefore, critically important. Mason also raised the issue of the digital divide, whereby the gap between the haves and the have-nots is increased by the have-nots' financial inability to purchase the equipment and training necessary to partici- pate in the information revolution. When the statistics are studied, there is clearly a gap between the economically disadvantaged in our communities and those with the financial means to purchase the equipment and training necessary to "get online." According to the latest statistics on the US Department of Education's Web site, only 31% of US families averaging less than US$20,000 in income have a computer at home, while 89% of families earning over US$75,000 have a home computer (NCES, 2003). From a global perspec- tive, there is a more general issue. Fully 41% of the individuals with online access are North American, despite the fact that this geographic region represents only 6% of the world's population (Digital Divide Network, http:/ /www.digitaldividenetwork.org/).

As the Internet becomes the major source of information for society, and as more and more economic activity moves online, this raises obvious ethical questions.

However, perhaps there is a focus on the wrong problem. When we view history, similar arguments were made regarding technologies such as the television and the telephone, yet almost all members of US society now have access to both. A case can be made that a similar situation will arise with access to the Internet. Certainly, there will be a cost involved with access, but it appears to be in the best interests of many corporations to ensure that we all are wired. When individuals cannot connect to the Web, they cannot purchase books from Amazon.com, for example. It is in Amazon's interest to ensure that all members of society are provided access to the Internet, thereby increasing the online consumer population. While clearly those without the current means to purchase the equipment and services necessary to go online are unable to purchase on the scale of the more affluent members of society, they still have a significant disposable income when compared to many people in the world, and the costs of providing access will eventually reach a point where a profit can be made. Perhaps a more interesting aspect to the digital divide is studying how this redistribution of profits will affect neighborhood shops, as opposed to those who currently access the Internet at home.

As technology becomes a more and more important part of our daily lives and a greater necessity in the ability to succeed, accessibility issues will remain an important and relevant point of discussion, as Mason proposed.

Saliency of Mason

Based on the above, it seems that Mason's four ethical issues still hold today, nearly 20 years after they were originally discussed. While some of the specifics of each of the issues may or may not have been realized as threats to information ethics, the four issues themselves can still be used in today's society to discuss information ethics. However, as has been already stated, much has changed in these last two decades. Computers are used today, both in businesses and in homes, in ways that Mason could not have dreamed in 1986. The Internet as we know it did not exist and massive databases were not accessible by individuals or businesses on a regular basis. Therefore, in order to "test" the saliency and applicability of Mason's four ethical issues to today's society, the issues must be examined and analyzed from a different perspective. They should be analyzed via an extreme example of information ethics — situations that are much less common than private information available via the Internet or identity theft or software piracy or even viruses and worms. If Mason's four ethical issues can serve to effectively discuss and analyze an "extreme" case of potentially (un)ethical behavior that exists today, then we can more confidently say that Mason's work is truly seminal.

The rest of this chapter will focus on a topic not commonly found in the mainstream literature: the idea of "justified" hacking. Most readers are familiar with the concept of hacking, a practice that is almost completely displayed in a negative light. However, there are other views, as the following paragraphs describe. While perhaps not readily apparent, there are privacy, intellectual property, and accessibility components to this interesting issue.

Hacking and 'Justified' Hacking

When access is provided to people's homes, it is inevitable that criminal elements will take advantage of that access. The same is true with computer systems. While the Internet provides us all with access to a wealth of resources, it also provides access for others to our own technology. Consequently, reported incidents of security violations have skyrocketed in recent years. CERT (2004), the Internet's most respected security watchdog, reported more than 137,000 incidents in 2003, up from 82,000 in 2002. It is important to note that these are *reported* incidents. Many more go unreported, as organizations are either unaware of the intrusion or too embarrassed to have the intrusion reported.

The press that hacking and hackers receive is predominantly negative. Hacking is often associated with computer crime, identity fraud, identity theft, denial of service attacks, political statements, and e-commerce disruptions. Hackers are often portrayed as societal outcasts with little or no care for the law (Timusk, 2001). In most countries, hacking is a crime, and when the perpetrators are caught, they are prosecuted accordingly.

While many instances of hacking and many hackers themselves fall into the above description, there is one aspect of hacking that may be viewed as legitimate, and even ethical – hacking for social justice, or "justified" hacking. This may occur when someone uses an otherwise illegal means for the greater good, such as an individual changing his/her social security number or other form of identification in order to evade a stalker, or when a doctor needs to begin again after several malicious and unproven malpractice suits threaten to ruin his/her career. Federal and state governments do not allow such changes, but the potential lifesaving advantages of being able to start over surely outweigh the illegality of the hack, or do they? Also, what about the cases that are not so cut-and-dry regarding the personal safety of the individual or the tarnished reputation? For example, would such an action be ethical if it were someone simply trying to start over financially after accruing excessive amounts of bad debt or even a bankruptcy?

Definitions

According to whatis.com (http://www.whatis.com), a hacker is defined as "a clever programmer," while a cracker is defined as "someone who breaks into someone else's computer system, often on a network; bypasses passwords or licenses in computer programs; or in other ways intentionally breaches computer security." Cracking is analogous to breaking and entering. While the content of this section of the chapter is more in line with the actions of crackers as opposed to hackers, "hackers" will be used as a term to cover both groups as one, as is often done in both the popular and trade presses. Hackers are known for their counterculture attitudes, their disdain of authority, and their technical skill. Hacking is sometimes seen as a game, or a one-upmanship contest, with each hacker trying to outdo previous hacks. Not all hacking is done with malicious intent, as the hack may simply be to show that a system is vulnerable or to prove the hacker's technical ability.

Sometimes hackers attack specific companies or organizations or specific software vulnerabilities. Sometimes hackers just attack. Hackers may be trying to show vulnerabilities, trying to infiltrate an organization's internal systems to gain access to valuable information in order to steal or alter it, or they may be trying to shut down Web sites through Denial of Service attacks (attacks that literally flood a Web site with requests to the point that the Web site is either unable to respond to these "hack" requests and legitimate ones, or must shut down entirely until the flood subsides). For more specific details and descriptions of hackers, hacking, cracking, and these types of attacks, see SEARCHSECURITY.COM (http://searchsecurity.techtarget.com/) and search on "hacking" or similar terms, or visit the Hacking Exposed Web site at http://www.hackingexposed.com/links/links.htm.

Theoretically, there is an unlimited list of actions that hackers can take, ranging from completely benign to catastrophically destructive (from the victim's perspective). One specific "use" of hacking occurs when an individual or group hacks to make a statement, usually political or ideological in nature. The intent of the hack is not to gain access to secure systems (though this is often necessary in order to accomplish their goal), but to send a message about a specific cause or idea. This form of activism, when performed via hacking, is called "hacktivism," and is not so far removed from the common act of defacing buildings with political or social posters or graffiti. The ethical nature of the hack depends on the actions being protested, the violation of another organization's property, and the resulting damage done.

Most often, an organization's Web site is compromised and the regular content of the site is replaced with a message or statement put there by the hacker. In many cases of hacktivism, the general public or the specific users of the attacked organization's Web site are the first to notice that something is awry, since the organization's Webmaster and likely most of the organization's employees do not necessarily use or see the public Web site on a daily basis. Even if the organization has Web-based or Web-enabled internal systems, the employees using these systems usually have a different access page than the general public. The embarrassment factor associated with having your Web site defaced and/or altered by an outsider (the hacker) is quite high, and can lead to a loss of confidence in the organization's security systems by both employees and customers.

"Justified" hacking refers to a specific type of hack where the intent of the hack is not to exploit software vulnerabilities, steal proprietary data, or shut down Web sites. The purpose of the hack is to provide an individual with a new identity or a new credit record, and often both, in order to start life over without some aspect of the past following the individual. These hacks are carried out with a sense of social justice, of righting some wrong. The hackers are completing the hacks as a service to other individuals, often for a fee. The question remains as to whether these hacks are indeed justified from an ethical perspective. Consider the following:

Scenario 1 – Stalking

Many people have a very difficult time relating to and understanding the difficulties and hardships (emotional, psychological, physical, etc.) faced by someone who is being stalked. Stalking cases are not common news stories, but when they do appear, the story often has an unfortunate ending. One of the most famous stalking cases took place in 1989, when Rebecca Schaeffer, a television star on the show *My Sister Sam*, was stalked. After three years of sending letters and attempting to meet her, the stalker found her address through the Department of Motor Vehicles (DMV), rang her doorbell posing as a delivery man, and then killed her when she answered the door. He confessed to the murder and was convicted. Since then, the DMV has changed its policies regarding the availability of private information in order to prevent such incidents from happening again.

Not all stalking cases involve actresses or famous personalities. The stalker may be sending threatening letters, showing up at work or other places to pester the individual, or even attempting to break into the victim's home. There are, unfortunately, many ways to stalk someone. Just as unfortunate is the fact that, until the stalker is caught, tried, and put in jail, the victim has very little recourse. The ability to change identities, relocate, and start anew may seem like an extreme step to take, but to a victim of a stalker, being able to avoid the stalker for good, with no way of being followed, can be an appealing option. Enter the "justified" hack.

This is not to say that such actions should be taken lightly or even should be taken at all. Changing your entire past and starting life anew will create difficulties and hardships of its own. Old friends, hangouts, and even relatives will never be seen again. Even with the changes, you may be constantly watching your back and afraid that someone, somehow from your past will recognize you. However, given the abilities of hackers to alter personal identification information, create new identities, and give someone a "new" life, the option does exist. Finding the right person to do all of this work may not be easy, but if an individual looks hard enough and in the right places, such services can be found.

Interestingly, such actions are not unprecedented. The police, FBI, and other state and federal government agencies are legally able to change personal information and give people new lives. Programs such as witness protection may go to such lengths to protect vital witnesses who fear for their safety both before and after criminal trials. However, these same agencies have yet to offer their services to those being stalked. The Appendix contains two additional scenarios.

Discussion

One of the questions that must be asked is whether the individual benefiting from the "justified" hack has a right to control his/her life in such an intimate way. In other words, is what they have done or have had done for them really wrong? Was anyone or any organization harmed by the actions of the hacker or the wishes of the beneficiary of the hack? How much of our own privacy and property are we willing and able to protect?

As previously mentioned, some of the situations have similarities to the well-established and legitimate witness protection and witness relocation programs. However, "justified" hacking is not supported by the local, state, or federal governments and, therefore, individuals must resort to illegal means to achieve similar results, although an illegal act is not necessarily unethical (e.g., the classic case of it being illegal to hide Jews in WWII Germany, despite the fact that it was clearly the ethical thing to do).

The stalking scenario is likely, though not always, going to affect women more so than men. The bankruptcy and malpractice scenarios (see Appendix) are gender-neutral. In addition, the bankruptcy scenario is less likely to be a result of external influences. In other words, stalking and erroneous/unsubstantiated malpractice suits are the result of someone else intruding into an individual's life. The victim is trying to get away from a situation that he/she did not get into on his/her own accord. However, bankruptcy avoidance is more often a result of one's personal decisions and actions and less a result of others, although this could be the case.

From a purely practical perspective, none of the "justified" hacking actions are legal. Individuals are not allowed to change their legal identification and "destroy" any links from the old identity to the new identity, or have others change it on their behalf. Doing so is a crime. However, no one was harmed by the actual hack in the stalking and malpractice scenarios and, in fact, lives could be saved. This may not be the case for the bankruptcy scenario, as this situation involves someone trying to avoid his or her responsibilities. As a result, legitimate debtors are left without their due payments when the bankruptcy is avoided.

The ethical implications of such actions are much more difficult to ascertain, and every individual will arrive at his/her own opinion. From a purely deontological perspective (i.e., the belief in universal "rights" and "wrongs"), none of these "justified" hacks can truly be justified. The private property of others is violated, and the act is a clear form of deception. However, from a consequentialist perspective (i.e., the belief that the ethical solution is the one that leads to the greater good), a good case can be made for the stalking and malpractice hacks, as no one is truly harmed, and the victim, who has done nothing "wrong" prior to the hack, certainly benefits. Any damage done is outweighed by the relief of the victim. The consequentialist perspective will have difficulty justifying the bankruptcy hack, due to the harm done to the debtors.

For most individuals, corporations, organizations, and governments, the act of hacking and the hackers themselves are viewed as "evils" of the computer and Internet era. Hacking exists in a semi-underground world with its own language and culture. Yet there are people who have received great benefits as the result of "justified" hacking, and have done so without causing physical, emotional, or monetary harm to others. By bringing issues such as this to the forefront, and by presenting them in an unbiased manner, information technology (IT) professionals, academics, and decision-makers will have a better understanding of the consequences of designing and creating the latest and greatest technologies.

"Justified" hacking, as described and discussed above, incorporates itself quite easily into Mason's four ethical issues of privacy, accuracy, property, and accessibility. In other words, Mason's issues hold and remain salient, even under this extreme example of (un)ethical behavior. Intellectual property rights are impacted, as the hacker is altering information under the control of another entity. Who owns this information? Is it the entity that gathers and stores the data, or does the person represented by the data have a right to alter it? Accuracy is also an issue. By falsifying data, an inaccurate record has been created. This is not necessarily what Mason envisioned, in his original framework (technology has changed the focus of the accuracy issue), but the act does fit neatly into Mason's four issues. Similarly, privacy becomes an obvious issue. The hack itself is committed to protect an individual's privacy. Finally, accessibility is a concern. How much access should an individual have to information stored about him or her in another entity's system? This is closely related to the property argument, described above. Even in an extreme situation that could not have possibly been envisioned by Mason in 1986, his framework provides a very useful way to discuss and analyze the issue, proving its worthiness even in today's information age.

Other Issues

In a field as prone to change as information technology, it is not surprising that several new ethical issues are now being faced by society. Many of these are well-known and often discussed in the popular press. For example, viruses and worms are now common terms among computer users. In August of 2003, it is estimated that computer viruses caused a record US$32.8 billion worth of damage. The Sobig virus alone was responsible for almost US$30 billion of that figure (Mi2g™ Ltd., 2004)

Similarly, the near monopoly position of Microsoft has been a common topic of discussion. Is it best for society to allow one company to consistently maintain a dominant market position in an industry that impacts our lives on such an everyday basis? The open source movement, and specifically Linux, may eventually provide some nontraditional competition for Microsoft and other industry leaders, but currently there is no stopping the Windows operating system juggernaut, despite legal challenges in both the United States and Europe. A similar issue is playing out in the mainstream media, where fewer and fewer outlets of information exist, as corporate titans such as Rupert Murdoch and Disney Corporation consolidate their holdings in the industry. These monopolistic situations gained through legal business practices could, in coming years, find themselves in conflict with the best interests of society.

However, there are issues that are often not covered in the popular press, and of which most readers will be unaware. Barger and Crowell, in Chapter IX, bring to light the fascinating issue of parasitic computing, and Mathieson, in Chapter III, discusses the use of information technology to develop a "moral support system," designed to aid individuals in understanding and dealing with moral dilemmas.

Conclusions

This chapter is meant to provide the reader with a framework from which to approach the rest of the book. The changes of the past two decades have altered the discussion and given rise to new ethical challenges. However, the discussion and contributions presented in Mason's seminal 1986 work are still relevant, despite the incredible growth of the use of IT in business and society, or perhaps because of this growth. This book attempts to update the discussion by providing the reader with a thorough debate of the major ethical issues, specifically in the areas of privacy and intellectual property rights, facing all of us living in today's information society.

References

CERT (2004). *CERT/CC statistics 1988-2003*. Retrieved from: *http://www.cert.org/stats/cert_stats.html*

IFPI (2003). *The recording industry commercial piracy report 2003*. International Federation of the Phonographic Industry, London.

Mason, R.O. (1986). Four ethical issues of the information age. *MIS Quarterly, 10*(1), 5-12.

Mi2g™ Ltd. (2004). Retrieved from: *http://www.mi2g.com*

Moore, G. (1965). Cramming more components onto integrated circuits. *Electronics, 38*(8), 114-117.

NCES (2003). *Computer and Internet use by children and adolescents in 2001* (NCES 2004-014). Washington, DC: National Center for Education Statistics.

Simon, H. (1960). *The new science of management decision.* New York: Harper & Row.

Timusk, P. (2001). *Computers: Ethical and Unethical Actions.* Retrieved from: *http://www.ncf.carleton.ca/~at571/page1.html*

World Privacy Forum (2004). *An open letter to Google regarding its proposed Gmail service.* Retrieved from: *http://www.privacyrights.org/ar/GmailLetter.htm*

Appendix

Scenario 2 – Medical Malpractice

Medical doctors, psychologists, and others pay substantial amounts of money every year for malpractice insurance. When these individuals are sued for malpractice, the insurance covers the legal costs and, if found guilty, the resulting payments.

No one ever wants to be sued for malpractice. The effects of a successful suit will have obvious negative effects on the person's career. The record of the suit will never go away, and avoiding it in the future will be difficult at best. Even if the suit fails (the defendant is found not guilty or perhaps the suit is thrown out of court), the stigma of having been sued for malpractice is quite substantial. Although the doctor, psychologist, etc., will be able to rightfully say that he/she was found not guilty or that the suit was dismissed, having to talk about such lawsuits will hurt business and reputation alike. Future patients will be second-guessing their decisions and always wondering in the back of their minds if the lawsuit really had merit or if "not guilty" was the right determination.

Now, consider what might happen if there were more than one such malpractice lawsuit. This can only serve to raise doubts in the minds of current and potential patient, no matter the legitimacy of the suits. Perhaps the suits are the result of an overzealous lawyer trying to make a name for himself (and some commissions along the way) or, perhaps, there is a legitimate reason to suspect malpractice. This uncertainty will surely affect the reputation and continued success of the medical professional in question.

As these lawsuits, no matter the outcome, stay with his/her professional record forever, how can a person who has successfully defended himself/herself from frivolous malpractice lawsuits ever expect to make a living and earn the trust and respect of his/her patients? Many people would say that this is unlikely. Enter "justified" hacking and the opportunity to start anew with a clean record and a clean reputation.

Scenario 3 – Debt and Bankruptcy

Corporations filing for bankruptcy are fairly common events. With the recent dot.com bust and the subsequent downturn in the US (and world) economy, many businesses have been left with no choice but to declare bankruptcy. Hopefully, given the opportunities and time that this declaration provides under the law, the businesses are able to turn things around and return to profitability.

Individual bankruptcy is also fairly common. However, individual bankruptcies do not make compelling news stories, so the public is much less aware of them. Bankruptcy laws allow individuals to start over financially, but there are consequences to credit ratings that affect credit cards, loans, and bank accounts for years to come. Many people try to avoid bankruptcy when their debt is large due to these consequences.

Whether bankruptcy is avoidable or not, when someone has such a large amount of debt that bankruptcy appears to be inevitable, "justified" hacking may be another option. Being able to start over with a new identity, a clean financial record, and no debt history could seem very inviting to some people.

Chapter II

Moral Psychology and Information Ethics:
Psychological Distance and the Components of Moral Behavior in a Digital World

Charles R. Crowell
University of Notre Dame, USA

Darcia Narvaez
University of Notre Dame, USA

Anna Gomberg
University of Notre Dame, USA

Abstract

This chapter discusses the ways in which moral psychology can inform information ethics. A "Four Component Model" of moral behavior is described involving the synergistic influences of key factors including sensitivity, judgment, motivation, and action. Two technology-mediated domains, electronic communications and digital property, are then explored to illustrate how technology can impact each of the four components believed to underlie moral behavior. It is argued that technology can create a kind of "psychological distance" between those who use technology for communication or those who acquire and use digital property (e.g., software or music) and those who may be affected by such uses (e.g., e-mail recipients or digital property owners). This "distance" potentially impacts all four components of moral behavior in such a way that the usual social or moral constraints operative under normal (non-technology-mediated) circumstances (e.g., face-to-face communication) may be reduced, thereby facilitating the occurrence of unethical activities like piracy, hacking, or flaming. Recognition of the potential deleterious impact of technology on each of the four components leads to a better understanding of how specific educational interventions can be devised to strengthen moral sensitivity, judgment, motivation, and action within the context of our increasingly digital world.

Introduction

We ignore ethics and computing at our peril!

Rogerson & Bynum, 1995

Unethical behavior is pervasive and timeless, as is the question of why people do bad things. What makes some people behave morally or ethically and others not? Psychologists interested in moral development have attempted to answer such questions by examining the psychological components of morality, the elements that work in concert to bring about moral behavior (Rest, 1983). Emerging from this work is a model of moral behavior that identifies the joint action of four psychological processes: sensitivity, judgment, motivation, and action (Narvaez & Rest, 1995).

Certainly, the "information age" has been accompanied by its share of technology-related ethical issues and challenges. Interestingly, many (if not most) of these challenges are not fundamentally new (Barger, 2001). Although there may well be exceptions, information technology appears to have created new and different ways to engage in the same kinds of unethical behaviors seen throughout history, from stealing property to invading personal privacy (Johnson, 2001). Because these issues have been studied and analyzed for years in other contexts, it is all the more important for Information Science (IS) researchers and practitioners to be well acquainted with general principles of moral and ethical development. Indeed, it is now well-attested that our perceptions of the moral landscape are influenced by developmental and social-cognitive factors (Lapsley & Narvaez, 2004). In order to plan educational interventions that help technology users develop appropriate ethical attitudes and behaviors with respect to their use of information technology, educators can take advantage of a wealth of knowledge about moral development from the field of moral psychology.

The purpose of this chapter is to acquaint those working in the field of Information Science with a psychological perspective on moral or ethical behavior. In this chapter we examine key psychological processes that are critical for moral behavior, discuss the function of these processes in the domain of technology, and suggest strategies to enhance education related to information ethics.

At the outset, it is important to draw attention to our use of certain terms. While we make no substantive distinction between the terms "moral" and "ethical," there is an important difference between what may be considered "moral" and what is "legal," or conversely between what is "immoral" and what is "illegal." To be "legal" is to conform one's behavior to the laws established by the societies in which we live. Morality, on the other hand, is a matter of conformity to "divine law" or codes of conduct derived from principles of right and wrong that transcend societal strictures. There is no automatic correspondence between that which is "legal" and that which is "moral," or vice versa. That is, depending on the society, what many would consider immoral practices may be considered legal (e.g., prostitution in Nevada), while some illegal practices (e.g., harboring Jewish fugitives in Nazi Germany during World War II) may be quite moral.

Four Component Model of Moral Behavior

The Four Component Model (Narvaez & Rest, 1995; Rest, 1983) represents the internal "processes" necessary for a moral act to ensue: moral sensitivity, moral judgment, moral motivation, and moral action. These components are not personality traits or virtues; rather, they are major units of analysis used to trace how a person responds in a particular social situation. The model depicts an "ensemble of processes," not a single, unitary one. Therefore, the operation of a single component does not predict moral behavior. Instead, behaving morally depends upon each process and the execution of the entire ensemble. Each process involves cognitive, affective, and behavioral aspects that function together in fostering the completion of a moral action.

Collectively, the following processes comprise the Four Component Model and are presented in logical order: (1) *Ethical sensitivity* involves perceiving the relevant elements in the situation and constructing an interpretation of those elements. This first component also includes consideration of what actions are possible, who and what might be affected by each possible action, and how the involved parties might react to possible outcomes. (2) *Ethical judgment* relates to reasoning about the possible actions and deciding which is most moral or ethical. (3) *Ethical motivation* involves prioritizing what is considered to be the most moral or ethical action over all others and being intent upon following that course. (4) *Ethical action* combines the strength of will with the social and psychological skills necessary to carry out the intended course of action. This fourth component, then, is dependent both on having the requisite skills and on persisting in the face of any obstacles or challenges to the action that may arise.

When considering moral or ethical behavior, a post-hoc analysis of the situation is often most helpful. In this way, we can point out where the processes might have failed. Consider the young adult who is tempted to download copyrighted music that has been illegally placed on a file-sharing system in violation of the owner's rights. Let's call this young adult, "Jim," and examine the four component processes in an effort to understand what might happen. Moreover, let's assume that downloading music for which one has not paid under these circumstances is both illegal and immoral.

Ethical Sensitivity

To respond to a situation in a moral way, a person must be able to perceive and interpret events in a way that leads to ethical action. The person must be sensitive to situational cues and must be able to visualize various alternative actions in response to that situation. A morally sensitive person draws on many aspects, skills, techniques and components of interpersonal sensitivity. These include taking the perspectives of others (role taking), cultivating empathy for and a sense of connection to others, and interpreting a situation based on imagining what might happen and who might be affected. Individuals with higher empathy for others and with better perspective-taking skills are more likely to behave for the good of others in a manner that is said to be "pro-social" (Eisenberg, 1992). So if Jim, our young adult, has highly developed ethical sensitivity skills, he takes the perspectives of all the people involved in producing the music. He feels empathy for their welfare and a sense of concern for them. He considers the ramifications of downloading copyrighted material including his and other people's welfare and reactions.

Ethical Judgment

After Jim has identified the "lay of the land" through an active set of ethical sensitivity skills, he must determine which action to take. Ethical judgment has to do with assessing the possible actions and determining which is the most moral. Hundreds of research studies have demonstrated that individuals (male and female) develop increasingly sophisticated moral reasoning structures based on age and experience, especially related to education (Rest, Narvaez, Bebeau, & Thoma, 1999). Jim could use one of several moral schemas (conceptual structures) in making a decision about what to do.

Rest et al. (1999) have identified three schemas individuals access depending on their level of moral judgment development. Using the *Personal Interests Schema* (common in high school students and younger), Jim would consider what benefits himself the most and perhaps choose to download the music from the file-sharing server. Alternatively, he might be worried about being caught and having to suffer the consequences, leading him to choose not to download. Based on recent threats in the news about how record companies intend to bring lawsuits against those who are participating in illegal sharing of copyrighted music files over the Internet, Jim's mother might have warned him about doing such things. That she may find out also might deter him, because he wants to be a good son. If his reasoning is even more sophisticated, he would be concerned about societal laws and social order (*Maintaining Norms Schema*). This would likely deter him, unless he subscribes to some other non-civil set of laws (e.g., cult norms). Yet even more sophisticated (*Postconventional Schema*) reasoning would lead Jim to think of ideal social cooperation. At this level, he could behave as an *Idealist* by seeking to take an action that he could demand of anyone in his position (Kant's Categorical Imperative), or he could adopt the view of a *Pragmatist* by choosing his actions according to "what would bring about the greatest good for the greatest number." In either case, at the postconventional level of reasoning, Jim is likely to resist downloading.

In fact, Friedman (1997) has shown that moral sensitivity and reasoning are critical to adolescents' decisions and opinions regarding the acceptability of taking actions such as violating copyright protection by making illegal copies of computer programs (i.e., pirating) or invading someone's privacy through unauthorized access to (i.e., hacking) his or her computer files. Friedman (1997) demonstrated that adolescents who viewed pirating and hacking as permissible did so not out of lack of respect for property and privacy rights in general, but because they judged computer property to be different than other types of property (see "Technology and Ethical Behavior" section below), suggesting that moral sensitivity (i.e., assigning moral relevance to some kinds of "property" and not others) was more at issue here than was moral judgment. The difference in question seems to be related to the relative lack of tangibility associated with digital instantiations of things like documents or songs (i.e., computer property) compared to things like bicycles or cars (i.e., physical property).

Ethical Motivation

After deciding that a particular action is the most moral, Jim must set aside other goals and interests to further its completion. He may have developed the necessary dispositional skills to maintain a sense of moral integrity such as the ability to distract himself from his original (impulsive) goal to download. Jim can more easily acquire these skills if he is already conscientious and has cultivated a sense of responsibility to others, or if he has a religious orientation in which he derives meaning from a power greater than himself. Research suggests that persons who chronically maintain moral standards as central to the self are more likely to interpret situations and react in ways that are consistent with these standards (Lapsley & Narvaez, 2004). So, if Jim has not developed these qualities, he may give in to his initial impulse to download at this point. In so doing, Jim would elevate other values (e.g., status, power, pleasure, or excitement) above the moral standards related to ethical action.

Ethical Action

The final component of the model is comprised of the skills that facilitate successful implementation of the moral action. Jim must know what steps are necessary to complete a moral action and possess the perseverance necessary to follow them. This component may be less salient in our hypothetical situation because it involves a singular personal decision to download or not download. But, imagine a more complex situation in which Jim has a friend who did illegally download copyrighted material on a campus computer. What should Jim do? If he decides to report the friend, he would need to know what steps to take and would need to have the motivation to follow through even if it costs him the friendship.

Recall that the Four Component Model is a set of processes that, working in concert, result in moral behavior. This implies that the course of moral behavior may fail at any point due to a weakness in one or more processes. Some people may function well in one process but may be deficient in another. For instance, Jim may demonstrate great sensitivity but poor judgment skills, or he might make an excellent judgment but fail in follow-through. We next examine the domain of technology to see how it potentially affects information ethics and the four component processes outlined above.

Technology and Ethical Behavior

While technology itself may not pose fundamentally new ethical challenges, it may well impinge in unique and important ways on one or more components of the model presented above. This, in turn, would be expected to affect ethical behavior. In this section, we will briefly review some of the known ways in which technology can exert such influences.

Technology-Mediated Communication and "Psychological Distance"

A growing body of evidence suggests that technology-mediated communications may differ in important ways from face-to-face or other traditional forms of interpersonal interactions. Kiesler, Siegel, and McGuire (1984) have elaborated on this possibility by identifying several ways in which e-mail (perhaps the most used means of computer-mediated communication) may differ from other forms of communication. For instance, e-mail can be relatively rapid and can be easily configured to reach just one or many recipients. Since it is predominantly textual, e-mail lacks the kinds of nonverbal cues that accompany face-to-face interactions and also is devoid of the information conveyed by voice intonations and inflections. In addition, e-mail can be viewed as a less personal medium of communication because the recipients are not actually present, leaving the audience either to be "imagined" by the sender or not envisioned at all. Thus, the normal triggers for empathy and interpersonal sensitivity that occur in face-to-face encounters are missing.

As Sproull and Kiesler (1991) have noted, the reduced audience awareness occurring during e-mail correspondence, due to the fact that participants neither see nor hear one another as messages are being sent or received, can have a variety of social-psychological consequences on both sides of the communication process. From the sender's perspective, unlike synchronous communications by phone or in person, there is no information available as the message is being composed and delivered to guide clarity or stimulate adjustment based on recipient reactions. This can reduce a sender's sensitivity to the "social correctness" of the message and likewise can reduce the sender's apprehension about being judged or evaluated by the recipient (Sproull & Kiesler, 1991). Similarly, the ephemeral nature of e-mail can render its recipients less sensitive to the sender's status or position and can compromise their ability to discern any affect or special points of emphasis intended by the sender, at least in the absence of special formatting or the use of "emoticons" (Kiesler et al., 1984; Sproull & Kiesler, 1991). Moreover, the accepted, regulating conventions and boundaries of more traditional communication do not necessarily apply to e-mail (Kiesler et al., 1984). This can blur distinctions of traditional importance (e.g., office vs. home, work hours vs. personal time) and can greatly diminish or abolish the use of commonly accepted communication protocols (e.g., letterheads) and other forms of etiquette (e.g., salutations). Also, those who correspond frequently using this electronic means may come to expect diminished response time to e-mail (Kiesler et al., 1984).

As a consequence of its altered social context and norms, computer-mediated communication may be distinctive in at least three important ways (Kiesler et al., 1984). When it is asynchronous, like e-mail, without the usual regulatory influences of the feedback inherent in real-time interactions, messages may be more difficult to understand and more challenging to compose with the desired level of clarity. Second, given a reduced sense of status among participants, electronic communications may be less formal and more like those characteristic of peer-to-peer interactions. Third, a reduced sense of audience may depress the self-regulation that is commonplace in more traditional communications, and may therefore render computer-mediated exchanges more open and less inhibited by normal social standards and boundaries.

Apparently, then, computer-mediated communication is less socially constrained than traditional forms of interpersonal interaction. In this way, the technological medium creates a kind of "psychological distance" between communicator and audience (Sumner & Hostetler, 2002). This factor has important implications for behavior within this medium. Of particular interest is the possibility that computer-mediated messages, exchanges, or discussions may be more open and frank than their traditional counterparts. That this might be true was strongly suggested by Weizenbaum's (1976) provocative observations of how people behaved with respect to "Eliza," a computer programmed to simulate a Rogerian psychotherapist. Weizenbaum noted that people appeared quite willing to reveal intimate issues to the computer, perhaps even more so than might be the case with an actual therapist (Sproull & Keisler, 1991). Subsequent research did in fact confirm that computer-mediated self-disclosure via an electronic survey is indeed qualitatively different—seemingly in favor of more open and honest responses–from that obtained with a paper and pencil questionnaire (Kiesler & Sproull, 1986), suggesting fewer social inhibitions. Sumner and Hostetler (2002) reported a similar finding in the context of e-conferencing. Moreover, comparing the efficacy of therapy using face-to-face, audio, and real-time video conferencing modes of communication, Day and Schneider (2002) found that clients participated more in the distance modes than in the face-to-face mode, although therapeutic outcomes were similar across all modes.

Decreased social inhibition may be the cause of a heightened tendency within computer-mediated communication to engage in behavior of a less than ethically desirable nature. For example, being less inhibited in electronic communications can lead to a behavior known as "flaming," in which one makes derogatory or off-color comments via e-mail or in a chat room that very likely would not be made in comparable face-to-face situations (Sproull & Keisler, 1991). Of course, a reduced threat of physical retaliation also could play a role in activating this behavior. In addition, electronic communications may facilitate another ethically questionable activity, spamming (Johnson, 2001), probably not just because e-mail makes it easy or cost-effective to do, but also because social inhibitions related to initiating unsolicited communications may be reduced. Finally, Johnson (2001) describes a whole category of "virtual actions," such as "cyber-stalking" and "cyber-rape," that probably are influenced at least to some degree by the reduced social constraints associated with computer-mediated communication.

With respect to technology-mediated communication, then, it seems quite reasonable to suppose that its altered social context will impinge importantly on one or more of the four components of the model described above. For example, a technological communication medium that reduces audience awareness likely will decrease Ethical Sensitivity (Component 1). In turn, Ethical Judgments (Component 2) and Ethical Actions (Component 3) associated with this medium could depart from those expected under more conventional modes of communication. However, the communication process is not the only aspect of human behavior where ethical behavior may be influenced by technology. Views of what constitutes "property" also may be affected as discussed in the next section.

Perceptions of Digital Objects and Materials

As noted above, Ethical Sensitivity (Component 1) relates to the question of how situations and objects are perceived. One way to think about the "psychological distance" associated with computer-mediated communication is as a form of altered "Ethical Sensitivity." This occurs because the interactive rules for face-to-face interpersonal communication are not as easily activated or applied in the cyberworld. Another way in which technology can impact Component 1 is by changing perceptions of what constitutes "property." Mounting evidence suggests that electronically encoded materials or objects are perceived differently than physical materials or objects. For example, Friedman (1997) reported the results of a 1988 study with high school students in which perceptions and ethical judgments about physical and digital objects were compared. Students made a clear distinction between physical objects that were private or not private. All students saw a trash receptacle on a street corner as not being private, while 97% saw someone's bicycle as private property. Interestingly, however, only 25% of the students believed that a commercially published and copyrighted computer program was private property. Friedman did not find the latter result to be readily attributable either to a general lack of computer experience among the students or to their lack of knowledge about applicable copyright policies. Instead, a certain domain-specific sensitivity appears to be lacking.

In further assessing the matter of privacy, Friedman (1997) examined student perceptions of different locations of information: an individual's computer files, the contents of a notice tacked on a school bulletin board, and a personal diary.

Almost all students (97%) regarded the diary information as private, whereas everyone regarded the bulletin board notice as not being private. In addition, a full third of the students also saw the contents of the computer files as not being private.

Teston (2002) was interested to determine if the perception of software as non-private property noted in the Friedman (1997) study also characterized the views of middle school students. In a sample of 264 seventh graders, Teston found the majority (55%) characterized software as being "public" property. In addition, over 58% believed that any property rights of the software developers were terminated at the time of purchase by a software user. Like Friedman, Teston also found that a majority of participants held this view despite recognizing the applicability of copyright laws. While the percentages of students holding these beliefs about software differed in the Friedman and Teston studies, the fact that the data in these respective studies were collected 10 years apart cannot be ignored. Nonetheless, taken together, these findings reveal that digital instantiations of objects (e.g., programs) or materials (e.g., computer files) are viewed differently than their physical counterparts (e.g., diaries).

Digital Objects and Ethical Judgments

The apparent differential perceptions of digital and non-digital materials reported by Friedman (1997) and Teston (2002) beg this question: How might ethical judgments (mediated by Component 2) differ with respect to these materials? One might expect that behavior considered ethically "wrong" in connection with tangible property or materials could be viewed differently when it comes to digital property or materials. That is, to the extent that digital objects or materials are perceived as being less private than their more tangible counterparts, a greater moral permissiveness is likely to be attached to behavior involving those objects or materials.

Both Friedman's (1997) and Teston's (2002) findings confirmed these suspicions. In terms of property, Friedman observed that none of the students in her sample thought it was alright to take someone else's physical property (a bicycle). In contrast, 77% felt it was okay to copy someone else's computer program (i.e., pirate it) for their own use; 47% said it was alright to pirate a program to give to someone else; and 40% even approved of piracy for purposes of making a profit by selling the copies. In addition, 62% also thought it was okay to pirate music to give away. With respect to materials, only 3% of the students said it was okay to read someone else's private diary, and only 10% said it was acceptable to read an open letter lying on someone else's desk. But when it came to materials in electronic form, 43% said it was fine to access someone else's computer files if you didn't read them, and 16% said it was okay to access and read someone else's files. Interestingly, however, no one in the sample approved of accessing and changing information in those files.

Teston (2002) found a similar pattern of results with younger adolescents. While only 10% of the students advocated taking someone else's bicycle, 52% thought it was okay to pirate software, and 65% found it all right to pirate music CDs. When the possibility of pirating digital objects via the Internet was explored, even greater latitude was observed. That is, 60% of the students said it was okay to pirate software from the Internet, and 85% found it acceptable to pirate commercial music files in MP3 format. The increased permissiveness associated with digital property was highlighted by Teston's (2002) overall finding that 88% of those who advocated software piracy were opposed to stealing a bicycle.

Thus, it seems that perceptions of digital objects and materials, as well as judgments about what constitutes appropriate behavior with respect to such materials, differ from those associated with more tangible objects. Just as was noted for computer-mediated communication, wherein the electronic medium seems to "distance" communicator from audience, digital instantiations of property (i.e., programs, music, or information) seem to "distance" users from property owners. Consequently, in both cases, a kind of increased permissiveness can arise resulting in situational behaviors (e.g., flaming, piracy) that may deviate from that which would be observed in non-technologically mediated circumstances (i.e., situations involving face-to-face communication or tangible property), wherein more accepted codes of conduct probably would be followed. An interesting question here relates to the extent to which "distance" and its possible ameliorating effects on normal inhibitions also may play a role in non-technology mediated forms of communication where sender and recipient are somewhat removed from one another (e.g., letters to the editor or a printed newspaper or magazine).

Digital World and Ethical Motivation

As intimated in the previous review, moral motivation (Component 3) can be altered in the digital arena. Whereas a bicycle connotes an "owner," software does not, and the usual rules concerning property rights do not engage. To the extent that people communicate in situations where the medium (e.g., technology) "distances" the person at the "other end" (e.g., software developer, message recipients), recognition of the need for adherence to usual norms or standards of conduct appears to be diminished. In turn, this "psychological distance" can alter the perception of consequences and harm to others, thereby increasing the motivational importance of personal interests.

So, what we have shown here, then, is that technology can influence the processing of morally relevant information by virtue of its distinctive effects on one or more of the processes that guide such behavior. Specifically, we have focused on two domains, communications and personal property, within which behavior seems to be influenced in unique ways when an electronic format is involved. In these cases, the electronic format acts as if it establishes a kind of "psychological distance" between communicators and their audiences as well as between people and property owned by others. This "distance" potentially impacts all four component processes involved in ethical action. *Ethical Sensitivity* can be reduced because the "distance" factor makes it more difficult to empathize with the audience or property owner who ultimately might be affected. *Ethical Judgment* may be altered because reduced empathy can reorder the priority of possible actions that could be taken such that what might be unethical in a different context (e.g., stealing a bike) now becomes more acceptable (e.g., pirating software). In turn, *Ethical Motivation* can change because the "distance" makes it far less obvious who is potentially harmed, thereby elevating personal goals over a concern for others, and the lack of immediate social sanction makes the cyberworld appear more like a lawless free for all. Finally, *Ethical Action* is influenced by a "no harm, no foul" mentality, which can lead to the occurrence of unethical behavior (e.g., flaming, cyber-rape, pirating, illegal downloading of MP3s, hacking into personal computer files, or plagiarizing from the work of others, etc.). Since some aspects of cyberspace, like the Internet, are in the public domain, the "problem of the commons" comes into play. Clearly, many can (and have been) hurt by the abuses of a few in the cyberworld. The recent rash of annoying or harmful computer viruses and worms are but one marked example of this abuse.

Two further points about the effects of technology on behavior should be noted here. First, we must acknowledge that technology may have many other influences on human action than those we have focused on here. We do not pretend to have offered an exhaustive look at all the possibilities in this regard. Second, not all of the consequences of technology are bad. Even in terms of the "psychological distance" factor we have identified, there are some instances in which enhanced self-disclosure or a reduced sense of evaluation anxiety mediated by a technological format may in fact be beneficial. For example, using technologically mediated communication channels, shy patients may feel more comfortable revealing important kinds of information to doctors or therapists. Similarly, students reluctant to participate in class might "open up" using electronic discussion boards or chat rooms.

Information Ethics Education

The field of information ethics is complex and multidimensional (see Johnson, 2001, for a review). We advocate, as have others (e.g., Smith, 1992), that this topic should be well represented in the curriculum of any program dealing with Information Science. At the same time, however, it is clear that IS majors/professionals are not the only people in need of information ethics education. The pervasive use of technology today by the general public, through the Internet, personal digital assistants (PDAs), and other means, strongly suggests that heightened awareness of information ethics should be engendered across the board. Although the exact ways by which this ambitious goal can be achieved are not immediately clear, the work of Friedman (1997) and Teston (2001) suggests that information ethics education should begin in the early grades.

Using the Four Component Model as a framework, we make the following suggestions for learning experiences that can enhance the development of each process within the domain of information ethics. These activities can be adapted for both pre- and post-secondary educational contexts. Due to space limitations, our treatment here is necessarily brief. For more detailed suggestions we recommend that you consult work by Narvaez and colleagues (Narvaez, in press; Narvaez, 2001; Narvaez, Bock & Endicott, 2003; Narvaez, Endicott, Bock & Lies, in press) who have parsed each component process into a set of specific skills. The learning experiences outlined below presume that a list of information ethics situations has been generated that can be used in discussions about each component, as has been done in other domains (Rest & Narvaez, 1994).

Developing Ethical Sensitivity

To increase ethical sensitivity, students should spend a lot of time practicing ethical problem solving in many contexts and with guidance from someone more expert, that is, someone who is familiar with the ethical landscape of the domain. Students also should spend time interpreting situations (e.g., determining what is happening, perceiving the moral aspects, responding creatively). For situations involving information technology, the gap between communicator and audience or user and property owner imposed by the technologically inspired "psychological distance" we have described above must be narrowed so that proper ethical sensitivity can be achieved. Here we would recommend exercises designed to enhance personal empathy skills, particularly as they relate to technology use. These exercises would focus on highlighting who is affected by personal technology use. Who is on the other end of that communication, or who really owns that resource? How would you react or what would you expect if you were in their position? Students might be encouraged to imagine the person on the other end of the communication as someone they know, as usually happens in instant messaging behavior with friends.

Developing Ethical Judgment

To increase ethical reasoning, students should discuss moral dilemmas (hypothetical and real) that will bring about cognitive conflict and challenge their thinking; they should discuss their reasoning with peers (especially peers with different viewpoints); and they should practice perspective-taking — both generally and within the technology domain — in order to learn to view the world from multiple perspectives (Lapsley, Enright, & Serlin, 1989). Ethical reasoning skills include reasoning about standards and ideals, using moral codes (e.g., discerning moral code application), understanding consequences (e.g., predicting consequences), reflecting on process and outcome (e.g., reasoning about means and ends, monitoring one's reasoning, making right choices), and learning to choose environments that support moral behavior. Exercises in this category should enhance the ability to recognize what is ethical from what is not and to reason about possible actions. Important in this effort would be creating an awareness of the relevant moral and ethical standards in question. For example, in terms of information ethics, students should be exposed to established codes of conduct like the "Ten Commandments of Computer Ethics" (Barquin, 1992). At the very least, such exposure should be accompanied by discussion of these codes in the context of an examination of what behavior is and is not consistent with them.

Developing Ethical Motivation

Ethical motivation skills include cultivating conscience (e.g., developing self-command), acting responsibly (e.g., meeting obligations, being a global citizen), valuing traditions and institutions (e.g., understanding social structures), and developing ethical identity and integrity (e.g., choosing good values, reaching for one's potential). In addition, students should be encouraged to build a self concept as an ethical person (Grusec & Redler, 1980) and learn about and be encouraged to adhere to personal, professional, and societal codes of ethics. In terms of technology use, these exercises should acquaint users with institutional "fair use" policies, which normally include statements related to the consequences of violations, and should allow for exploration of existing mandates (or laws) and consequences related to domains like privacy, intellectual property, and intellectual honesty.

Developing Ethical Action

Ethical action skills include planning to implement decisions (e.g., thinking strategically) and cultivating courage (e.g., standing up under pressure). To increase the ability to complete an ethical action, students need to develop ego strength (i.e., strength of will) and specific implementation skills. To increase ego strength, students should learn "self-talk" that allows them to encourage themselves towards a moral goal and distracts them from temptation. They should also know how to mobilize support from others for the ethical action. To increase implementation skills, students need to observe models implementing specific skills. They need to practice implementing, step-by-step, a particular ethical action in multiple contexts. For information ethics, a primary focus might be on identifying obstacles and challenges to ethical action: What tends to get in the way of doing that which is right and how can such challenges be managed? Of course, peer pressure often is a perennial challenge in this regard that should be considered at some length.

Conclusions

In this chapter, we have argued that information ethics can be informed by moral psychology: specifically, the Four Component Model of moral behavior. Moreover, we have examined some of the ways in which technology may impinge on the components of moral action through the creation of "psychological distance." Further research is needed to study such questions as how a sense of social embeddedness can be facilitated and how "psychological distance" can be reduced in the cyberworld. For example, in technology mediated communication, can "psychological distance" be reduced by incorporating visual representations of the audience through photos, video, or digital representations (i.e., avatars)?

There is no doubt that technology use will continue and even escalate with time. Therefore, it is imperative continuously to examine ways in which our understanding of technology's impact and implications for personal and societal behavior can be guided by principles derived from other fields of study. Establishing clear ties between the fields of moral psychology and information ethics is a good place to start.

References

Barger, R. (2001). Is computer ethics unique in relation to other fields of ethics? Retrieved September 9, 2003 from: *http://www.nd.edu/~rbarger/ce-unique.html*

Barquin, R.C. (1992). In pursuit of a 'ten commandments' for computer ethics. *Computer Ethics Institute.* Retrieved September 9, 2003 from: *http://www.brook.edu/dybdocroot/its/cei/papers/Barquin_Pursuit_1992.htm*

Day, S., & Schneider, P. L. (2002). Psychotherapy using distance technology: A comparison of face-to-face, video, and audio treatment. *Journal of Counseling Psychology, 49*, 499-503.

Eisenberg, N. (1992). *The caring child.* Cambridge, MA: Harvard University Press.

Friedman, B. (1997). Social judgments and technological innovation: Adolescents' understanding of property, privacy, and electronic information. *Computers in Human Behavior, 13*(3), 327-351.

Grusec, J., & Redler, E. (1980). Attribution, reinforcement, and altruism: A developmental analysis. *Developmental Psychology, 16,* 525-534.

Johnson, D. G. (2001). *Computer ethics* (3rd ed.). Upper Saddle River, NJ: Prentice Hall.

Lapsley, D. K., Enright, R. D., & Serlin, R. (1989). Moral and social education. In J. Worell & F. Danner (Eds.), *The adolescent as decision-maker: Applications to development and education* (pp. 111-143). San Diego, CA: Academic Press.

Lapsley, D., & Narvaez, D. (2004). A social-cognitive view of moral character. In D. Lapsley & D. Narvaez (Eds.), *Moral development: Self and identity*, pp. 189-212. Mahwah, NJ: Erlbaum.

Kiesler, S., Siegel, J., & McGuire, T. W. (1984). Social psychological aspects of computer-mediated communication. *American Psychologist, 39*, 1123-1134.

Kiesler, S., & Sproull, L. (1986). Response effects in the electronic survey. *Public Opinion Quarterly, 50*, 402-413.

Narvaez, D. (2001). Moral text comprehension: Implications for education and research. *Journal of Moral Education, 30*(1), 43-54.

Narvaez, D. (in press). The Neo-Kohlbergian tradition and beyond: Schemas, expertise and character. In C. Pope-Edwards & G. Carlo (Eds.), *Nebraska Symposium Conference Papers, Vol. 51.* Lincoln, NE: University of Nebraska Press.

Narvaez, D., Bock, T., & Endicott, L. (2003). Who should I become? Citizenship, goodness, human flourishing, and ethical expertise. In W. Veugelers & F. K. Oser (Eds.), *Teaching in moral and democratic education* (pp. 43-63). Bern, Switzerland: Peter Lang.

Narvaez, D., Endicott, L., Bock, T., & Lies, J. (in press). *Foundations of character in the middle school: Developing and nurturing the ethical student.* Chapel Hill, NC: Character Development Publishing.

Narvaez, D., & Rest, J. (1995). The four components of acting morally. In W. Kurtines & J. Gewirtz (Eds.), *Moral behavior and moral development: An introduction* (pp. 385-400). New York: McGraw-Hill.

Rest, J.R. (1983). Morality. In P.H. Mussen (Series Ed.), J. Flavell & E. Markman (Vol. Ed.), *Handbook of child psychology: Vol. 3, Cognitive development* (4th ed.), pp. 556-629. New York: Wiley.

Rest, J.R., & Narvaez, D. (Eds.) (1994). *Moral development in the professions: Psychology and applied ethics.* Hillsdale, NJ: Lawrence Erlbaum.

Rest, J. R., Narvaez, D., Bebeau, M., & Thoma, S. (1999). *Postconventional moral thinking: A neo-Kohlbergian approach.* Mahwah, NJ: Erlbaum.

Rogerson, S., & Bynum, T. (1995). Cyberspace: The ethical frontier. *The Times Higher Education Supplement, No 1179, 9 (June), p. iv.*

Smith, M.W. (1992). Professional ethics in the information systems classroom: Getting started. *Journal of Information Systems Education*, *4*(1), 6-11.

Sproull, L., & Kiesler, S. (1991). *Connections: New ways of working in the networked organization.* Cambridge, MA: MIT Press.

Sumner, M., & Hostetler, D. (2002). A comparative study of computer conferencing and face-to-face communications in systems design. *Journal of Interactive Learning Research*, *13*(3), 277-291.

Teston, G. (2002). A developmental perspective of computer and information technology ethics: Piracy of software and digital music by young adolescents. *Dissertation Abstracts*, *62*, 5815.

Weizenbaum, J. (1976). *Computer power and human reason.* San Francisco, CA: Freeman.

Chapter III

Designing a Moral Dilemma Support System

Kieran Mathieson
Oakland University, USA

Abstract

Information technology may be able to help people become better ethical decision makers. This chapter explores philosophical and psychological issues underlying the design of a Moral Dilemma Support System (MDSS). The effects of schemas, decision strategies, social information, and emotions on dilemma analysis are considered. MDSS features that would help people understand moral dilemmas, choose a response, and explain analyses are identified.

Introduction

Most of the chapters in this book are about the unethical use of Information Technology (IT). This chapter addresses a different issue: using IT to help people make better ethical decisions. For the purposes of this chapter, "better" does not refer to the particular action someone chooses in a situation, but to the process he or she uses to make the choice. People often disagree on what actions are morally right. However, most people would accept that someone who has thought deeply about a situation, considered who is affected, reflected on his or her own duties, and so on, will make a better choice than someone who makes a snap decision with little thought.

The chapter focuses particularly on issues underlying the design of a Moral Dilemma Support System (MDSS). An MDSS would help people structure their thinking about morally ambiguous situations. It would not tell people what they should do, but would make it easier for them to make better decisions. Just as a word processor can help authors write better stories, an MDSS's decision tools might help people make better ethical choices.

There's reason to think that systems for dilemma analysis could be worthwhile. There's considerable evidence that analyzing dilemmas improves people's moral reasoning ability (Schlaefli, Rest, & Thoma, 1985). Further, moral reasoning is an important precursor to ethical behavior (Rest, Narvaez, Bebeau, & Thoma, 1999). Finally, moral judgment is amenable to IT support.

Before building a system, it is important to know what it should do. That's what this chapter is about. Literature on ethical decision making is examined, with the goal of identifying the features an MDSS should have. The technical architecture of a system with these features is left for the future, as is testing its effectiveness.

The discussion makes some assumptions. First, MDSS users have access to appropriate technology, and possess basic literacy, technological, and abstract reasoning skills. This is not to dismiss the digital divide (Patterson & Wilson, 2000). However, it is important to investigate every approach to improving ethical reasoning, even those involving tools not available to the entire population. In fact, if IT can improve ethical choice, this is yet another argument for bridging the digital divide. Further, it is assumed that MDSS users *want* to make good decisions. If they do not, it will not matter how good the system is.

The final assumption is that competent adults have the right to make their own moral choices. This seemingly innocuous statement has important implications. People who think carefully about their lives — and this includes some IT designers — will have developed personal moral philosophies. This leads to the question: should designers promote their own ethical views when creating an MDSS? For example, I oppose radical relativism, the belief that morality is purely subjective. Should I ensure that anything I construct does not support radical relativism?

My visceral answer is "yes", but my considered answer is "no". I might explain why I think radical relativism is a bad idea, but should not prevent others from using it. Respect for people's autonomy is the most important reason for this stance, but there's another issue as well. Being intelligent, people know that information systems are built to achieve certain goals. If people think the goals offensive (e.g., they perceive attempts to manipulate their beliefs), they may not voluntarily use the system.

The discussion is limited to systems that have no hidden agenda. Not that an MDSS can be created without assumptions. For example, why build a system to help people make ethical choices if they do not have the right to do so? However, a system's assumptions should be honestly identified.

The chapter proceeds as follows. The first section explains what a moral dilemma is and gives an example used throughout the discussion. The psychological processes people use to think about dilemmas are then considered. The final section suggests how an MDSS could aid moral reasoning. As is common practice, "morality" and "ethics" are synonymous in this work.

Moral Dilemmas

Moral dilemmas involve a conflict between two ethical standards, both of which are right. An example is assisted suicide, which pits the sanctity of life against individual autonomy. Both are desirable, but only one can be chosen. Heinz's dilemma is one of the best known dilemmas in the literature:

> *In Europe, a woman was near death from cancer. One drug might save her, a form of radium that a druggist in the same town had recently discovered. The druggist was charging $2,000, 10 times what the drug had cost him to make. The sick woman's husband, Heinz, went to everyone he knew to borrow the money, but he could get together only about half of what it should cost. He told the druggist that his wife was dying and asked him to sell it cheaper or to let him pay later. But the druggist said no.*

We can add more ethical complexity, such as:

> *Heinz's wife knew she was dying. She told him she did not want*
> *him to do anything that might ruin his life, like stealing the drug*
> *or the money to pay for it.*

To qualify as a dilemma, every alternative action must violate at least one moral standard. For example, if Heinz steals the drug, property rights will be violated. If he does not steal the drug, his wife will die, violating the "sanctity of life" principle.

The contexts in which people encounter dilemmas affect the way they make decisions and, consequently, the way an MDSS might help them. Sometimes people encounter dilemmas in contexts specifically designed to raise ethical awareness, such as university business ethics courses or church-based spirituality workshops. The dilemmas used in these cases are often fictional, like Heinz's dilemma. People sometimes analyze these dilemmas individually and sometimes in groups. Often people are required to explain their analyses, in person or in writing.

People also encounter dilemmas in real life. However, in real life people often do not have time to think carefully. A soldier deciding whether to shoot a distant figure must act instantly and is under such emotional stress that rational thought is difficult. Instinct and training take over. However, military training includes instruction in ethics (Swift, 2001). It is in these classes that an MDSS might help soldiers hone their moral instincts.

Making Ethical Decisions

This section considers how people analyze moral dilemmas. These processes are not qualitatively different from those used in other domains (Narvaez, 2002). The same mechanisms operate, and the same constraints apply. This review is selective, of course. It focuses on important processes that an MDSS could support.

Schemas

A schema is a mental template for an object, idea, or process (Narvaez, 2002). For example, a marriage schema might include the elements "spouses," "love," and "fidelity." The schema's "slots" are instantiated for a particular situation. For example, "spouses" might be instantiated as "Ann and Kieran" when describing a specific marriage.

Schemas influence cognitive processes in various ways. First, schemas help people infer a situation's details from a few pieces of information. Suppose you read that "Harry punched Ellen." You might invoke a wife-beating schema, with all of its attendant consequences. However, if you learned that Harry and Ellen are boxers, you would use a different schema, inferring different things about the situation.

Schemas are implicated in social pathologies (Kunda, 1999). For example, the behaviors of someone with the schema "black men are thieves" might range from putting his hand on his wallet when a black man walks by, to denying black men housing, credit, and jobs. These behaviors need not be conscious. In fact, people are unaware of most of their mental activity (Narvaez, 2002).

The second way schemas affect cognitive processes is by setting goals. Suppose you see a robbery in progress. Your schemas for yourself might prompt you to call the police. This becomes a subgoal. Calling the police means finding a telephone. This is another subgoal, and so on. Schemas for sets of actions are sometimes called scripts (Narvaez, 2002).

Third, schemas affect people's judgments of the diagnosticity of information, that is, how relevant the information is in describing a situation. For instance, where Heinz lives (Europe, Africa, North America, etc.) does not change his dilemma from a moral perspective. That Heinz's wife does not want him to risk his future *is* important to decision makers who value autonomy.

Schemas are accumulated and elaborated throughout life. Task expertise is largely dependent on schemas. Experts have more and richer schemas than novices, use them more flexibly, and recall them more quickly (Narvaez, 2002).

In applying schema theory to dilemma processing, we find that many ethical schemas have been described. Some are analytical, derived largely from prescriptive moral theories. Western thought typically focuses on three types of moral philosophies: teleological, deontological, and virtue-based. Teleological theories like Mill's utilitarianism concentrate on outcomes. For example, if Heinz steals the drug, who gains and who loses, and by how much? Deontological theories, of which Kant is perhaps the best-known proponent, are concerned with duties and rights. What are Heinz's duties as a husband? As a citizen? Virtue ethics focuses on people's character. For example, Aristotle listed courage, wisdom, and compassion as attributes of a good person. If Heinz were courageous, what would he do? What action would be most wise? What would be compassionate?

In contrast to these prescriptive theories, there are descriptive, empirically derived theories that also identify schemas. Rest et al. (1999) list three schemas, derived in part from Kohlberg's (1976) work. The "personal interests" schema says, "A fair world is one in which people get what they want" (Narvaez, 2002). The "maintaining norms" schema says one should follow established rules set by legitimate authorities. The "postconventional" schema emphasizes moral ideals, like justice and compassion. Kidder (1995) identifies four schemas he believes underlie many dilemmas: truth vs. loyalty, individual vs. community, short-term vs. long-term, and justice vs. mercy.

Moral schemas help describe a dilemma's structure. Some writers also offer scripts for dilemma analysis, that is, schemas for the process of thinking about dilemmas. Figure 1 shows an example (Kidder, 1995). See Maner (2002) for a review.

Figure 1. Dilemma script

1. Recognize that there is a moral issue

2. Whose issue is it?

3. Gather the relevant facts

4. Test for right vs. wrong issues

5. Test for right vs. right issues

6. Apply the resolution principles

7. Study trilemma options

8. Make decision

9. Revisit and reflect

Decision Strategies

People manage to analyze complex moral dilemmas, despite having limited cognitive resources, like short-term memories and attention. How do we do it? First, we divide complex problems into smaller subproblems. This hierarchical structuring lets us focus attention on parts of the problem, one at a time.

Second, most knowledge is tacit and is used without conscious attention (Narvaez, 2002). For example, literate adults can answer the question "What is two times five?" with little effort. Cognitions performed without conscious effort are said to be automatic (Kunda, 1999).

Third, we reduce the amount of information we consider. We sometimes use satisficing to find a "good enough" answer from a large choice set (Byron, 1998). We often search for confirming evidence to decide whether a statement is true (Kunda, 1999). For instance, to decide whether more people die from murder or suicide, we simply might choose the one for which we recall more cases.

These methods introduce errors, of course. Someone might use a rule like "theists are more moral than atheists" automatically in every situation, even though a little thought would suggest it may not always be accurate. Satisficing leads us to choose the first option we encounter that meets minimal criteria, rather than the optimal alternative. Searching for confirming evidence is often less effective than searching for disconfirming evidence (Kunda, 1999). For instance, while murders in the US receive more attention from the press, suicides are more common, with about one and a half to two suicides for every murder over the last decade (US Census Bureau, 2002).

Social Information

Social information also affects dilemma analysis. Nucci (2001) differentiates between social conventions and moral values. Conventions are somewhat arbitrary standards that vary from culture to culture, like forms of address for men and women. On the other hand, moral values like "do not harm others" are relatively invariant across cultures. Piaget (1965) wrote that children learn values mostly from interaction with peers. For instance, they learn that equal sharing can avoid some disputes. Respected authority figures can be influential as well (Lind, 2002).

Social interaction also offers feedback on goal attainment. For example, social information is a primary source of feedback for those who crave social dominance. Other people being deferential suggests that social dominance has been achieved. People are also a source of knowledge about the world. If you have a question (e.g., is homosexuality "catching"?), there are people ready with an answer.

Social information can be misleading, of course. The social conventions of one culture can be misinterpreted in another. Someone with a hidden agenda might say that homosexuality spreads like influenza, even if empirical evidence suggests otherwise. People also engage in impression management, conveying a social image that helps achieve their goals (Frink & Ferris, 1998).

Social interaction is not all face-to-face. People also communicate via letters, telephones, e-mail, and so on. Virtual interaction may not be as emotionally rich as personal interaction, but some people develop meaningful relationships with individuals they have never met (Turkle, 1995).

Emotion

Emotions also influence dilemma analysis. Important moral emotions include guilt, shame, and empathy (Eisenberg, 2000), disgust (Haidt, Rozin, McCauley, & Imada, 1997), and elevation (Haidt, 2000).

Sometimes cognition serves emotion (LeDoux, 1996). For example, someone yearning for social dominance might create an elaborate plan to satisfy the desire. Developing and executing the plan will require significant cognitive effort. The individual might be willing to harm others and violate his or her duties to achieve social dominance, without even noticing the emotional motivation. Developing emotional awareness can be difficult, but, without self-examination, the roots of one's actions can remain obscure.

Finally, emotions sometimes cloud people's judgment. Emotional arousal can overwhelm cognitive processing (Derryberry & Tucker, 1992). Further, LeDoux (1996) suggests that much of the information in our memories has somatic markers, providing quick "good/bad" evaluations of objects and actions. They are the "gut feelings" that guide so much behavior. Some people rely on gut feelings in even the most complicated situations, despite there being little reason to think they are veridical.

MDSS Features

The previous section considered how schemas, decision strategies, social information, and emotions influence dilemma processing. This section suggests how an MDSS might support dilemma analysis, while helping decision makers (DMs) address the cognitive and emotional issues described above. For the purposes of discussion, dilemma analysis is divided into three subtasks: understanding the dilemma, choosing a response, and explaining the choice. The tasks are interdependent, of course, and DMs move freely between them.

Understand the Dilemma

In a practical sense, to "understand" a dilemma means to identify or infer information that helps DMs decide what to do. An MDSS could offer various types of assistance. First, it could offer scripts DMs could use to understand a dilemma (Kidder, 1995). Recall that a script is a schema for a process (Figure 1). The MDSS could explain how to use the scripts, and offer samples of completed scripts. The system could create document templates based on these scripts, making it less likely that DMs will forget important issues.

Second, the MDSS could offer DMs schemas they could use to understand conflicts. The system could also help DMs instantiate them. Figure 2 shows a deontological schema instantiated for Heinz's dilemma. Figure 3 shows a teleological description of a hit-and-run traffic accident (this is not a dilemma, since there is no "good versus good," but the idea of a teleological description applies).

Third, the system could show DMs how other people analyzed the same dilemma. It could store the description in Figure 2, for example, for other DMs to examine. Not only could DMs learn from other people's solutions, they could also offer feedback to each other. A threaded discussion board for each dilemma would be one way to implement this.

Fourth, the MDSS could help DMs learn schemas and scripts. For instance, it could describe Kidder's (1995) schemas, then offer a short quiz the DM could use to test his or her knowledge. The system could also offer to repeat the quiz in the future, to make sure the schemas are not forgotten.

Fifth, the MDSS could raise questions about the schemas the DM is using. For example, many people might use a "Scrooge" schema to describe the druggist

Figure 2. Describing a conflict in duties

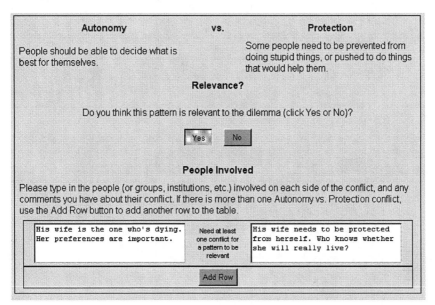

in Heinz's dilemma, thinking him a heartless man only interested in wealth. The dilemma's text does not say that, however. Could there be other reasons the druggist refused Heinz? Perhaps there is not enough of the drug to go around, and the druggist has already promised all he can produce to other people.

Sixth, the MDSS could help DMs find relevant documents on ethics and other subjects. The system could ask DMs to rate documents on criteria like usefulness and readability to help others find the best material. The MDSS might offer summaries of long works, like Aristotle's *Nichomachean Ethics*. Recall, however, that DMs schemas affect the information they consider important. Someone reading Aristotle's work from a virtues perspective might remember different things from someone reading it from a utilitarian standpoint. The MDSS might store more than one summary of the same document, created by people with different points of view.

Seventh, the MDSS could highlight similarities and differences between dilemmas, particularly as summarized by experienced DMs. This would help DMs identify diagnostic elements of dilemmas, that is, information that is particularly important in choosing a response.

Eighth, the MDSS could help DMs become more aware of their emotional reactions to a dilemma. The system could, for example, prompt DMs to

Figure 3. Describing outcomes

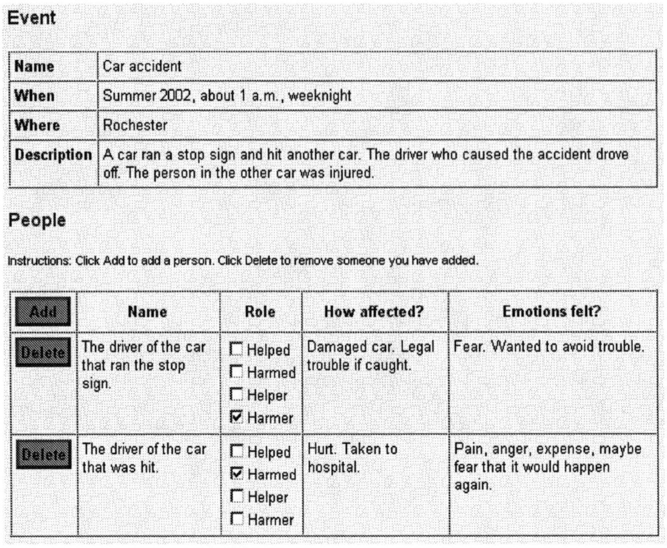

Event

Name	Car accident
When	Summer 2002, about 1 a.m., weeknight
Where	Rochester
Description	A car ran a stop sign and hit another car. The driver who caused the accident drove off. The person in the other car was injured.

People

Instructions: Click Add to add a person. Click Delete to remove someone you have added.

Add	Name	Role	How affected?	Emotions felt?
Delete	The driver of the car that ran the stop sign.	☐ Helped ☐ Harmed ☐ Helper ☑ Harmer	Damaged car. Legal trouble if caught.	Fear. Wanted to avoid trouble.
Delete	The driver of the car that was hit.	☐ Helped ☑ Harmed ☐ Helper ☐ Harmer	Hurt. Taken to hospital.	Pain, anger, expense, maybe fear that it would happen again.

describe their emotions, and think about the effects emotions have on their decisions. Were they angry at the druggist in Heinz's dilemma? Did they want to punish him? Did they pity Heinz's wife? Would their emotions change if they learned that her cancer was caused by smoking, a behavior with well-known risks?

Choose a Response

Once the DM understands the dilemma, he or she must choose a response. DMs are sometimes given specific responses to evaluate (e.g., should Heinz steal the drug?). Sometimes they are free to recommend other solutions (e.g., perhaps Heinz can promise to work for the druggist part-time to pay for the drug). In the latter case, an MDSS could identify responses the DM might not have considered, perhaps by aggregating options other DMs have thought about.

Second, the MDSS could help the DM describe and evaluate the possible consequences of each response. If Heinz steals the drug, he might get caught, or he might not. The MDSS could gather arguments from different DMs on the likelihood of each consequence. One DM might say that burglars are usually not caught if they are careful. Another could point out that Heinz is known to have a motive, and would attract police attention. The system could also offer more objective information on, say, FBI estimates of the probability that a first-time burglar will be caught.

Eventually the DM has to make a choice. The MDSS could help the DM review his or her work, perhaps identifying missing information, and summarizing the analysis in an easy-to-read report. The system could help the DM rank potential actions. Once a choice has been made, the system could help the DM record the reasons for the choice, and perhaps show what other DMs chose.

The MDSS could help the DM avoid processing errors. It could reduce satisficing by asking the DM to make comments about each potential action, rather than simply choosing the first one that is minimally satisfactory. This might also reduce unwarranted automaticity, since DMs would be explicit about the reasons they accepted or rejected each option. Having the DM record and analyze each potential action also adds hierarchical structure to the problem. When evaluating a particular action, the DM can concentrate on that option, assured that the MDSS is saving his or her previous work.

Explain the Analysis

Sometimes DMs must explain their analyses to others, like peers, managers, or graders. The MDSS could offer templates for reporting an analysis to others, perhaps as a Web page, a presentation (PowerPoint, Impress), or some other format. The system could include features like spell checking. As DMs analyze dilemmas, the MDSS could remind them to think about how they would explain their thoughts to others, encouraging them to be careful and explicit in their analyses.

Conclusions

Computers may be able to help people become more effective moral decision makers. This chapter considers the features a Moral Dilemma Support System (MDSS) might have. An MDSS cannot help people *want* to be moral, but it can help them work out *how* to be moral.

This chapter focuses on an artifact, the MDSS. Ultimately, however, systems must conform to the environments in which they are used. For instance, a system might be designed to support ethical discussions inside a company. That context adds constraints, like anonymity and confidentiality. To be useful, an MDSS must comply with the social, operational, financial, and other constraints present in its environment.

Supporting dilemma analysis does not exhaust the potential of IT in the ethical domain. People's moral perspectives reflect their personal histories, their loves and hates, disappointments and triumphs, chance meetings, and systematic thought. Computer technology can help people integrate their ideas to explore life's larger questions. It can help them examine their values, map their life histories, and interact with people who have similar concerns.

Using computers to help people fully realize their humanity almost seems oxymoronic. Yet it does appear to be feasible. It is an exciting thought that system designers could make such a contribution to human flourishing.

References

Byron, M. (1998). Satisficing and optimality. *Ethics, 109,* 67-93.

Derryberry, D., & Tucker, D. (1992). Neural mechanisms of emotion. *Journal of Consulting and Clinical Psychology, 60,* 329-337.

Eisenberg, N. (2000). Emotion, regulation, and moral development. *Annual Review of Psychology, 51,* 665-697.

Frink, D., & Ferris, G. (1998). Accountability, impression management, and goal setting in the performance evaluation process. *Human Relations, 51,* 1259-1283.

Haidt, J. (2000, March 7). The positive emotion of elevation. *Prevention and Treatment [online],* 3(7). Retrieved from: *http://journals.apa.org/prevention/volume3/pre0030003c.html*

Haidt, J., Rozin, P., McCauley, C., & Imada, S. (1997). Body, psyche, and culture: The relationship of disgust to morality. *Psychology and Developing Societies,* 9, 107-131.

Kidder, R. (1995). *How good people make tough choices.* New York: William Morrow and Company.

Kohlberg, L. (1976). Moral stages and moralization: The cognitive-developmental approach. In T. Lickona (Ed.), *Moral Development and Behavior: Theory, Research and Social Issues* (pp. 31-53). New York: Holt, Rinehart and Winston.

Kunda, Z. (1999). *Social cognition.* Cambridge, MA: MIS Press.

LeDoux, J.E. (1996). *The emotional brain.* New York: Simon and Schuster.

Lind, G. (2002). *Moral dilemma discussion - The Konstanz method.* Presented at the meeting of the Association for Moral Education, Chicago, November 7-10, 2002. Retrieved from: *http://www.uni-konstanz.de/ag-moral/pdf/Lind-2003_Konstanz-Method_Colombia.pdf*

Maner, W. (2002). Heuristic methods for computer ethics. *Metaphilosophy, 33*, 339-365.

Narvaez, D. (2002). Incorporating cognitive science into moral psychology. Working paper. Retrieved from: *http://www.nd.edu/~alfac/narvaez/Cognitive%20Sciencehandout.pdf*

Nucci, L. P. (2001). *Education in the moral domain.* Cambridge, UK: Cambridge University Press.

Patterson, R. & Wilson, E. J. (2000). New IT and social inequality: Resetting the research and policy agenda. *Information Society, 16*, 77-86.

Piaget, J. (1965). *The moral judgment of the child.* New York: The Free Press. (Original work published 1932).

Rest, J. R., Narvaez, D., Bebeau, M., & Thoma, S. (1999). *Postconventional moral thinking: A neo-Kohlbergian approach.* Mahwah, NJ: Erlbaum.

Schlaefli, A., Rest, J., & Thoma S. (1985). Does moral education improve moral judgment? A meta-analysis of intervention studies using the Defining Issues Test. *Review of Educational Research, 55*, 319-20.

Swift, J. (2001). The teaching of morality in warfighting in today's officer corps. Maxwell Air Force Base: US Air Command and Staff College. Retrieved from: *http://handle.dtic.mil/100.2/ADA407876*

Turkle, S. (1995). *Life on the screen.* New York: Touchstone.

US Census Bureau (2002). Statistical Abstracts of the United States. Retrieved from: *http://www.census.gov/prod/www/statistical-abstract-02.html*

SECTION II:

INTELLECTUAL
PROPERTY RIGHTS

Chapter IV

Intellectual Property Rights – or Rights to the Immaterial – in Digitally Distributable Media Gone All Wrong

Kai Kristian Kimppa
University of Turku, Finland

Abstract

In the light of three major ethical theories, Lockean liberalism, consequentialism, and Kantian deontology, it seems that the intellectual property rights in digitally distributable media — be it software or other — have not been derived correctly. The three theories and their implications are reviewed and handled individually and conclusions based on each will be presented. Many aspects of these theories do not match with the current copyright and patent laws affecting digitally distributable media in western societies. A different, less restricting approach is offered.

Introduction

In today's globalized world of enhanced information and communication technology (ICT), the rights to the immaterial — generally understood as Intellectual Property Rights (IPRs) — are a central issue. The common usage of the term "intellectual property rights" already implies that the immaterial can be owned. Contrary to many expectations during the earlier decades of ICT, copyright is extending and thus limiting dissemination of information and knowledge into our societies. Laws such as the US Digital Millennium Copyright Act (DMCA) of 1998 and its European counterpart the European Copyright Directive of 2001, are limiting access to information further. Similar restrictions can be seen in the trend in the United States towards the patenting of software features — a trend that is expected to be taken up in Europe in the not too far distant future.

Considering the enlarging of markets, the growing speed of dissemination of the marketed items — especially in the digital form — it is somewhat surprising that the protection of the immaterial should need to be strengthened, particularly with regard to the time extension now in place. Instead, one might surmise that the benefits of the growing markets and speed of dissemination would make the time needed for a limited monopoly to gain back its investment shorter rather than longer. After all, the idea of IPRs is not to grant an effective monopoly to the item but to ensure the bringing forth of new inventions and fine arts and to ensure their dissemination to the general public. After the investment (with some decent profit, maybe) has been regained, the idea surely is not to limit the functioning of the markets. Considering the strength and length of current IPR law in most western nations (and increasingly in other nations), it seems that most patent and copyright-protected digitally distributable media (DDM) is covered by IPR protection longer than its expected lifetime.

The main purpose of this chapter is to critically analyze the benefits individuals and societies actually gain from intellectual property rights in digitally distributable media, be it software, journal articles, children's books, etc. An alternative solution to the current regime is also offered.

The chapter will look into liberalist (mainly Lockean), consequentialist (or utilitarian), and deontological (mainly Kantian) arguments pro but especially con intellectual property rights. It will analyze what benefits and drawbacks intellectual property rights can offer from the selected perspectives. The traditional positions for IPRs are not introduced comprehensively, but rather only named. It is presumed that the reader is at least somewhat familiar with the current justifications for IPRs, since they are presented quite often, even in the mainstream media. The reason for choosing these particular ethical theories is their undeniable influence reflected in the social foundations and laws of our societies in the Western world. Liberalist and consequentialist arguments have especially been used in the Anglo-American traditions and are clearly visible in the laws in Great Britain and the constitution of the US. On the European continent, deontological theories have had great influence and are thus of importance to the topic at hand.

Each of the previous views will be discussed separately and then, based on the discussions, some conclusions will be drawn. In addition, some differing views, such as Free and Open Source Software (F/OSS) will be introduced and handled as alternatives to current proprietary views on digitally distributable media. No conclusions regarding which view is "the best" will be presented; the intention is rather to stimulate critical reflection on the part of the reader.

The theoretical contribution of the chapter is to analyze the field of IPRs at a more theoretical level based on sound ethical theories rather than the bottom-up approach rising from the field and applications, which seems to be the norm in most (although arguably not all) information technology ethics today.

Contributions to practice are two-fold. First, the issues in IPRs related to ethical theories are presented for the specialists in the areas involved. This will benefit people in information science, information ethics and law, and the layperson, be they representatives of government agencies or interested citizens or even business executives (after all, F/OSS software has proven to be also a marketable good). Secondly, it is proposed that the current trend of expanding the protections of digital media and software is not necessarily preferable for the individual or society at large. Rather, a weaker or shorter — and in some cases no — protection scheme might be more viable.

History and Ethical Positions to IPRs in DDM

In this chapter, I will consider what has happened so far in the field of IPRs in general and IPRs in DDM in particular. I will also consider the philosophical justifications behind the story.

Ever since the introduction of IPRs, they have gradually become legally stronger. Copyright — the right of the person who ordered the artwork — in Genoa was originally held by force of the purchaser of the work of art. The US, for example, did not grant copyright to foreigners until 1891 (Alford, 1995), that is, as long as the US was a net benefactor of material copyrighted elsewhere. In Britain, the original patent was aimed at bringing into the country new practical inventions to be utilized during the industrialization of the country. Not just any so-called inventions could get protection, only those that benefited the growing industry. The protection times were also relatively shorter than they are today (not necessarily in years), due to the longer usability of inventions in general (and of course if compared to DDM, in particular). The protection was also regional not global as it now most often is. If, as seems to be the case, the original forms of IPRs were based on national needs rather than the rights of the authors, creators, or innovators, the rationalizations later proposed for IPRs are at least *prima facie* suspect.

Lockean Liberalist Position to IPRs Revisited

Of the Immaterial

Locke's Second Treatise on Government (TTG II, 1690) is often cited when considering individual rights to property. How IPRs can be derived from it has been widely discussed (see e.g., Kramer, 1997; Long, 1995; Simmons, 1992), but whether IPRs can be derived from it at all seems to have been mostly ignored. The right to property in Locke stems from the need to preserve oneself. To ensure this, one must be able to appropriate things for one's benefit. According to Locke, everyone has property in themselves, in that they have the right to "life, liberty, and estate". The method to appropriate things for oneself is to mix labor in them. When one mixes one's labor in what one works with, one does not lose one's work, but rather gains what is worked upon (Kimppa, 2003a; Locke, 1690).

In liberalist discourse, the value of work is considered to be the factor that gives one a right to ownership of what one has worked upon (see e.g., Kinsella, 2001; Kramer, 1997; Simmons, 1992). It has been seen that the labour gives the laborer a right to any and all things worked upon, whether they are material or immaterial. The reasoning for this is that we need ownership of the results of the labour, because there is only a limited amount of material to be owned. The items owned cannot be shared by (very) many at the same time. Thus, labour gives one rights to (material) property (Kimppa, 2003a).

The immaterial does not suffer from this restriction. It can be owned by as many as have a need or want to own it at the same time. The immaterial can be traded, given, or sold to another without any less being left to one. One can discover, invent, or create the exact same thing as others without lessening them of their ownership. Therefore, we do not seem to need ownership of the immaterial for the same reasons as for the material, that is, because it can not be shared by many at once. If this is accepted, it follows that owning the immaterial because of scarcity becomes difficult to justify (Kimppa, 2003a).

If someone uses a method, say picking of acorns or apples (Locke, 1690), to acquire something for oneself, the results (i.e., acorns or apples) of using that method (i.e., work) become that person's. This, however, says nothing about the method becoming owned by the one who uses it. In all of Locke's examples of how the unowned becomes owned, he seems to take for granted that the method can be used by others in addition to the first user at their will. Thus the use of a method is not what should be considered one's work. It is not "ownable" since using the method does not detract from another's possibility to use the same method. If the other would take the method away from the first, it would limit the rights of the first, but this is not the case with the immaterial. Thus, it can be argued that instead of the limited immaterial commons (like the limited material commons), Locke presumed an unlimited immaterial commons from which one could draw new ideas and methods as one pleases (Kimppa, 2003a).

The immaterial commons can be seen as unlimited in two different ways. It can be seen, as has traditionally been interpreted, as satisfying Locke's proviso that "as much and as good" is left in any case, since the immaterial undoubtedly is infinite. This interpretation suffers from a fault, however. "As much" is necessarily left, when talking about an infinite amount of things, be they material or immaterial. "As good" does not satisfy as easily, however (for similar argument, see e.g., Friedman, 2000). Since no one would be directly worse off by not granting rights to the immaterial, such rights should not be given, for it would mean that by not using the immaterial it would, in a Lockean sense, spoil and not benefit others. If one does not share what is shareable and what one cannot use oneself, one is to blame for leaving it to spoil. For some problems, only some solutions are as good as others. When one solution is reserved for one party through IPRs, less good options only may be left for others to use. But if we return to why ownership is needed, we note that it is needed to protect property when ownership is limited naturally. This is not the case with the immaterial. Instead in granting ownership to the immaterial, we artificially deprive others from what they could own at the same time as the first. This affects how much equally good is left, and thus does not satisfy the Lockean proviso of as much and as good being left to others. In the material realm, this is unfortunately necessary, but it is not necessary in the immaterial (Kimppa, 2003a). This can be clarified through an example. Let us consider one-click shopping through World Wide Web (WWW) pages. There really is only one way to do one-click shopping, and if it has been patented, others could not use it. If there only is one IPR (patent, in this case) for one-click shopping, all others must use "less good" methods to incorporate their WWW shopping systems. This then would not meet the requirement "as much and as good" being left to others.

Of Joining Societies

The reason for people to join societies (or commonwealths, as Locke uses in TTG II) is to better their condition compared to the natural state. If the legislative does not further this end, it must, according to Locke, be changed. Any laws passed by the legislative of the society must further the ends of the members of said society. If they do not, they are not just laws. It would be absurd, if people were to join societies to worsen their conditions in comparison to their state in the state of nature. It follows, then, that should it be the case that if IPRs do not enhance the conditions of the members of the society, they ought to be reconsidered (Kimppa, 2003b).

According to Locke (1690) one cannot transfer to another — be it a person or a collective of persons, such as a society in large — more power than one has over oneself. Since one is composed of ones own "life, liberty, and estate" (TTG II), over which one does not have arbitrary power, one cannot transfer that power to others. Thus, the legislative of a society cannot pass a law that would contradict one's ownership to what one possesses. IPRs give arbitrary power over one's possessions to an outside party, the IPR holder. If it could be clearly shown that IPRs better the condition of those joining in the society, they could be justified. This, however, does not seem to be the case (Kimppa, 2003b).

The case of programs today is very different from that of books a hundred years ago. The fact that the easiest way to copy a program is from one neighbor to another, the fact that a program has both source code and object code which are distinct, and the fact that a program is used rather than read and enjoyed, combine to create a situation in which a person who enforces a copyright is harming society as a whole both materially and spiritually; in which a person should not do so regardless of whether the law enables him to. (Free Software Foundation, 1993)

Thus, IPRs as transferable rights ought to be reconsidered. It seems, as is shown in the next chapter, that at least many of the claims on how IPRs better the condition of those joining in the society are theoretically weak, ad hoc rationalizations, false, or a combination of the previous.

Consequentialist Position to IPRs Revisited

From the previous discussion, we have seen that it is not necessary for a liberalist theory to presume ownership of the immaterial, although this has been widely presumed in the liberalist tradition (for a contradictory view, see, for example, Spinello, 2003). Were we to accept that, however, some consequentialist concerns are raised. What kind of consequences would a system with no ownership of the immaterial produce? Would we be left without most, if not all, software, were IPRs in DDM abolished?

Utility has been defined as happiness (for example, Johnson, 2001) or, more recently, in greater and greater amount as money or profit. This does not seem to do justice to consequentialism or utilitarianism. Traditionally, consequentialism and utilitarianism have aimed to produce "as much good as possible for as many as possible." The "as much good as possible" seems to have been misunderstood and the "to as many as possible" seems to have been forgotten or has been claimed to be irrelevant (for example, Feldman, 1992) (Kimppa, 2004).

The "as much good as possible" seems to be understood in a way that maximizes the quantitative but at the same time ignores the qualitative. This is due to the qualitative being difficult to measure in money and profit (for example, Svatos, 1996). The more innovations we get, the better, seems to be the argument irrespective of whether the innovations are as good as possible. The current IPR system encourages protection early and often, whether the innovation itself has any value or not; at least it can be used to stop others from following that path or to force them to pay royalties for doing so. This produces innovations that can be marketed, not necessarily innovations that are needed or wanted by the public. If we were to abolish IPR protections, the innovations would spring from a source from which people best come up with ideas, that is their own needs — be that need for themselves, their close ones, society, or even – for some hopelessly ideological people — mankind as whole. This kind of innovation is hardly promoted by the current system, however. The reason for this is that the IPRs granted effectively reduce the possibility to innovate based on them — unless the innovator is in a position to acquire licenses to the current innovations (for example, Spinello, 1995). The basis of consequentialism and utilitarianism is to produce "as much good for as many as possible," not "as much quantitatively, or easily countable, good for as many as possible" (Kimppa, 2004).

The "to as many as possible" seems also to have been forgotten. The aim is to get as much good as possible, irrespective of what the distribution of it is. Feldman (1992) has presented a reasoning why the "to as many as possible" should not be taken into account. According to him, taking it to account would introduce several variables that would not be dependent on one another. This would cause it to be difficult to measure the utility. This justification seems ill justified. Only the total amount of innovations would be counted, even if they mostly fall in the hands of select corporations and distribution organizations and thus would not benefit the society at large. This seems to be the case within countries as well as between them (Kimppa, 2004).

In connection to the "as many as possible," one of the main claims has been that if we have IPRs in place, the innovations will end up at everyone's use eventually (when the 'limited' monopoly ends, if not sooner). It is widely acknowledged that the trickle down is slow. In human scale, innovations such as medicines might trickle down too slowly. Say, AIDS medicine that could be produced cheaply but is expensive due to patents might (and often does) trickle down to those who would most benefit from it when it is already too late (i.e., the beneficiaries are dead) (see, for example, Himanen, 2002). This effect is in another way also present in DDM, and especially software. Since software has IPR protection, claimed to be limited, it cannot be further developed or distributed without the consent of the rights holder even though it is not rivalrous. Taking into consideration the time software is actually usable or practically can be developed further, this means that most software will be considered unusable and unable to be further developed by the time their IPRs end (for example, Drahos, 1996; Wreen, 1998). I have yet to find a developer or a programmer who would want to continue development for actual use (and not just for the fun of it) a program that would be over 70, or even only over 20, years old — which in the case of proprietary software is the earliest possible timeframe if open source or free source software licenses are not issued to the software at some point. During the time it takes for software to fall out of IPR protection, the societies with high IPR amounts can distance themselves further from those having low amounts of IPRs. On top of this, the population of those societies with few IPRs will have grown (if population growth predictions hold), thus ending up in a situation in which the number of those with less access to public domain IPRs has actually grown and not lessened (Kimppa, 2004).

As pointed out by Grove (2003), even learning from the current IPR-protected proprietary software is difficult. The current protections, which cannot be bypassed even for research, fault search, or security issue purposes, limit the possibility to access the software (Pike, 2004). One of the main problems with this is that the parties willing to crack through the protections will do so regardless of IPR protections. Meanwhile, the user is left at the mercy of the IPR holder as to whether software upgrades to patch security holes are produced or not and whether they hold against hostile attacks or not. This problem is not dependent on the IPR holder with F/OSS (for example, Kimppa, 2004). Another of the main problems is that further research based on the created is stifled even more than just by the normal (limited) monopoly granted by the IPRs.

Even if IPRs would create a net benefit locally in one country, they still might globally cause net losses (Drahos, 1996). Access to information is crucial if we want to equalize the world's living conditions. Access to basic information is not enough; access to applied information must also be available, lest the weaker never catch up with the stronger. Application advances need to be understood and the possibility to further develop them needs to be available, else the gap between the rich and the poor countries can never be bridged, and the relative, and likely also the actual distance will continue to grow rather than abate (Kimppa, 2004).

At least the consequentialist justifications for the need of IPRs handled seem to be lacking. If this is the case, the burden of proof that the justifications offered actually benefit the society, and societies should fall to those claiming the need for strong IPRs, not to those claiming that no IPRs should be granted. This is especially true if, as has been pointed out in the previous chapter, IPRs cut into the natural rights of the people.

Kantian Deontological Position to IPRs Revisited

The familiar Kantian categorical imperative has been presented in many forms. Kant himself considered at least two different forms of it (CI1 and CI2 henceforth) to be different formulations of the same issue. CI2 states "an act is morally right if and only if the agent, in performing it, refrains from treating any person merely as a means." CI1 states that "an act is morally right if and only if the agent of the act can consistently will that the generalized form of the maxim of the act be a law of nature" (Feldman, 1992). These formulations of the categorical imperative have been used to justify the creator's rights to the immaterial. The form the justifications have taken can be presented in a following manner: "since the creator of immaterial is an end in themselves, they ought to be revered for what they are and thus granted rights to the immaterial they have created" and "the (limited) monopoly rights to the immaterial are justified because everyone is treated the same in respect to their creations" (Drahos, 1996). Both of these justifications sound justified *prima facie*. However, neither stands too well to closer examination.

Unfortunately for the creators of the immaterial, CI2 applies also to them (Drahos, 1996). They ought not to consider the buying public as only a means to an end (be that end recognition or profit). The public, of course, has responsibilities towards the creators of the immaterial, for the creator too is to be considered an end to him/herself, but whether such consideration demands (limited) monopoly to the creations of the creator is not clearly evident, especially since it strikes into the rights of the public. Recognition, however, is clearly required of the public to not treat the creator of the immaterial as merely a means to an end.

CI1 fares no better under closer scrutiny. The formulation offered to justify the (limited) monopolies of the creators of the immaterial suffers from the fault that it is misrepresented. Rather, it ought to be: "anyone who creates immaterial may shut others from it for a (limited) period as they wish." Unfortunately, this fails to take into account CI2, as presented in the previous paragraph. It treats others as means and not as ends in themselves. That is clearly not agreeable in Kantian terms.

Conclusions Based on the Theories Handled

The liberalist position can be understood in various ways, not only the way it has been understood so far. It seems that the reason for property has been forgotten along the way to property in the immaterial. Also, the current consequentialist view seems to suffer from problems, mainly from the lack of ways to understand what "as much good to as many as possible" actually means. Finally, also the deontological position seems to have been misunderstood in the favor of a few instead of in the favor of all — which in itself fails to satisfy the requirements of categorical imperatives, no matter how they are formulated.

In spite of this, it seems that the intellectual property rights in the western societies — and largely elsewhere as well — are gaining in strength rather than lessening, which, it could be argued is what is needed (Kimppa, 2004). Limited monopolies in software and DDM seem to have become unlimited, if not de jure then at least de facto. The expectations of easier and wider dissemination of knowledge through DDM in general and Internet in particular do not seem to be satisfied, not because the technology would not make it possible, but because laws that hinder it are put in place.

The problems seem similar within societies. There is no need to own the immaterial — due to it being unrivalrous (Moore, 1998). The right to command other people's possessions is falsely deducted from the liberal tradition. The limited monopolies — created for the benefit of the public or for a misunderstood sense of ownership in something that needs none — have de facto turned into unlimited monopolies in DDM and software. The digital distribution forms currently used are antiquated before the IPRs in them expire. The software now created is unusable and is not worth developing by the time the IPRs in it expire (compare, for example, the operating systems (OSs) made for some of the first personal computers, IBM PC 8086 in 1981 and Apple MacIntosh in 1984 — the IPRs in the OSs have yet to expire, yet no one in their right mind would think of these OSs as software for further development now). A lot of small steps might, in the end, be better than a few large leaps decided by the corporations. Although the requirement for respect for the creators of applications is unquestionable, so is the respect for and rights of the users. Different factions within and between societies share different ethical values and social conditions. These ought to be taken into account when deciding a form of protection for the immaterial. Exceptions far surpassing the current ones should be introduced instead of further limiting the ones already in place. The right to copy to a friend should be widened instead of stifled to satisfy the need and moral obligations of the people of the society (Birsch, 2003).

Where Are We Going and Where Should We Be Going?

IPRs are closing the public domain ever further, both within societies and between them. The legal measures put in place — such as DMCA and its European counterpart, the lengthening and strengthening of copyright, the extending of patent law to cover things within the sphere of software — try to see to it that the further development and sharing of software and DDM becomes as difficult as possible. These draconian measures, along with persecution by organizations such as Recording Industry Association of America (RIAA), aim to stifle any copying and further development of software and DDM. For now, it seems that the future of the public domain is grim. It is ever diminishing and losing strength (for example, Grove, 2003).

Fortunately, we have a counter movement in Free and Open Source Software. It can be pointed out, that F/OSS is already competing with the proprietary software, so we have no need to lessen the IPR protections. However, these too are under stress of late because of software patents and DMCA. The software patents and DMCA limit the free development of decrypting software for certain DDM, which is sure to block the law-abiding public from using these products due to their inability to offer certain services. Now that these protections have been in place for a short while, we already see examples of how they limit the development of F/OSS. Were it so, that such future development in the proprietary realm becomes increasingly common, it will likely become impossible to compete with it with F/OSS. The reason for this is that reverse and even forward engineering of the protected features is illegal if the software has any kind of digital protection in place (Kimppa, 2004; Simons, 2000).

Future Choices

The views to IPRs are divided among different factions. A way to handle them that would satisfy all parties is unlikely to be found. Three directions remain: (1) to go where we are led, that is, stronger IPR protection and more and more draconian legal measures of hunting down those invading IPR holders' "property"; (2) a compromise that would benefit the public, society, and likely the creators of DDM and would lessen the control of distributing organizations and create less work for lawyers and law enforcement (Hettinger, 1989, for example, has proposed a time for patents that would be in effect for the time an independent then starting research group would need to complete the research); or (3) to abolish IPRs all together (which does not appear likely, at least not in the near future) which would be sure to lead to at least temporary setbacks in IPR development but might in the long run be the best alternative.

References

Alford, W. P. (1995). *To steal a book is an elegant offence: Intellectual property law in Chinese civilization.* Stanford, CA: Stanford University Press.

Birsch, D. (2003). Copying computer programs for friends. *Proceedings for Computer Ethics – Philosophical Enquiry* (pp. 61-66). June 25-27, Boston College, Chestnut Hill, MA.

Drahos, P. (1996). *A philosophy of intellectual property.* Sudbury, MA: Dartmouth Publishing.

Feldman, F. (1992). *Introductory ethics.* Englewood Cliffs, NJ: Prentice-Hall.

Free Software Foundation. (1993). The GNU manifesto. Retrieved February 15, 2004 from: *http://www.gnu.org/gnu/manifesto.html*

Friedman, D.D. (2000). *Law's order: What economics has to do with law and why it matters.* Princeton, NJ: Princeton University Press. Also available online [cite 15 Feb 2004] at: *http://www.daviddfriedman.com/laws_order/index.shtml*

Grove, J. (2003). Legal and technological efforts to lock up content threaten innovation. *Communications of the ACM*, *46*(4), 21-22.

Hettinger, E.C. (1989). Justifying intellectual property. *Philosophy & Public Affairs*, *18*(1), 31-52.

Himanen, P. (2002). Open source, open mind. *Time Europe*, March 18, *159*(11), p. 14, 1p.

Johnson, D.G. (2001). *Computer ethics* (3rd ed.). Englewood Cliffs, NJ: Prentice-Hall.

Kimppa, K. (2003a). Intellectual property rights in software: Justifiable from a liberalist position? The free software foundation's position in comparison to John Locke's concept of property. *The Sixth Annual Ethics and Technology Conference*, June 27-28, Boston College, Boston, MA.

Kimppa, K. (2003b). Redistribution of power from government to intellectual property rights owners and organizations looking after their interests: Justifiable from a liberalist position? The free software foundations position compared to John Locke's concept of distributable rights. *Risks and challenges of the network society*, August 4-8, Karlstad University, Sweden.

Kimppa, K. (2004). Consequentialist considerations of intellectual property rights in software and other digitally distributable media. *Ethicomp 2004, Challenges for the Citizen of the Information Society*, April 14-16.

Kinsella, N.S. (2001). Against intellectual property. *Journal of Libertarian Studies*, Spring, 15(2), 1-53, Ludwig von Mises Institute, Available online [cite 15 Feb 2004] at: *http://www.mises.org/journals/jls/15_2/15_2_1.pdf*

Kramer, M.H. (1997). *John Locke and the origins of private property: Philosophical explorations of individualism, community, and equality*. Cambridge, UK: Cambridge University Press.

Locke, J. (1690). *Two treatises of government*. Originally published in 1690, various publishers used. London: Everyman. Second treatise of government (TTG II) also available online [Cite 15 Feb 2004] at: *http://www.swan.ac.uk/poli/texts/locke/lockcont.htm*

Long, R.T. (1995, Autumn). The Libertarian case against intellectual property rights. *Formulations,* 3(1. Libertarian Nation Foundation. Also available online [Cite 15 Feb 2004] at: *http://www.libertariannation.org/a/f3l1l.html.* NOTE: in the URL, the sequence of "111" is actually "one," "letter 'L' in lower case," and "one."

Moore, A.D. (1998, October). Intangible property: Privacy, power, and information control. *American Philosophical Quarterly*, *35*(4), 365-375.

Pike, G.H. (2004, January). New international IP laws on the horizon. *Information Today*, *21*(1),17, 2p.

Simmons, A. J. (1992). *The Lockean theory of rights*. Princeton, NJ: Princeton University Press.

Simons, B. (2000). To DVD or not to DVD. *Communications of the ACM*, *43*(5), 31-32.

Spinello, R.A. (1995). *Ethical aspects of information technology*. Englewood Cliffs, NJ: Prentice-Hall.

Spinello, R. (2003). The future of intellectual property. *Ethics and Information Technology*, *5*(2), 1-16.

Svatos, M. (1996). Biotechnology and the utilitarian argument for patents. *Social Philosophy & Policy*, *13*(2), 113-144.

Wreen, M. (1998). Patents. *Encyclopedia of Applied Ethics, 3*, 435-447.

Chapter V

Intellectual Property Rights, Resource Allocation and Ethical Usefulness

Bruno de Vuyst
Vesalius College and the Institute for European Studies,
Vrije Universiteit Brussel, Belgium

Alea M. Fairchild
Vesalius College, Vrije Universiteit Brussel, Belgium

Abstract

Intellectual property rights (IP) are established through the Trade Related Aspects of Intellectual Property Rights (TRIPS) Agreement (part of the Uruguay Round Agreements creating the WTO) as global and uniform. This absolute IP may provide such opportunities for rent-seeking that misallocations may occur, resulting in a perception of IP as ethically unuseful.

Introduction

Material property rights have been increasingly limited as a result of social and cultural pressures and are exercised according to societal values, with a view toward ethical usefulness. Intellectual property (IP) is still stated in absolute terms and, via the Trade Related Aspects of Intellectual Property Rights (TRIPS) Agreement, part of the WTO/GATT Uruguay Round Agreements, in a globalized way.

This contribution suggests that the exercise of absolute intellectual property rights, given their basic difference from material property rights, provide such opportunities for excessive rent-seeking that misallocations may have been made and are continuing to be made, resulting in a perception of fundamental injustice of intellectual property rights as they are exercised beyond societal values, that is, in an ethically unuseful way. The chapter questions whether the debate on IP and free access to information should not be restated as a debate on excessive rent-seeking, and whether allocations of resources in IP are ethically useful vis-à-vis societal values.

Material Rights: Roman Origins and Enlightenment Views

In Roman law, the first possessor of a thing became the owner by right of occupancy ("Res nullius fit primi occupantis"). Occupancy was defined as a person taking physical possession of something, which at that moment was the property of no man ("res nullius"), with the view of acquiring property in it for him. In certain cases, that intention was required to be established through formal acts instituting "appropriation." Roman law viewed occupancy as a natural process, a normal mode of acquisition by which the earth and its fruits, originally held as a common good, became the legitimate property of individuals.

Medieval and Enlightenment societal views recognized the acquisition of property through occupancy and possession as a form of natural law, acknowledged in common law as appropriation. As William Blackstone (1765) indicated: "When mankind increased in number, it became necessary to entertain conceptions of more permanent dominion, and to appropriate to individuals not the immediate use only, but the very substance of the thing to be used".[1]

A similar concept of natural law as a basis for individual property ownership is reflected in John Locke's *Two Treatises on Government* (Locke, 1720). The system he set forth held that each human should have full and free disposition of himself, subject to no other. As an owner of his own person, humans have a right to own anything that they remove from the common, from nature, doing so by mixing their labor with it, so as to create and maintain, legitimately, private property.

Evolution of Material Rights

Material property rights as formulated by the 1804 *Code Civil* started out, ostensibly at least, as being as total and absolute as current intellectual property rights. Their natural law origins, however, did not bear out such absoluteness, stressing appropriation by way of labor, and thereby inherently recognizing already that there was a social factor to justify ownership by appropriation. Nevertheless, by the end of the 18th and the beginning of the 19th century, ownership rights, perhaps out of a defensive political concern, were posited as absolute.

It is a fact that The Declaration of the Rights of Man and the Citizen of August 26, 1789, influenced by the American Declaration of Independence, states in its Article 17: "Property being an inviolable and sacred right, no one can be deprived thereof, unless it be for a public need, legally acknowledged, evidently required, and on condition of a just and prior indemnity" (p.5) (all translations are the authors').

This statement echoes the almost contemporary (proposed by Congress on September 25, 1789) last sub-sentence of the Vth Amendment to the US Constitution.

Also revealing are the statements found in the *Declaration of the Rights of Man and the Citizen*'s Articles 4 and 5:

> *Liberty consists of being able to do all that does not harm another: thus, the exercise of the natural rights of each man is based on those that ensure the other members of society the benefit of these rights* (pp.1-2).

These bases can only be determined by law ... ." (Article 4, p.1)

And *"All that is not prohibited by law may not be stopped, and nobody may be constrained to do what the law does not order"* (Article 5, p.2).

Doctrinal writings on the *Code Civil* (1804) written in the early 19th century stressed, however, a view which is summed up by Morin's (1920) statement:

The Code, adopting the strong notion of Roman dominium, makes of individual property an absolute right, conferring to the holder prerogatives which he can use freely as he wishes. The proprietor has the possibility to leave a thing unproductive, to destroy it or even to use it to be a nuisance to another. (p.7)

That this is a blatant overstatement is attested to, even in the Napoleonic period, by Locré (1832), secretary of the Conseil d'Etat, writing:

If I undertook to report all the limitations on property and its use, it would require me to transcribe those concerning ways, constructions of buildings, the alignments, the use of woods, hunting, fishing, rural police, the sail of grains and the markets, and a large number of volumes would not suffice. (p.5)

Today's planning and zoning ordinances, environmental protection regulations, or rules on good neighborly behavior bear out that material ownership must be exercised in a way that is ethically useful for the happiness of participants of society.

In Search of the Underpinnings of IP

While the underpinnings of material property rights are clear, those of intellectual property rights appear clouded (Radin, 1982; Schnably, 1993; Yen, 1990). All theories have difficulty explaining the dichotomy between absolutist views in intellectual property rights and the checks and balances, social and economical, weighing on material property rights (Gordon, 1993; Hettinger, 1989). Indeed, the most common explanation for this situation today does not emanate from philosophical theory, but is based on economic pragmatism: intellectual property rights are stated to be what they are because they are based on, and fundamentally about, incentives to create and invent. The United States Supreme Court, in *Marer v. Stein* (1954)[2], summed it up:

> *The copyright law, like the patent statutes, makes reward to the owner a secondary consideration" United States v. Paramount Pictures, 334 US 131, 158. However, it is "intended definitely to grant valuable, enforceable rights to authors, publishers, etc., without burdensome requirements: "to afford greater encouragement to the production of literary [or artistic] works of lasting benefit to the world" Washington Pub. Co. v. Pearson, 306 U.S. 30. The economic philosophy behind the clause empowering Congress to grant patents and copyrights is the conviction that it is the best way to advance public welfare through the talents of authors and inventors in "Science and useful Arts". Sacrificial days devoted to such creative activities deserve **rewards commensurate with the services rendered**." (emphasis added)*

This approach, however, does not satisfactorily explain the recent growth of IP and its corollary, the withering away of the public domain, as well as the absolute nature of IP ownership.

IP Extensions

Intellectual property rights have seen perceptible, indeed substantial extensions in the last decade alone. In patent law, there have been extensions into biotechnology, including into plant tissue and animals, into the protection of software through patent rights, and into the protection of "business methods."[3] Trademark law was extended to include the protection of smells, sounds, and colors.[4] In the area of copyright, extensions were rendered to software and to formats.[5]

New intellectual property rights saw the light of day for semiconductors[6] and for data banks.[7] At the same time, European Community rights were created for trademarks[8] and designs,[9] and a European Community patent is under way as of this writing (2003).[10] A European Directive was adopted on the legal protection of biotechnological inventions.[11]

Domain names have recently become property, making the world of property laws and liabilities applicable to the virtual world of the Internet.[12] All of these lead to the consideration of what is left, in the world of creation, of pure liberty: "Look at every aspect of intellectual property and the evidence is plain: the public domain, like the mighty rainforests of South-America, is being whittled away almost while we watch it" (Philips, 1996, p.429).

With the advent of the Uruguay Round Agreements and the WTO, TRIPS provides for a monolithic global framework for treating IP. The emphasis is on absolute power to the IP owner. Few exceptions are available and these are restrictively interpreted (Ginsburg, 2001).

Basic Differences Between IP and Material Property Rights

The fact that IP is created as a (temporary) monopoly, and that material property rights are not, or no longer without ethical usefulness held or exercised, may not offer a totally suitable explanation. Certainly a 19th century liberal view of material rights ownership was as absolutist as current IP ownership thinking. That IP has been developed in a common law atmosphere is not entirely correct — while much expansion has originated there, it is now global — and cannot in itself explain the extension of IP.

Perhaps a systems science approach may be beneficial to an understanding of the differences and a basis for further analysis, as well as a structure on which to build. Systems science, as pioneered by Ludwig von Bertalanffy (1973), is a transdisciplinary approach that focuses on the dynamics of intra- and inter-organizational interaction. It views an entire system of components as a unified entity rather than simply an assembly of individual parts whereby each component is designed to fit properly with the other components rather than to function by itself. Systems science, which focuses on organized complexity, is thus concerned with the identification, modeling, analysis, design, and control of systems. It describes and analyzes the evolution of a system's growth, its maintenance and sustainability, and its decline. It may therefore be useful as an approach in explaining legal systems, in particular, in this case, ownership rights and how material and intellectual property may fit within a system of ownership. In a systems perspective, inputs (goods, ideas) being processed (labor) create outputs (materials or intellectual findings) that are sustained by legal concepts of ownership. Finding the basis for such ownership may elucidate the basis for ownership rights.

The Roman Grundnorm of ownership and philosophical teachings all stress appropriation of a good from the commons and, by using one's labor to transform it, earning the right to individual ownership. The system of ownership rights is thus based on two elements, a conjunction thereof, and the logical conclusion: inputs and a process lead to an output.

First, there is a common thing (C) that is appropriated by an individual. Mere occupancy may warrant individual ownership. It is clear, however, from the review of history and teachings that this occupation alone fails to warrant sustainable, legitimated ownership. Indeed, it requires the process of labor (L) to transform occupancy to appropriation-legitimized ownership (O), creating an ownership rights system: $C + L = O$. This appears as a basis for a material ownership system.

IP is, however, distinguished from it, as it does not build upon the same components. Indeed, what is at first glance striking about IP is that it originates not from occupancy of a thing originally held in common, but that it sprouts from the human mind itself. In other words, the factor C does not enter into the formula. Labor — the labor of the mind — alone is at the basis of ownership. If for material ownership $C + L = O$, for IP one stands before $L = O$. The input includes the process.

The differentiation becomes perceptibly clearer as one looks at the demise of ownership rights. A material ownership right is perpetual unless otherwise stipulated. Hence, in principle and systemically, material ownership, once acquired, does not end except by destruction of the thing or incorporation into another. Intellectual property ownership, however, is always temporal, that is, restricted in time and at some point coming to an end, whereafter ownership falls within the public domain. In material ownership, appropriation implies individualizing and defining individual ownership rights, in principle forever, in intellectual ownership the reverse occurs. Through intellectual labor, an individual may appropriate his work individually for a defined period and become the single owner. His ownership rights end, however, at the end of a stated monopoly period, whereafter the fruits of his labor will be shared with all in common.

Is the intellectual-philosophical basis for material and intellectual property ownership the same for material property and IP? It appears not from a systemic viewpoint. Indeed, the former involves drawing from a common; the latter ultimately gives to a common. The former belabors a thing from the common to validate individual ownership; the latter belabors the mind alone.

The difference in systemic-philosophical basis may be the explanation for the temporal ownership monopoly, which is so striking in IP (and, thus, the temporal ownership is not the explanation for the systemic difference). As it is based on human labor itself and alone, and not on drawing from a common good, as belabored, it may warrant keeping this ownership to the individual, at least for a while. Indeed, the systemic-philosophical basis may also explain why the creation of the mind called IP falls, after a period of monopoly right to its owner, into the common.

Does this mean that intellectual property ownership, when a monopoly to the owner, is bereft of any societal dimension, that is, ethical outlook? *Marer vs. Stein* (1954), quoted above, provides an answer that appears to be straight out of the utilitarian school but also echoes Roman era *Grundnorm* and Enlightenment writings: the decision speaks of "to advance public welfare... Sacrificial days devoted to such creative activities deserve rewards commensurate with the services rendered" (p.201).

A tentative understanding of the different bases of material and intellectual property rights leads to an appreciation of a key consideration of IP. Intellectual property rights are stated to be what they are because they are based on and fundamentally about incentives to create and invent. Hence, it appears that economic incentives are the key drivers in the granting of intellectual property protection. But are these incentives really necessary to ensure and sustain creation and invention?

Resource Allocation and the Role of Technology

If IP rights are incentives needed to create and invent, how these IP rights as a resource are allocated and how objects that contain intellectual property are distributed are both important issues to sustain the economic value of IP protection. Technology can play a role in both of these issues in that it can assist in maintaining the records of who gets paid for what, and in distribution, technology can be a tool to protect IP rights through proper usage.

In terms of allocation for the production and distribution of objects containing IP goods to be economically viable for all parties concerned, there must be some mechanism for recovering costs for these resources. In the case of many artistic creations, this collection of royalty payments and other remuneration schemes is done via trade associations or societies such as the Belgian Society of Authors, Composers and Publishers (SABAM) or the UK's Mechanical Copyright Protection Society (MCPS) that licenses a writer's copyright for sound recordings. How an artist or composer is paid depends on the allocation of the object. For example, in the UK, payment for live performance is straightforward in that no new IP rights are created. The venue where the performance takes place pays performers or their agents directly, and the song owners are paid through the venue license.

But the use of the Internet as a distribution medium has caused some challenges for collection on resource allocation. Although new technology makes it faster, easier, and cheaper for the end user to acquire objects containing IP, the use of technological tools (watermarking, read-only documents, public key infra-structure, etc.) to limit the usage to correlate to the royalty received by the creator of the IP has been inadequately implemented. Therefore, as ease of global distribution has increased, as seen by Napster with MP3 files, the need for IP protection to appropriately compensate for usage has become easier to justify.

Needed: An Ethical Usefulness Justification for Measurable IP Protection

Brainpower supposedly drives the post-modern economy. Technology change makes it harder to protect ideas. Globalization made IP spread, and one might fear that in a variant of Gresham's Law, nations that do not protect IP will drive down global standards. Still, current IP may not be suitable as a monopolistic global system. If the case for intellectual property rights is to be maintained, correctives will need to be introduced that require IP to be exercised in an ethically useful way.

In the battle over intellectual property rights, owners, even in the developed world, may not maintain their rights if they go further than what society considers justifiable. For example, when ASCAP sent thousands of letters to Girl Scout groups, demanding royalties for songs presumably sung around the campfire, the public relations disaster that ensued made them refrain from collecting a full profit, which was their due under black letter law. The popular reaction, deeming ASCAP's demanding excessive—say, ethically unuseful—made ASCAP relent from a full application of the law and instead made them charge the Girl Scouts one US dollar per group per year (Zittrain, 2002).

Indeed, if intellectual property owners do not see reason, it may hinder their more patently reasonable claims for due compensation. This is the more so as the value of intellectual property rights creation as ethically useful is being questioned by an eminent jurist, Judge Richard Posner (2002):

> *Granting property rights in intellectual property increases the incentive to create such property, but the downside is that those rights can interfere with the creation of subsequent intellectual property (because of the tracing problem and because the principal input into most intellectual property rights is previously created intellectual property). Property rights can limit the distribution of intellectual property and can draw excessive resources into the creation of intellectual property, and away from other socially valuable activities, by the phenomenon of rent seeking. . .*

> *Striking the right balance, which is to say determining the optimal scope of intellectual property rights, requires a comparison of these benefits and costs — and really, it seems to me, nothing more.*

> *...*

> *We do not know how much intellectual property is in fact socially useful, and therefore we do not know how extensive a set of intellectual property rights we should create. For all we know, too many resources are being sucked into the creation of new biotechnology, computer software, films, pharmaceuticals, and business methods because the rights of these different forms of intellectual property have been too broadly defined. (p.12)*

The socio-economic measurement that Judge Posner (2002) proposes may appear to set a daunting task, but it points to correctives that may sustain the case for intellectual property rights. Indeed, there appears to be a need for measuring the impact of intellectual property rights to determine its optimal scope vis-à-vis societal values, that is, to determine its ethical usefulness.

Excessive expression of intellectual property rights appears to correlate with excessive rent seeking by owners. For example, it appears unacceptable if Girl Scouts are being harassed for more than a symbolic dollar for their campfire songs. This excessive rent seeking may in turn correlate — as Posner (2002) suggests — to a misallocation of resources. Even within intellectual property rights themselves elements of this misallocation might be detected. For example, an explanation is required as to why subsequent copyright term extensions are not matched by patent term extensions. One explanation might be the power of the media industry lobby. Still, this appears unsatisfactory if one considers the size and might of the pharmaceutical industry. Might the expected rapid return on investment in rapsters — exceedingly more rapid than the pharmaceutical industry's return on investment in cancer drugs — provide for an explanation?

Indeed, if studies of returns on investment would indicate that returns on investment in a rap group are exceedingly higher than those in research and development of a cancer drug or other forms of investment, then one might seek confirmation that such returns would drive investors/owners (1) to pour more resources into such investments, disregarding the societal and ethical usefulness of such investments, and (2) to seek maximum rent for such investment.

If such exceedingly higher (than in other investments) returns occur for certain kinds of IP, they might be indicative not only of "excessive" allocation of scarce resources, but they might also lead to a conclusion by the general public that the maximized rent seeking for such investment is "excessive," that is, ethically not useful.

Conclusions

Taken to the full consequence, IP appears based on the human mind alone, as distinct from material property rights which are linked to appropriation of a common through labor. Therefore, IP's protection structure appears to rigidly protect the owner, at least for a stated period, so as to preserve the incentive to create.

This rigidity, as currently conceived, might become a driver for over-investment in that it is of little use to society's welfare because of possibilities of excessive rent seeking that are ethically unacceptable.

The adoption of the global and monolithic TRIPS intellectual property rights system was perhaps the high water mark of absolute intellectual property ownership. The system is already being challenged by both libertarians and developing countries. What is perhaps required is an understanding that what is being fought over may perhaps be the symptoms rather than the disease.

Indeed, perceived excessive rent-seeking opportunities may point to excessive returns on investment that may in turn point to misallocation of resources into societally less valuable investments. If the current intellectual property rights system would be found to be, by its nature, distortive — driving to investment in rapsters rather than roads — then mainstream society may need to act, to correct, on equitable and ethical grounds. [13]

The question hence arises whether the debate on IP and free access to information should not be restated as a debate on excessive rent seeking, socially unfruitful investment, indeed, on ethically unuseful allocations of resources in IP.

Directions for Further Research

IP appears to have a distinctively different systemic-philosophical basis from that of material rights ownership. This may reflect in, that is, be the reason for, a temporal monopoly right for IP owners and for the transfer of IP to the public domain, the common, thereafter. Clearly, more reflection is required to study these phenomena and their bases.

Addressing the optimal and the good of IP, that is, the basis for a right to individual ownership and ownership rights, creates obvious problems of evidencing "excessive" rent seeking, and currently posits the issue of ethically useful ownership and ownership rights without defining it other than in rent-seeking terms or as ethically unuseful, "because we know it to be so."

Much empirical work is needed to measure IP, cost/benefits of IP and rent seeking, and to assess IP in terms of social-ethical justification. If one wishes to advance towards an ethical usefulness assessment, it will be key to frame such empirical work in a firm methodological basis, so as to progress in assessing IP for ethical soundness and social justification from a current situation akin to Justice Byron White's crude assessment methodology for pornography: "I know it when I see it."

References

Bertalanffy, L. von (1973). *General system theory*, London: Penguin.

Blackstone, W. (1979). *Commentaries on the laws of England* (volume 2). Chicago, IL: University of Chicago Press. (Original work published 1765).

Declaration of the Rights of Man and the Citizen, August 26, 1789, *http://www.yale.edu/lawweb/avalon/rightsofm.htm*. The authors' translation is from the French original text.

Farcy, J.-C. & Wijffels, A. (2004). Code Civil 1804-2004. *Toutes les versions du Code Civil Depuis deux siècles*, Litec/Editions Jurisclasseur, Paris, France, CD-Rom.

Ginsburg, J.C. (2001). Toward supranational copyright law? The WTO panel decision and the "three-step test" for copyright exceptions. *Revue Internationale du Droit d'Auteur*, *187*(3), 17-19.

Gordon, W. J. (1993). A property right in self-expression: Equality and individualism in the natural law of intellectual property. *Yale L. J.,* 102, 1533.

Hettinger, E.C. (1989). Justifying intellectual property. *Phil. & Publ. Aff.*, 18, 31.

Locke, J. (2000). *Two Treatises on Government*. Birmingham, UK: Palladium Press (Original work published 1720).

Locré, J. (1827-1832). *Législation civile, commerciale et criminelle de la France.* IV, 5, Paris.

Morin G. (1920). *La révolte des faits contre le Code*. VII, Paris: Bernard Grasset.

Philips, J. (1996). The diminishing domain. *European Intellectual Property Review*, 8, 429.

Posner, R.A. (2002). The law and economics of intellectual property. *Daedalus*, 5, 12.

Radin, M.J. (1982). Property and personhood. *Stan. L. Rev.*, 34, 957.

Schnably, J. (1993). Property and pragmatism: A critique of Radin's theory of property and personhood. *Stan L. Rev.*, 45, 347.

Trade Related Aspects of Intellectual Property Rights (TRIPS) Agreement, annex 1C of the Marrakesh Agreement establishing the World Trade

Organization, signed in Marrakesh, Morocco on August 15, 1994, *http:/ /www.wto.org/english/tratop_e/trips_e/t_agmO_e.htm*

Yen, A. (1990). Restoring the natural law: Copyright as labor and possession. *Ohio St. L. J.* 51, 517.

Zittrain, J. (2002). Calling off the copyright war. *The Boston Globe*, November 24.

Endnotes

[1]   Quoted in the 1979 edition, *Commentaries on the laws of England*, 75 (Vol. 2). Chicago, IL: University of Chicago Press.

[2]   Marer v. Stein, 347 U.S. 201 (1954).

[3]   The European Patent Office (EPO) issued on May 13, 1992 a patent application covering a process/method for producing a genetically engineered mouse that would develop cancer (the so called "Harvard-onco-mouse"). The Harvard-onco-mouse could be used as a tool to study the effects of anticancer treatments and products [EPO Patent N° 0169672, *Official Journal EPO*, 1992/10, 588]; The Technical Board of Appeal (TBA) of the EPO decided on July 1, 1998 in the *IBM* case that "a computer program claimed by itself is not excluded from patentability if the program, when running on a computer or loaded into a computer, brings about, or is capable of bringing about, a technical effect which goes beyond the 'normal' physical interactions between the program (software) and the computer (hardware) on which it is run." [*See*: TBA, July 1 1998, T 1173/97, *Official Journal EPO*, 1999/10, 609. (cons. 13)]; In the *Pension Benefit* case TBA of the EPO had to decide if a method of controlling a pension benefits program by administering at least one subscriber employer account on behalf of each subscriber employer's enrolled employees each of whom is to receive periodic benefits payments claims to methods and systems for performing business methods are excluded or not form patentability (i.e., a business method) was patentable. The TBA decided that "all the features of this claim are steps of processing and producing information having purely administrative, actuarial and/or financial character. Processing and producing such information are typical steps of business and economic methods. Thus the invention as claimed does not go beyond a method of doing business as

such and, therefore, is excluded from patentability" [*See*: TBA, September 8, 2000, T 95/0931, *Official Journal EPO*, 2001/10, 413 (cons. 3)].

4   On February 11, 1999 the Second Board of Appeal Office of the Harmonization for the Internal Market (OHIM), the EC Trade Mark Office, decided in the *Vennootschap Onder Firma Senta Aromatic Marketing* case that an application to register as an olfactory Community Trade Mark (CTM) "the smell of freshly cut grass" for tennis balls was an adequate representation of the mark that the applicant was intending to apply these goods. The Board decided that: "The smell of freshly cut grass is a distinct smell which everyone immediately recognizes from experience. For many, the scent or fragrance of freshly cut grass reminds them of spring or summer, manicured lawns or playing fields, or other such pleasant experiences" [*See*: Second Board of Appeal, February 11, 1999, R 156/1998-2, *Official Journal OHIM*, 1999, 1239 (cons. 14)]; In *Orange*, the UK company *Orange Personal Communications Services Ltd.* applied on March 1, 1996 for the entry of the color mark "orange" in the trade mark register for a large number of goods in class 9 and services in class 38. In the application form, the applicant had ticked, under the heading "Type of mark," the box "other" and had specified as the other type of mark "Color mark." For a description of the trademark, it had referred to an attached sheet on which it stated that the mark consisted of the color "orange." The applicant had not enclosed a reproduction of the specific color shade or indicated a code number. Following a request by the examiner, the applicant filed subsequently a graphical representation of the color on a separate sheet of paper. The Third Board of Appeal of the OHIM confirmed that a single color is in theory registrable as a CTM, although it must be distinctive (i.e., capable of indicating the origin of the goods or services for which registration is sought). [*See*: Third Board of Appeal, February, 12, 1998, R 7/19997-3, *Official Journal OHIM*, 1998, 641]; In 1994 the Dutch company *Shield Mark B.V.* applied for a Benelux Trade Mark consisting sounds (Beethoven's *Für Elise*) in class 9 and 16. The trademark was described as follows: "THE TRADE MARK CONSISTS OF THE NINE FIRST TONES OF FÜR ELISE" [translation from Dutch]. The trademark was accorded by the Benelux Trade Mark Office (BTO) [*See*: *Official Journal BTO*, 02/1995, Reg. N°: 551849].

5   See Council Directive 91/250/EEC of 14 May 1991 on the legal protection of computer programs, *Official Journal*, L/122, 17 May 1991, 42,

amended by Council Directive 93/98/EEC of 29 October 1993, *Official Journal*, L/290, 24 November 1993.

[6]   Council Directive 87/54/EEC of 16 December 1986 on the legal protection of topographies of semiconductor products, *Official Journal*, L/024, 27 January, 1987, 36-40.

[7]   Directive 96/9/EC of the European Parliament and of the Council of 11 March 1996 on the legal protection of databases, *Official Journal*, L/077, 27 March 1996, 20-28.

[8]   Council Regulation 40/94/EC of 20 December 1993 on the Community trade mark *Official Journal*, L/011, 14 January 1994, 1-3, amended by Council Regulation 3288/94/EC of 22 December 1994, *Official Journal*, L/349, 31 December 1994, 83; and First Council Directive 89/104/EEC of 21 December 1988 to approximate the laws of the Member States relating to trade marks, *Official Journal*, L/040, 11 February 1989, p.1, amended by Council Decision 92/10/EEC of 19 December 1991, *Official Journal*, L/006, 1 January 1992, 35.

[9]   Council Regulation 6/2002/EC of 12 December 2001 on Community designs, *Official Journal*, L/003 , January 5, 2002, 1-24; and Directive 98/71/EC of the European Parliament and of the Council of 13 October 1998 on the legal protection of designs, *Official Journal*, L/289, 28 October 1998, 28-35.

[10]   Proposal for a Council Regulation on the Community patent (COM/2000/0412 final), *Official Journal*, C/337 E, 28 November 2000, 278.

[11]   Directive 98/44/EC of the European Parliament and of the Council of 6 July 1998 on the legal protection of biotechnological inventions, *Official Journal*, L/213, 30 July 1998, 13-21.

[12]   As decided *in Kremen v. Cohen*, 03 C.D.O.S. 6565 (9th U.S. Circuit Court of Appeals, July 25, 2003).

[13]   See for examples of this debate in the legal field: Anawalt, H. C. (2002). Internet distribution of intellectual property protected works in the United States, in Japan, and in the future, 18 Santa Clara Computer and High Technology Law Journal, 207; Newton, J. (2001). Global solutions to prevent copyright infringement of music over the Internet: the need to supplement the WIPO Internet Treaties with self-imposed mandates, 12 Indiana International and Comparative Law Review, 125; Rajzer, A. (2000). Misunderstanding the Internet: How courts are overprotecting trademarks used in metatags, *The Law Review of Michigan State University*, Detroit College of Law, 427.

Chapter VI

Software Piracy:
Possible Causes and Cures

Asim El-Sheikh
The Arab Academy for Banking & Financial Sciences, Jordan

Abdullah Abdali Rashed
The Arab Academy for Banking & Financial Sciences, Jordan

A. Graham Peace
West Virginia University, USA

Abstract

Software piracy costs the information technology industry billions of dollars in lost sales each year. This chapter presents an overview of the software piracy issue, including a review of the ethical principles involved and a summary of the latest research. In order to better illustrate some of the material presented, the results of a small research study in the country of Jordan are presented. The findings indicate that piracy among computer-using professionals is high, and that cost is a significant factor in the decision to pirate. Finally, some potential preventative mechanisms are discussed, in the context of the material presented previously in the chapter.

Introduction

Software piracy takes place when an individual knowingly or unknowingly copies a piece of software in violation of the copyright agreement associated with that software. Despite the best efforts of industry organizations, such as the Business Software Alliance (BSA) and the Software and Information Industry Association (SIIA), and extensive legislation in many countries, piracy is rampant in most parts of the world. While illegal copying has decreased in the past few years, most likely due to the activities mentioned above, it is estimated that piracy cost the software industry a combined US$13 billion, in 2002 alone. Thirty-nine percent (39%) of all business application software installed in 2002 was pirated (BSA, 2003).

This chapter will discuss the current state of the research into software piracy, focusing specifically on potential causes and cures. The results of a study of software piracy in the country of Jordan are presented, both to demonstrate the extent of the problem outside of the typically studied Western world, and as a basis for discussion of the theories and data presented in the rest of the chapter. It is hoped that this chapter will make the reader aware of the major issues involved in preventing piracy.

Background

The growth of the importance of software in both the personal and professional worlds has led to a corresponding increase in the illegal copying of software. While academic research often splits illegal software copying into "software piracy" (the act of copying software illegally for business purposes) and "softlifting" (the act of copying software illegally for personal use), this chapter will use the term "software piracy" to encompass both activities, as is often done in the popular press. The following provides an overview of the ethical issues involved in the decision to pirate and the results of previous research.

Ethics of Piracy

The ethics of piracy are not as cut and dried as it may first seem. By definition, when piracy is committed, the copyright agreement or software license is violated, clearly breaking the law. However, does that make the act unethical? Obviously, the fact that something is illegal does not necessarily make it unethical, and vice versa (many laws have been overturned when their unethical nature became apparent, such as laws governing slavery). Also, in the case of digital products, such as software, we are faced with the unique situation where the product can be replicated at virtually no cost and without "using up" any of the original version. So, while software piracy is technically stealing, it is quite different in nature than the stealing of a material item, where the original owner is then denied the usage of the item taken.

In the case of illegal software copying, several ethical issues come into play. In one of the few studies utilizing ethical theory to study the piracy problem, Thong and Yap (1998) found that entry-level IS personnel use both utilitarian and deontological evaluations to arrive at an ethical decision regarding whether or not to pirate. The authors concluded that efforts to encourage ethical behavior in IS personnel should include training in ethical analysis and enforcement of an organizational code of ethics. From a utilitarian or consequentialist perspective, where the focus is on the results of the action more so than the action itself, arguments can be made that an individual act of piracy is not unethical. Assume that an individual can significantly improve his or her productivity in the workplace by installing a pirated copy of Microsoft Excel. While the employee completes the same amount of work in a single day, he or she is now able to leave work earlier and spend more time with his or her family, thus increasing their happiness. If the organization was not going to purchase the software under any circumstances, it is difficult to claim that Microsoft is financially damaged, as no sale would have taken place. In any case, one further sale of Excel would do little to impact Microsoft's overall profits and most likely would not outweigh the good created by the employee playing with his or her children for an extra hour or so each day. In the end, the individual and his or her family benefit, while the creator of the software is not significantly harmed. The organization, and even society, may also benefit, as the individual and his family will be happier and the employee will be under less stress to complete things on time. From a utilitarian viewpoint, the benefits of this single case of piracy may outweigh the costs, implying that the act is ethical in nature.

Some researchers have claimed that software piracy may even benefit software companies, as individuals who would never have been exposed to a software product are given the opportunity to try the software at no cost, which may lead to future purchases of the product if it benefits the user (Givon, Mahajan, & Muller, 1995). This is similar to the concept of providing trial versions of products. If this is the case, the utilitarian arguments defending piracy behavior are strengthened, although further study of this claim is required.

However, what if everyone pirated software instead of just one individual? The situation now changes dramatically. Software manufacturers would see a drastic reduction in income and would eventually have to either go out of business or greatly reduce their activities. The rapid pace of technological growth seen over the past two decades would slow down significantly. Open source products, such as Linux, have demonstrated that a non-profit software industry can still lead to technological advancement, but it is hard to imagine the advance continuing at the same pace with no profit motive in place. Even programmers have to eat.

Therefore, a single act of piracy in a situation where the software would never have been purchased seems the easiest to defend from an ethical standpoint. However, if the piracy is replacing a potential legitimate purchase, the equation is changed. Any large scale commitment of piracy of this type would lead to serious damage to the software industry which, in turn, would negatively impact future software development. It could certainly be argued that the costs would outweigh the benefits.

From a deontological perspective, things are somewhat clearer. Deontologists argue that the act itself is ethical or unethical, regardless of the outcomes. In the case of piracy, the facts are clear — the software corporation has expended its research and development money to create the software, usually for the purposes of recouping the development costs and creating an income stream. These corporations legally create software licensing agreements into which purchasers enter voluntarily when they purchase the software. Those agreements, in most cases, prohibit the unauthorized copying of the software for purposes other than backing up the software. As the purchase is voluntary and certainly not a necessity of life, one has to argue that the purchaser is ethically bound to abide by the licensing agreement. The fact that so many individuals and organizations have voluntarily purchased software and abided by the licensing agreements, without major complaint, is further evidence that these licenses are generally accepted to be fair and ethical. Therefore, allowing for that, copying software in violation of the agreement is unethical — it is the same as breaking any other contract where both sides, in full knowledge of the situation, voluntarily enter into an agreement to abide by a set of rules. Breaking those rules, especially unbeknownst to the other party, is clearly an unethical act, as it violates the other entity's trust. It may not be stealing in the material sense, but it is a violation of a voluntary contract, nonetheless.

Looked at another way, using Immanuel Kant's Categorical Imperative, we want people to act in a way that is universally applicable (i.e., the way in which we would want all people to act, in that situation). In the case of standard legal business agreements, we certainly cannot envision a situation where we would want all people to violate those agreements, especially in secret. Therefore, it must be unethical to break the software licensing agreement by copying the software illegally or using an illegally copied version of the software against the software creator's wishes.

One interesting caveat to this discussion is the role of cultural norms. In the Western world, it is commonly accepted that the creator of intellectual property is granted rights to exploit that property for financial gain, if he or she so wishes. The foundations of copyright and trademark law are based on the view of ownership. Just as material items can be owned, so can intellectual property, and the right of ownership can be protected by legal and ethical means. Given that the technology industry developed primarily in the United States and Western Europe, it is not surprising that the legal concepts of intellectual property rights were developed in parallel.

However, in many other cultural traditions, most notably in Asia, the concept of individual ownership of intellectual property is not as common. For example, while in the Western world artists are rewarded and recognized for creating unique works and often criticized for "copying," in many Eastern traditions, success can be gained through the replication of works and styles created by previous masters. In another major difference, the focus in many Eastern societies is on the collective, as opposed to the individual. In the US, in particular, individualism is encouraged and rewarded. Uniqueness is seen as a strength, in many cases, whereas in Asian culture, it is much more important to assume the proper role in the group. Individualism is often seen as a negative, and people strive to become part of the whole; individualism is sacrificed for the benefit of the group. In a culture such as this, it is easy to see how the concept of individual ownership of a virtual property, especially one that can be copied and distributed at no cost to the originator, can be difficult to establish. Hence, it is not surprising to see that countries such as Vietnam (95%), China (92%), and Indonesia (89%) lead the world in terms of software piracy rates (BSA, 2003). The cultures of these countries have a different concept of intellectual property than the cultures of Western Europe and North America.

This leads to the idea of cultural relativism, which states that ethics are based on a society's culture. Therefore, individuals in cultures with different attitudes and norms can undertake completely opposite acts, although both could be acting ethically. While the concept of intellectual property in Western culture makes it easy to claim that piracy is unethical, it may be that cultural norms in societies like those found in Asia are such that the act of piracy is simply not seen as unethical. As the global marketplace becomes a reality, and Western business concepts are embraced across the international spectrum (witness China's recent admission into the World Trade Organization), it seems inevitable that Western concepts of intellectual property will have to be accepted by other cultures and their corresponding legal systems. However, it may be a slow process and will require well-developed educational programs. Until the time that intellectual property rights are fully understood and accepted into non-Western cultures, the initial rush to judgment regarding the unethical nature of software copying in those societies must be tempered with an understanding of the cultural traditions in which those ethics were developed.

Previous Research

In recent years, a small research stream has developed in the academic literature regarding the causes and potential cures of piracy. Not surprisingly, initial studies focused on the extent of the problem. Shim and Taylor (1989) found that more than 50% of managers admitted to copying software illegally, consistent with a later study of computer-using professionals by Peace (1997). Several other studies found piracy to be common among college students (e.g., Oz, 1990; Paradice, 1990). Males have been found to commit piracy more often than females, while age has been found to be negatively correlated with piracy (i.e., younger people copy software illegally more often than older people) (Sims, Cheng, & Teegen, 1996). When combined with the yearly reports by the BSA and SIIA, it is evident that a significant percentage of computer users are pirating software and that the software industry faces billions of dollars in lost sales each year.

In recent years, studies have focused more on the causes of piracy. In one of the initial attempts to build a model of piracy behavior, Christensen and Eining (1991) utilized the Theory of Reasoned Action (TRA). TRA posits that a person's behavioral intention is the leading predictor of whether or not the person will carry out that behavior. In other words, if someone intends to do something, then he or she probably will. Intention, in turn, is predicted by the individual's subjective norms (i.e., the perception of pressures from the external environment, such as peer norms) and the individual's attitude towards the behavior (positive or negative, based upon the perceived consequences of the behavior). The authors found that attitude and peer norms are directly related to piracy behavior (although they did not utilize a construct for intention, in their study).

TRA has been expanded to include the concept of perceived behavioral control; the individual's perception of his or her ability to actually undertake the behavior in question (Ajzen, 1991). The resulting theory is known as the Theory of Planned Behavior (TPB), and it has been empirically tested in many situations, with successful results. In the most recent major study of piracy behavior, Peace, Galletta, and Thong (2003) used TPB as a base for the development of a more complete model of piracy behavior (Figure 1). Economic Utility Theory (EUT) and Deterrence Theory were utilized to identify the antecedents of the main TPB constructs, including the cost of the software, the severity of potential punishment (punishment severity), and the probability of being punished (punishment certainty). Each was found to be an important factor in the decision to pirate, and the model was found to account for 65% of the variance in piracy intention.

Research into software piracy has come a long way from its humble beginnings in the late 1980s. The model developed by Peace et al. (Figure 1) is a major step forward from the first attempts to identify the factors that lead to the decision to pirate. We will return to the discussion of these factors and what they tell us about piracy prevention, later in the chapter. The next section details a study of software piracy in the little analyzed country of Jordan.

Figure 1. Model of software piracy behavior (Peace et al., 2003)

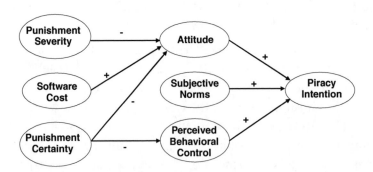

The Jordan Story

Almost all academic piracy research to date has focused on the industrialized nations of Europe, Asia, and North America. To add interest to the discussion of software piracy's causes and potential cures, the authors undertook a small study of piracy behavior in the country of Jordan. Jordan entered the World Trade Organization in 2000 and signed a free trade accord with the United States in the same year. An association agreement was signed with the European Union in 2001, leading to increases in trade and foreign investment. Eighty-three percent (83%) of the workforce is employed in the services industry, and approximately 212,000 of the country's population of 5.5 million have regular Internet access (CIA World Factbook, 2004).

Background

The BSA's statistics indicate that software piracy is prevalent in the Middle East, although there have been signs of significant improvement over the past several years. From a high of 84% in 1994, piracy rates have decreased to 50% in 2002, representing a dollar loss to the software industry of US$141 million (BSA, 2003). This is a small number, when compared to the nearly US$5.5 billion in losses sustained in the Asian market, or the US$2.2 billion lost in North America, which perhaps accounts for the lack of detailed research into software piracy in Middle Eastern countries.

Jordan has a small but growing information technology industry, currently employing approximately 10,000 people and generating US$167 million in annual revenue (Usaid.gov, 2004). The government has placed a clear emphasis on developing this sector, and also on reducing piracy. In 1999, Jordan's parliament amended the country's 1992 Copyright Law and passed various regulations to better protect intellectual property. Two years later, King Abdullah received a special award from the BSA for his efforts to enforce the country's copyright and trademark laws. Largely due to these efforts, software piracy in Jordan has seen a steady decline since 1994, when rates reached 87%. By 2002, piracy rates had dropped to 64%, although the total losses to the software industry had risen, from US$2.2 million in 1994 to US$3.5 million in 2002 (BSA, 2003).

Method

For the purposes of this study, questionnaires were distributed to a sample of adults taking graduate-level evening classes at the Arab Academy for Banking and Financial Services in Amman, Jordan. Engineers and programmers in the telecommunications industry in Amman were also surveyed. No incentives were given for completing the questionnaire, and all respondents were promised anonymity. Almost all of the respondents were employed. This sample was chosen as it provided an available group of business professionals with the ability, opportunity, and knowledge to use computer technology. All of the respondents indicated some training with computers during their education, and 53% stated that they worked with computer technology on a daily basis.

Results

One hundred and two questionnaires were distributed and 98 were returned. However, 12 surveys were deemed unusable, as those respondents indicated that they did not use computers, either at work or at home, leaving 86 surveys for a usable response rate of 84.3%. 86% of the respondents were male, which is not surprising given the make-up of the workforce in both the software industry and the Middle East in general, each of which are male dominated. 24 (28%) respondents ranged in age from 20 to 25 years old, 37 (43%) respondents ranged in age from 25-30 years old, and the remaining 25 (29%) were older than 30 years of age, at the time of the survey. The sample was well educated, with 58% of the respondents holding a bachelor's degree, and a further 37% holding a master's degree or higher. The majority of the respondents (64%) were employees in industry, 20% were students only, and 15% were either university personnel or privately employed. 46 (53%) of the respondents had a computer at home, 18 (21%) used a computer at work, and 22 (26%) had computers available both at home and in the workplace. Almost half of the respondents had used computers for more than six years, while all respondents had used computers for at least one year.

When asked about their knowledge of the laws regarding software copying, 86% reported understanding the concept of software piracy, while 13% reported no knowledge of the issue. Of those who reported an understanding of the subject, 24% reported learning about piracy at school, 41% from media reports, and 34% reported knowledge from both sources.

Rather surprisingly, the respondents were very open about their software copying habits. A troubling 80% of the respondents admitted to using illegally copied software. When asked for the main reason behind their usage of pirated software, price was the number one issue raised. Sixty-one percent (61%) of the respondents listed the cost of software as the main reason for committing piracy. A further 18% responded that they simply saw no reason for paying when the software was available for free. Seventy-eight percent (78%) stated that they were satisfied with their decision to pirate software, while the remaining 22% admitted to some dissatisfaction or guilt associated with their choice.

The respondents were asked to list the source of their pirated software. Eighty-six percent (86%) received software from friends or colleagues both within and outside of their organization. Surprisingly, 17% stated that their pirated software came with the PC that they had purchased, and 3.5% claimed to have received pirated software from a software industry professional, indicating that the problem is inherent in the supply chain. This may relate to the discussion of cultural relativism, described above.

When their attitudes were studied further, 76% stated that it is "fair" to be asked to pay for software, since software companies had expended effort to produce the product. Also, 74% thought that it was necessary to require the purchasing of software, in order to sustain the software industry. However, only 3.5% of the respondents stated that they had personally purchased legal software from a technology company in the past.

Discussion

The most obvious result of the survey confirms the findings of the BSA. Piracy is a serious problem in the Middle East, and the act of piracy is not seen in a negative light. The piracy rate found in this survey is much higher than the 64% found by the BSA, most likely due to the sample utilized — computer-using professionals who have the knowledge, skills, and opportunity to pirate. While the Middle East is not a major user of software, when compared to the industrialized nations of Europe and North America, the numbers are still significant and indicative of the work that must be done to combat illegal software copying. Perhaps most disturbing is the fact that 78% of the respondents seemed to show no remorse, despite the fact that 86% claimed to understand the concept of piracy, indicating that they knowingly committed an illegal act. It is also interesting to note that the majority of the software pirates believed that being asked to pay for software is fair, and even necessary to maintain the software industry, showing an obvious conflict between their views and actions. There is clearly a lot of work to be done if piracy is to be fully understood and prevented in the future.

Potential Cures

The SIAA and BSA have undertaken a two-pronged approach to reducing the problem of piracy: enactment and enforcement of applicable laws (i.e., punishment as a deterrent), and education of organizations and individuals as to the ethical and legal implications of pirating. There is evidence from the academic literature that each of these efforts is useful. In particular, punishment is an important factor. Peace et al. (2003) found that the level of punishment is directly related to the individual's attitude towards piracy — the higher the perceived level of punishment, the more negative the individual's attitude, and the more unlikely the individual will be to intend to pirate. In fact, punishment levels are quite high. In the US, for example, punishment can include jail time and fines of up to US$250,000. However, do people truly believe that they, personally, will incur these punishments? High punishment levels are not enough; the individual must *perceive* the levels to be high, and they must also perceive that pirates are likely to be caught. When looking at the case of Jordan, the fact that 80% of the individuals surveyed freely admitted to copying software illegally gives the impression that they do not perceive the risks of being punished to be high. In reality, while the efforts of the BSA and SIIA to bring pirates to justice have led to some highly publicized convictions, the fact is that most pirates are not caught and freely commit the crime with no negative consequences.

The perceptions of punishment severity (the level of punishment) and punishment certainty (the chance of incurring punishment) relate to the education efforts of the industry trade groups. While the unethical nature of the act is important, making potential pirates aware of the possible punishments has been a main focus of the BSA. One look at its Web page (http://www.bsa.org) quickly makes the individual aware of the organization's tactic to publicize the potential punishments that pirates face and the fact that some individuals and organizations are actually being caught. There is a clear goal of increasing the individual's perception of the levels of punishment certainty and severity. In the case of Jordan, over 73% of the respondents indicated that they had become informed of the issue of piracy at least partially through the media, which indicates that that the campaign of industry groups is working — the word is being spread. However, with over a quarter of respondents claiming no information from the media, and 13% claiming to have no knowledge of the issue at all (keeping in mind that many of these respondents work in the technology industry), there is still work to be done.

On an organizational level, punishment severity and certainty can also be useful tools. Companies wishing to reduce piracy can use punishment effectively; auditing can be carried out to find pirated software, and those committing piracy can be punished. Similarly, research shows that peer norms are a factor in the decision to pirate (e.g., Peace et al., 2003). Establishing a corporate culture that promotes only the legal use of software, combined with punishment for those that do not comply, can greatly reduce piracy in an organization. As suggested in the literature, corporate codes of conduct can aid in this endeavor (e.g., Thong & Yap, 1998).

Software cost is a more interesting aspect of the problem. As can be seen in the study results, cost is a significant factor in the decision to pirate. Sixty-one percent (61%) of those admitting to piracy listed software cost as the major reason. It would not be surprising to find that cost is more of an issue in a country such as Jordan, with an annual per capita GDP of US$4,300, as opposed to the US, where per capita GDP is a much greater US$33,600 (CIA World Factbook, 2004). Peace et al.'s (2003) model also found that price plays a significant role in the piracy decision. Some interesting suggestions have been made in this area. Clearly, incomes differ in various parts of the world. Therefore, the importance of the cost of the software may vary on a regional level, based on things such as per capita GDP and income. Researchers, such as Gopal and Sanders (2000) and Moores and Dhillon (2000), have suggested that price discrimination strategies could be used as a tool to combat piracy. In countries with lower per capita incomes or GDPs, such as Jordan, reduced prices could be used to limit the incentive to pirate. This is an area very deserving of future study.

Another area much deserving of future research is the impact of local culture on piracy. As stated above, cultural relativism in the area of ethics is a potential issue, as some cultures do not have a history of protecting intellectual property rights, and the concept of intellectual property ownership is mainly a Western ideal. Also, most major research to date has focused on the industrialized countries of Europe and North America. Gopal and Sanders (1998) have called for further study of the cross-cultural aspects of piracy, and a fruitful research stream awaits for those willing to focus on this area of the problem.

Conclusions

This chapter provides an overview of the topic of software piracy, including the results of a study of illegal software copying in the country of Jordan. Piracy costs the software industry billions of dollars each year, but through the two pronged approach of education and enforcement, industry groups such as the BSA and the SIIA have managed to greatly reduce piracy worldwide. However, the issue of software cost appears to be a major factor in the decision to pirate, indicating that price discrimination strategies may have to be used to truly impact illegal software copying in much of the world, and cultural relativism may make changing habits difficult, in some societies.

Looking into the future, the case of software piracy provides insight into what is quickly becoming a larger intellectual property rights issue: the illegal downloading of both music and video files via the Internet. Not including Internet downloads, it is estimated that piracy of CDs and cassettes cost the entertainment industry US$4.6 billion in 2002 (IFPI, 2003). There are many similarities between software piracy and entertainment piracy, and the lessons learned in the software arena can provide insight into how to deal with this new issue. With the spread of technologies such as Kazaa and bittorrenting, the ability to copy any digital product quickly, easily, and almost anonymously threatens the value of the intellectual property that has created great wealth for Bill Gates and David Bowie alike. It is imperative that the ethical, legal, and technological factors involved are studied further, so that prevention and protection strategies can be devised to protect the rights of those creating intellectual property.

References

Ajzen, I. (1999). The theory of planned behavior. *Organizational Behavior and Human Decision Processes*, 50, 179-211.

Business Software Alliance (BSA) (2003). *Eighth Annual BSA Global Software Piracy Study.* Washington, DC: Business Software Alliance.

Central Intelligence Agency (CIA) (2004). *CIA World Factbook* (2004). U.S. Central Intelligence Agency. Washington, DC. Retrieved from: *http://www.cia.gov/cia/publications/factbook/*

Christensen, A., & Eining, M. (1991). Factors influencing software piracy: Implications for accountants. *Journal of Information Systems, 5,* 67-80.

Givon, M., Mahajan, V., & Muller, E. (1995). Software piracy: Estimation of lost sales and impact on software diffusion. *Journal of Marketing, 59,* 29-37.

Gopal, R., & Sanders, G. (1998). International software piracy: Analysis of key issues and impacts. *Information Systems Research, 9*(4), 380-397.

Gopal, R., & Sanders, G. (2000). Global software piracy: You can't get blood out of a turnip. *Communications of the ACM, 43*(9), 83-89.

International Federation of the Phonographic Industry (IFPI) (2003). *The recording industry commercial piracy report 2003.* London: International Federation of the Phonographic Industry.

Moores, T., & Dhillon, G. (2000). Software piracy: A view from Hong Kong. *Communications of the ACM, 43*(12), 88-93.

Oz, E. (1990). The attitude of managers-to-be toward software piracy. *OR/MS Today, 17,* 24-26.

Paradice, D.J. (1990). Ethical attitudes of entry-level MIS personnel. *Information & Management, 18,* 143-151.

Peace, A.G. (1997). Software piracy and computer-using professionals: A survey. *Journal of Computer Information Systems, 38*(1), 94-99.

Peace, A.G., Galletta, D.F., & Thong, J.Y.L. (2003). Software piracy in the workplace: A model and empirical test. *Journal of Management Information Systems, 20*(1), 153-178.

Shim, J.P., & Taylor, G.S. (1989). Practicing managers' perception/attitudes toward illegal software copying. *OR/MS Today, 16,* 30-33.

Sims, R.R., Cheng, H.K., & Teegen, H. (1996). Toward a profile of student software piraters. *Journal of Business Ethics, 15,* 839-849.

Thong, J.Y.L., & Yap, C.S. (1998). Testing an ethical decision-making theory: The case of softlifting. *Journal of Management Information Systems, 15*(1), 213-237.

Usaid.gov (2004). USAID supports Jordan's information, communication and technology sector. Retrieved from: *http://www.usaid.gov/locations/ asia_near_east/countries/jordan/ict-jordan.html*

SECTION III:

TECHNOLOGY'S IMPACT ON ETHICS

Chapter VII

Does 'Public Access' Imply 'Ubiquitous' or 'Immediate'?

Issues Surrounding Public Documents Online

David W. Miller
California State University, Northridge, USA

Andrew Urbaczewski
University of Michigan - Dearborn, USA

Wm. David Salisbury
University of Dayton, USA

Abstract

In the information age, various entities (e.g., citizens or business concerns) are now able to access and gather large amounts of publicly available information online, which has obvious benefits. However, there are perhaps unfavorable consequences to this information gathering, and little attention has been paid to these. This chapter highlights the various issues that are created by having unfettered access to documents online, as well as the ability of citizens and investigators to compile databases of personal information on individuals. We cite existing laws to support the position of having limits on the freedom of access, and we propose several strategies for consideration in balancing the rights of the public to access public information while yet protecting and celebrating individual privacy. While the majority of this paper deals with American laws and history, international examples are also noted. In the post-9/11 world, a great deal of reasonable concern has been raised by governmental information gathering. We suggest that equal attention should be paid to ubiquitous access to public records, even by individuals and non-government agencies, and potential concerns for individual privacy that this access might raise.

Introduction

New advanced information technologies (mainly the Internet and large-capacity databases) have enabled governmental agencies to make public documents more accessible and cheaper to store. Through various e-government initiatives, many agencies are now moving their public records access to an online format. This seems to make a great deal of fiscal sense; paper documents are difficult and costly to store and archive and rather labor-intensive to make available to the public. In electronic format, the documents are cheaper to store and access can be made near-universal (i.e., to anybody with access to the Internet). Further, since the documents are public records anyway, there should be no privacy concerns with posting them online.

However, as Mason's (1986) prescient essay indicates, with every piece of information that is made available, a tiny thread is created that can eventually grow to form a tangled web. Making information ubiquitously available, even that which is by purpose and design public information, can eventually have previously unforeseen implications. For example, in 1997, publicly available pending arrest warrants in Maryland were used by law firms to attract new clients. The attorneys searched the online database and informed suspects that there was a pending warrant for their arrest, in essence using that information as a marketing tool (Pan, 1997). Obviously such a practice would have potential to endanger police officers as they served the warrants. Other examples of potential misuse occur when state department of motor vehicle offices (DMVs) make their lists available, often to create revenue streams. In several cases, women who are victims of abuse have been tracked down by their abusers using information gathered by purchasing state DMV records (cf. Chandrasekaran, 1998). While the provision of the limited data available in a database such as the DMV's (name, age, appearance, and address) may be in itself innocuous, that data, when combined with data from other databases, may lead to an inadvertent erosion of individual privacy. Accurate DMV information could, for instance, be combined with other data to reveal the home addresses of public officials, thereby making their homes targets of public protest and possibly threatening the safety of their families.

This chapter examines conflicts that arise at the nexus of individual privacy and public disclosure. We propose that unforeseen cross-checking among multiple databases, even by well-meaning agencies, can subvert individual privacy. With this in mind, we offer suggestions for the level of accessibility appropriate for public information that contains sensitive data on individual citizens. Our proposals are intended to illustrate means for providing access to public records that is fair to both the individuals on whom data is kept and those that wish to access that data. We conclude our discussion with a look at what the future may hold for access of public information and whether the notion of public information should be changed or reconsidered. We believe that in the post-9/11 era, understanding the implications of ubiquitous access to public information takes on even greater importance.

Definition of Information Privacy

We advance a perspective on privacy that focuses on the rights of the individual tempered with the practical limits of functioning within the society. This tension has always existed. To participate in a society, individuals have to come in contact with one another as they go about their daily lives. And, individuals will have to reveal some facts about themselves in order to engage others within the society (e.g., we need to positively identify ourselves in order to accomplish many daily transactions). As such, we do not take an absolute position with respect to the definition of information privacy, which would ascribe privilege to one's right to be left alone (cf. Warren and Brandeis, 1890). Rather, we suggest that while active participation in a society means that one cannot presume to be left entirely alone, individuals should enjoy a claim of privacy in society such that they may determine what information about themselves should be known to others, unless there is some probable cause that they have engaged in illegal activity. This claim of privacy should also apply to social groups and other associations (Westin, 2002). Freedom to select one's associations is a basic tenet of the US Constitution, and we believe that this right should extend to one's personal information.

Background

Concerns over the accumulation of private information held by public entities are hardly new. Warnings of this potential in advancing technologies was addressed four decades ago in such exposés as Benton's (1964) *The Privacy Invaders*, Packard's (1964) *The Naked Society* and Westin's (1967) *Privacy and Freedom*. Reports at the time indicated that there was no immediate cause for concern as the high cost of storage for very large databases and insufficient technologies to search the databases precluded any real encroachment on privacy (Westin, 2002). However, it was clear that the rate of technological advancement would at some point jeopardize information privacy; a concern that was reflected in the passing of the Privacy Act of 1974.

The ability to remotely access many types of public records is not new either. For over thirty years, the LexisNexis™ online research system has provided access to full-text legal documents. However, the service was only available to subscribers and so, generally, only those with a specific need to know the information available in this type of document subscribed to the system. The cost of access created a natural limitation to accessibility of the documents. In addition, subscription was restricted to professionals (such as lawyers) who had a vested interest in maintaining confidentiality of the documents. In our discussion, it is not the access of documents per se that is of concern. Rather, the cause for concern is unfettered access by individuals and organizations whose purpose in accessing the documents is unknown.

Privacy vs. Disclosure

An implicit assumption of a democratic society has always been the tension between the needs of the individual against the need to provide disclosure of information necessary for the rational and responsible conduct of public affairs and fair dealing in business affairs (Westin, 2002). In a related vein, we have seen these tensions brought forward in the ongoing debate of individual rights balanced against the need for security in the post-9/11 world. Some level of disclosure is necessary in the conduct of social life to maintain public order. However, there is a point at which disclosure makes unreasonable intrusions into people's private affairs. Database and data-mining technologies that allow the easy accumulation, storage, processing, and retrieval of even minute details of an individual's private data have brought these needs into conflict. Prior to these technologies, the accumulation and aggregation of data at the individual level from diverse sources was not practical (Westin, 2002). New technologies have created a need to examine how to balance the competing needs of privacy and disclosure.

The dilemma of balancing concerns of privacy with those of disclosure was demonstrated in the case of requests for the release of the autopsy photographs of professional race driver, Dale Earnhardt. A few print and online news media organizations requested the photographs, considering them public information (Kelly, 2001). Attorneys for the Earnhardt family filed suit to block the release of the photos stating that the release would be a violation of privacy. The Earnhardt family eventually settled, allowing a newspaper's medical examiner to view the photos with the understanding that the photos would not be published or made available online. The judge eventually ruled that the photos would not be released, citing the harm which could come to the Earnhardt family as sufficient reason to take this action. The Florida legislature quickly enacted a law that removed autopsy photos from the public domain. While many of us would agree with the apparent invasion of privacy the judge proclaimed this to be, many others, particularly members of the news media, disagree (Marcano, 2001). A concern was expressed that this is an erosion of the "rights of the public" (Marcano, 2001, p. 4). It is clear that the issue of balancing the needs for privacy and public disclosure will not be easily or quickly resolved.

In the US, interests of privacy are assured primarily through the Privacy Act of 1974 and its subsequent amendments (Relyea, 2001). The interest of disclosure is assured primarily through the Freedom of Information Act (FOIA) of 1966 with its subsequent amendments. The Privacy Act of 1974 seems to indicate a realization by the government of the potential dangers of "super data warehouses" that could be exploited to the detriment of citizens and for that reason instituted barriers to data being used in this manner. The FOIA requires that certain disclosures be made by agencies of the federal government (Strickland, 2003). Under this act, individuals have the right to request information about themselves or the activities of government agencies. The FOIA does provide some exceptions to disclosure of information related to the matters of privacy. Any files that would lead to an invasion of personal privacy if released are exempted from disclosure under the FOIA.

Into this discussion come the capabilities offered by advanced information technologies such as large-capacity databases and the Internet. These technologies offer nearly ubiquitous and immediate access to government-collected public records. This is potentially troubling for at least two reasons. First, there is the notion that those who provide information do so with at least some assumption the information collected by the government will be used only for governmental purposes. Citizens often express shock that this is not necessarily the case (cf. Slane, 1998). To illustrate, an online address book at a university, compiled by the university intending to enable students and faculty to contact each other, could easily be accessed by a credit-card company for targets to solicit. Second, in the case of government records, there is the notion that citizens are compelled to provide personal information (Slane, 1998). For instance, an accurate residential address and telephone number are required on many states' driver's licenses, as well as a full-face photograph. The need to provide this information was tested in Florida and upheld in 2003 (CNN.com, 2003).

Compulsory Disclosure and Trust

Whenever individuals provide personal information to any organization, including government agencies, there is an implied reliance on that organization to handle the information appropriately. When dealing with a private business, if individuals feel that their information will not be kept confidential, they may refuse to participate in the exchange. For instance, if an online shopper for a book is not confident that his or her shopping information will be kept confidential, he or she may either choose not to purchase the book, or choose to buy the book from an online seller that provides such confidence.

On the other hand, individuals who believe that their government is not taking appropriate safeguards with their personal information cannot simply select a competitor for the service (outside of changing citizenship) as would be the case in dealing with a private business. The citizen is not presented with these kinds of market choices; governments face no competitive pressures to correct agencies that misuse private information. Citizens are forced to trust government agencies to protect their information from unreasonable disclosure to private entities or even other government agencies. As a consequence, it would seem incumbent upon the agency to disclose potentially sensitive information to others only with the express knowledge of the individual. However, this is often not the case. Indeed, some DMVs sell driver's license information to marketers (Chandrasekaran, 1998). While it is laudable that government agencies are seeking to reduce their dependence on tax revenue to fund their operations, they should not use citizens' personal information contained in their databases to generate revenues.

Indeed, the government already has a significant image problem when it comes to its perceived ability to secure personal information. A recent survey (Shutter & de Graggenreid, 2000) found that barely more than one-third (35%) of e-commerce users trust the government to keep personal information confidential. The rate was even worse among nonusers of e-commerce (20%). On the other hand, these same citizens seem to understand the need for government agencies to share information in a democratic society. Sixty-one percent agree or strongly agree that government agencies should share information in order to identify wrongdoing or misrepresentations. So it seems that while individuals would like the government to be more dependable in securing personal information, they recognize the need for at least a degree of openness.

There is a tendency for us to trust in the institutions with which we associate, particularly employers and the government (Slane, 1998). As a result, we may give away sensitive information unwittingly. A case in point involves one of the authors. In the midst of preparing this chapter, he was presented with a commuter transportation (i.e., rideshare program) form from his employer. Among other information, the form requested the author's name, home address (physical address only, post office box numbers were not acceptable), contact phone number, work hours, department, and mode of transportation. The form included a cover letter signed by the head of the institution expressing that this year's goal was to achieve a 100% response rate. The delivery of the form to the author's employee mailbox was preceded by an e-mail message informing him that the forms were being placed in the mailboxes and that a 100% response was *required*. Accordingly, the author completed and returned the form. Only upon reflection did he realize what sensitive personal information he had entered and how that information could conceivably be used. He further noticed that there was a statement at the bottom of the form thanking participants for their cooperation. That statement seemed to imply that completion of the form was not mandatory. The conflicting messages (the e-mail versus the form and cover letter) left him perplexed over whether he had to provide the information or not. Despite the statement on the form that it was not mandatory, he felt somewhat compelled to complete and return the form, which he did. He accepted the assurances stated in the form and cover letter that the sensitive personal information would be used and safeguarded in an appropriate manner.

The language used in the cover letter and the e-mail message that preceded it gave the impression that completing and returning the form was required, when indeed it was not. The author can be assumed to have a relatively heightened awareness of the issues regarding the provision of such information and its possible use. Yet, he provided the information with little reflection as to the possible implications of providing such information. One may assume that others, less aware of these implications, routinely provide this type of information. Requestors of information need to be aware of how their requests are perceived. Individuals should not be led to believe that voluntary provision of sensitive information is required of them. Conversely though, individuals should understand the sensitive nature of the information they provide and need to be aware of how that information can possibly be used.

Means to Balance Privacy and Disclosure

It seems reasonable to assert that some uses of public information (e.g., DMVs selling lists) go beyond "fair use" and "informed consent." Governments have responded by indicating a willingness to impose barriers and limits on information use intended to protect the privacy of individual citizens. For example, federal regulations currently prohibit most U.S. businesses from compelling the use of a potential customer's Social Security Number (SSN) as a condition of doing business. This is similar to stipulations in the Privacy Act of 1974 that explicitly forbid local, state, and federal governments from denying any "right, benefit, or privilege provided by law" based on a refusal to provide a SSN, and in 2002 this law was expanded to assert "an individual's name and address may not be sold or rented by an agency unless such action is specifically authorized by law" (US Department of Justice, 2002). Hence, at least at the federal level some concern does exist as to unnecessary disclosure and release (at least for sale or rental) of public information. However, this law perhaps leaves a legal avenue for telemarketers and others to capture this information by further stipulating that "this provision shall not be construed to require the withholding of names and addresses otherwise permitted to be made public." These apparently opposing principles for treatment of sensitive information suggest a need for further discussion of means to secure sensitive information while allowing adequate levels of public disclosure. Various means of securing private information or restricting access to it are discussed below.

Registration of Searchers

One solution would simply be to require registration of individuals seeking to access information. This could be done through the creation of identification and authentication schemes. While this would not necessarily deter individuals from continuing to do mass searches and data collection, it would at least add to the public record of who is looking at the information. Such user identification is currently required in many libraries, although this is usually in the context of protecting the copyright holder of the material being accessed and ascertaining that the user is indeed one who is entitled to use the material (e.g., a student using a university library). The adaptation of this concept to protect privacy could be analogous to a suggestion from a report on this issue in British Columbia (Flaherty, 1995) that government databases be redesigned to capture access information (i.e., who accessed what records, and how many times). We do not advocate this type of system for researching activities of governmental agencies or even publicly held corporations. We suggest it merely for searches on information about individual citizens. Perhaps part of an individual's record would be a listing of every access made against his or her information. As part of an FOIA search, an individual could be provided with information about every access of his or her records, much the same as can be done for requests made against credit reports.

Examination of Data

We hold to the notion extended in the US Department of Health, Education, and Welfare Fair Information Practices (HEW, 1973) that all citizens should have access to information any entity has about them and the ability to correct errors (Westin, 2002). However, individuals are often not aware that certain data has been accumulated about them (Slane, 1998). It should be incumbent upon the holder of the data to inform each individual contained within that database of the existence of the information and the intended use of the database. On the one hand this might seem an onerous request, but if it is easy to put information together, it should certainly be easy enough to make this information available. The individual should then be made aware of any access that had been made to that information and who accessed the information. Perhaps this could be set up as an automatic operation that forwards an e-mail message — for those having e-mail access — when someone has accessed the data; those without e-mail access could receive notice by post. Alternatively, the industry could be required to provide a means (e.g., a Web site) that individuals regularly access for what information about them is stored and what entities have sought or accessed that information.

However, this suggestion raises an interesting and related discussion found in Mason's (1986) notion of access. At the point where one accepts the premise that the information should be completely, immediately, and ubiquitously available to all citizens, the issue becomes this: How we can be sure that this level of access is available to all citizens? If one is unable to afford the device to connect to the information infrastructure, is not that person being deprived of a right; that is, if unfettered and ubiquitous access is indeed a right (O'Harrow, 1998)? Of course others (cf. Pan, 1997) would suggest that "public" does not imply "ubiquitous" and "electronic." However, to indicate that one should inform individuals about the existence of information about them in a computerized database implies that access to this notification may well be done in an electronic format. In this situation, those with limited access to the Internet could conceivably be seen as being denied a basic right. Clearly this discussion should be ongoing.

Remove Certain Lists from Distribution

Since citizens have no choice to provide personal information to governmental agencies such as DMVs, such agencies should not be permitted to distribute lists that can identify individuals. Such lists can be quite valuable to marketing firms, for no other reason than their relative completeness. One can well imagine how valuable it would be to have an accurate list of *all* drivers in the state with their current home addresses and phone numbers, since such information may not be available elsewhere. While it is laudable that agencies wish to reduce their dependency on tax revenues, selling lists to marketing firms blurs the traditional notion of government agencies. Indeed, selling lists may even be seen as another form of taxation, since it involves making a choice for individuals to give up something about themselves of value. Each agency must be cognizant that disclosure of even the most innocuous information may not be considered so harmless when combined with other information. At the very least, the agency should have individuals "opt-in" or "opt-out" before distributing the data.

"Opt-In" and "Opt-Out"

Consent should be given by individuals through opting-in or opting-out of distributed information lists. We further believe that the preference should be toward "opt-in," where one's information cannot be placed on the list until the individual has made a conscious choice to allow the information to be included. Which strategy should prevail would depend on the nature of the information being released (Westin, 2002) and the association the individual has with the institution (Sturdevant, 2003). Opt-in strategies are those in which an individual must be notified of and authorize transfer of personal information to parties with whom the individual has no prior association. For instance, California's recently enacted law (SB1) requires financial institutions to get an individual's authorization before selling or sharing personal or financial information to third parties (Sturdevant, 2003). An opt-out strategy is one in which the individual must block the movement of personal information to third parties. Such strategies allow individuals to have their information removed from a list shared with others.

Opt-in and -out strategies are based in the notion that individuals must consent to release and distribution of their information. The notion of consent, however, has become rather muddled in recent years (Garfinkel, 2000). Collectors of sensitive data have adopted the belief that an individual's willingness to provide data in itself indicates the individual's consent to use and distribute the information as the collector wishes. It is often claimed that individuals are aware that they have given blanket consent to allow their information to be distributed and that the consent is perpetual. Consent is also often given under circumstances of duress such as a patient being expected to sign a consent form before being treated.[1] The entities collecting sensitive information should make it abundantly clear that information may be released to others and that individuals have the right to block that release without a reduction in the services that the entity is providing.

Withholding "Voluntary" Information

Government and other entities should make it quite clear when provision of sensitive information is voluntary. Consider the case of the author unwittingly providing information for the rideshare program. Nowhere in the cover letter or on the form was it stated that participation was voluntary. It should be noted that the author is confident that the information contained in the form will be kept confidential and will be used only for the purposes for which it is collected. The point of the example is to point out how someone who should be aware of potential misuse of sensitive information yet provided it without considering the consequences. Entities should be careful not to use language in their requests for information that can lead individuals to believe that the information is required of them or that pressures individuals to provide the information (i.e., such as suggesting a sense of camaraderie).

Charge Fees

Another potential barrier to dissuade marketers would be simply to charge a higher premium for the information they access. The changes to the definition of public information with this example are obvious, but in many cases this model already exists with the fees hidden as "duplication charges" or "supervisory fees" (ISU OUC, 2003). The scheme for charging could be applied in such a way that it is a very minor factor to the average person seeking a specific piece of information but a large barrier to those who are trying to create large databases. The fee should be sufficient to discourage those wishing to create a large resource, while leaving the information accessible to those with a legitimate and reasonable need to know the information, or those who are making a limited search for a specific entity or individual. While electronic methods of delivery of data may be acceptable, there is no reason why that access must be "free" or immediate. Charging a fee for requested documents, even a nominal one, may be sufficient to discourage the merely curious. When asked if they would conduct a transaction such as renewing a drivers' license online for a fee, the percentage of citizens willing to do so dropped dramatically, to nearly zero, as the fee increased from $1 to $10 (Shutter & de Graggenreid, 2000). While a nominal fee may not represent an undue burden for a single piece of information, it may be sufficient to dissuade those who are searching with the intent of building large, detailed databases about individual citizens.

A tangential means of applying this system would be to reduce the bandwidth available to information seekers for every successive kilobyte requested, thus making it potentially cost-prohibitive for an information seeker to create such databases. Moreover, individuals could be limited to a certain number of kilobytes or pages requested per day. If users then need more information, they could be required to go in person to the records office to see and access such information. Similarly, online searches could be limited to cursory information such as case numbers or the names of the involved parties. Users would then have to go to the records office to view or acquire copies of the full documents.

There are other possible controls that a fee system may offer. An electronic payment system (e.g., similar to PayPal) would require the searchers of the information to identify themselves and leave an electronic paper trail that could be followed if any nefarious activity were noted relating to the individual on whom the data was acquired. The other control that the fee system provides is an answer to the ubiquity question. Online searchers are able to take advantage of a system that is not available to all citizens. That advantage is enjoyed only by the technology enabled. Those who are not enabled with online access or the knowledge to use the technology would be compelled to use traditional methods to acquire the desired information including paying a fee for the reproduction of the document. Since there seems to have been no adverse effect in the past with charging a fee for the documents, it seems reasonable to charge a similar amount to support the system that allows online access to the document. We do not feel that such a fee would be in violation of the provision of the FOIA that allows government bodies to charge reasonable fees for reproducing requested documents. We believe that, though the marginal cost of providing the document electronically is essentially zero, there is a cost in developing and maintaining the means to provide the document that is reasonable to pass on to users of that system.

Hurdles to Access

The ability to access public information is not new. Citizens and organizations have been able to access needed information for a long time. It is the convergence of technologies that have aggregated data and made access abundantly, perhaps excessively, available to anyone—even those who do not have a clear need for the information. If the level of access that was available before the availability of the technologies was acceptable, then perhaps a means that provides similar levels of access as the traditional means yet provides the desired economies would be acceptable. For instance, a traditional limitation of access to paper documents was that the one seeking the information had to visit the agency possessing the document. Why then, would it not be possible to continue to require information seekers to visit the agency for the documents? The agency could simply provide the documents only through a closed, electronic information system available in onsite reading rooms. Users could look up the desired document and read it there or make a printed copy — for a fee — to take with them. Again, this means of constraining access serves to discourage the merely curious while making the documents at least as accessible as they had been while allowing the agency to enjoy most of the benefits of reducing the documents to electronic format.

Future of Privacy

The issue of access to public records will persist as data warehousing and data-mining techniques advance and the cost per unit of storage continues to decline. Legislative bodies at both the federal and state levels are aware of the issues and are moving with unusual speed to address them. While the legislatures and courts have moved rapidly to reconcile the conflicting interests of openness and privacy, the swift pace of technological advances shows that it is unlikely that laws will be able to keep up with the capabilities of the technology. Collectors and users of information and the developers of the technologies that handle the information will continue to face ethical questions of how much access is appropriate.

It is encouraging to see that some information technology firms are addressing the access versus privacy issue. For instance, Systems Research and Development of Las Vegas has developed software that can search for a term in two lists from different sources without having to merge the lists (Mollman, 2003). Its software can search for the name of a terrorist on a government watch list in a hotel reservation system without either entity having to hand over its list to the other. The question remains whether governmental bodies will adopt such a technology. Within the realm of foreseeable technological developments, it is unlikely that there will be a single technical solution to the privacy and access issues associated with electronic public information.

Opt-in and opt-out lists have received some challenges from marketing firms. The opt-out list of the FTC's National Do Not Call Registry (FTC, 2003) has received legal challenges from the Direct Marketing Association (DMA). A judge has recently ruled that the list is an unconstitutional violation of freedom of speech, while the Federal Trade Commission and Federal Communications Commission continue the struggle to enforce it. The DMA does, however, encourage its members to honor the names on the list created through the registry (DMA, 2003). Further, it is unclear whether this system can be circumvented by multinationals that could simply build their call centers offshore. We believe that it is reasonable to expect that some form of opt-in and opt-out lists will be utilized. While some states such as California are enacting laws requiring institutions to provide a means of opting out of the lists, the future will likely see institutions adopt a voluntary system of permitting individuals to opt-out of the lists. While this would seem to diminish the value of the lists since they are no longer complete, the lists are reduced to only those individuals with an interest in participating. Opt-out policies actually act as a filter of the lists, leaving only those individuals that present the greater prospects for the institutions acquiring the lists. The difficulty for system providers will be managing the accuracy of the opt-in/opt-out lists. The lists will have to constantly be updated and reconciled against the institution's databases. It is helpful that some government agencies have indicated a willingness to manage lists as evidenced in the FTC's continuing efforts with the National Do Not Call registry.

Increasing globalization will affect issues of privacy and access as well. As corporate boundaries become increasingly international and worldwide marketing, trade, and communication become ever more commonplace, opposing views on access to personal information and its transfer across national boundaries will become of critical importance. This chapter has presented the issues of privacy, disclosure, and access to personal information from a decidedly US-centric position. It should be pointed out that other nations and governing bodies do not share the US view of privacy. The European Union (EU), for instance, holds a much more stringent view of the protection of sensitive personal information (Westin, 2002; cf. Scheer, 2003). The EU has mandated that private information may not be transferred to countries that do not adhere to the standards set forth in EU Directive 95/46/EC (1995). The EU's data protection policy is seen as more rigorous than that of the United States. As U.S. firms wish to continue and increase business within Europe, it is possible that there will be a tendency towards organizational data protection policies resembling the stricter EU rules that apply for all personal data (Scheer, 2003).

Little has been said so far about the responsibilities of the individual on whom information is collected. As previously discussed, individuals should have the ability to opt-out of lists that contain information about them; or, they should be able to prevent the distribution of their personal information outside of the agencies for which it was collected. This will require citizens to be aware of both the potential sensitivity of the information they provide and the means to opt-out of provision of that information. While we contend that the agencies have an obligation to inform citizens of their ability to opt-out, this should not remove a level of responsibility that rests upon individuals to be knowledgeable regarding their own sensitive information. That said, we do not advocate a continuation of the sense of caveat emptor that prevails regarding the provision of personal information. The current mood is that individuals are aware that the information that they provide is made available to others. It has been shown that citizens are often unaware and shocked to discover that their personal information can be viewed by others (Pan, 1997). There must be some type of informed consent; it should no longer be assumed that individuals are aware of the potential uses of their personal information. However, citizens cannot continue in ignorance to rely on the agencies to guard their personal information.

Conclusions

Advances in information technologies that accumulate, store, and data mine information will continue to present ethical challenges for system managers, users, and citizens. It will be difficult to reconcile the conflicting interests of privacy and disclosure in the turbulent social and political environment of the early 21st Century. This chapter has focused primarily on the documents and other information that are held by government agencies and are accessible to the public. The overriding question has centered on whether it is appropriate for there to be unfettered, anonymous, and immediate access to such information. We offer evidence and discussion to suggest that it is not. Access to public information can and should be limited to those demonstrating a need for that information. While we have not determined the threshold for that need, we acknowledge that it is at least reasonable to discourage the merely curious from accessing data. Agencies already have the power within the purviews of the

Privacy Act of 1974 and its subsequent amendments and the exceptions within the Freedom of Information Act of 1966 to protect certain private and sensitive information from public view. Agency managers must be cognizant, however, that seemingly innocuous information can be combined with other similarly innocuous information in such a way that creates an infringement on individual privacy. This possibility will require information managers to consider information that is well beyond that which is stored in their databases. We believe that future legislation should more specifically consider the future capabilities of the technology to aggregate data from disparate sources and data mine masses of data in order to allow specific agencies to control access to otherwise innocuous information. Since it is uncertain which form future technologies will take, legislation should be technology neutral and phrased in general terms (FTC, 2000). Thus, the definitions set forth in such legislation should be broad enough to provide sufficient flexibility in their implementation that the agencies involved will be able to regulate currently unforeseen circumstances.

This chapter has also suggested a number of means that may be considered in order to control access to information without reducing the availability of that information. It is our position that access to public records does not mean that the access be immediate. Our stance is that the documents must be accessible, but that there is no reason that the documents need to be immediately available. Neither do the documents need to be absolutely without cost to the user, nor does the access need to be anonymous. We do however feel that access to publicly available information should not be constrained from citizens. The access provided should be such that all citizens may have equal access. No special access should be granted to those who are able to afford the technological means to acquire the information online. Some of the means of limiting access that have been suggested in this chapter also address the issue of the equal access. Policies and procedures that slow the access or restrict access to a physical location render a similar if not identical level of access for those who do not possess the means to acquire the documents online.

In the end, we propose that there is not a need to redefine public information. There is no need to place increased restrictions on public documents and other information that have traditionally been available to the public, that is, as long as availability to the information is limited to those same levels of access. If the means of access to public information is permitted to fully exploit advances in information technologies, then the definition of *public information* will have to be readdressed. Information managers must be vigilant in protecting the privacy of individuals within our society while providing sufficient disclosure. Society will have to continue balancing the reasonable need for disclosure within a democratic society with the need to protect individual privacy. Finally, individuals should become increasingly aware of the growing risks to their privacy and what means are available to them through opt-in and opt-out programs to avoid relinquishing personal information.

We believe that Mason's original concern about privacy in the context of tying together public records is relevant and well considered. The advent of more advanced technologies to sift through the information and an increased willingness of governments to engage in various e-government initiatives will only make the issues more relevant. Hence, this chapter casts a more critical eye upon the underlying assumptions that drive the move toward having more and more public records online, and has offered some suggestions for how these concerns may be addressed. We identified abuses that could occur and indeed have occurred. We presented suggestions as to how the access could be slowed yet still be public, if this is indeed desirable. Much as the "QWERTY" keyboard was designed to actually slow typing speed because of unforeseen difficulties with fast typists and limitations of the mechanical typewriters of that generation, we suggest that there are many societal, legal, and technical issues to be addressed regarding the electronic availability of public information, and perhaps that the race toward electronic, total, and ubiquitous access to information should be slowed as well.

References

Benton, M. (1964). *The privacy invaders*. New York: Coward McCann.

Chandrasekaran, R. (1998). Doors fling open to public records. *The Washington Post*, March 8, p. A1.

CNN.com. (2003, June 10). Judge: Woman can not cover face on driver's license. Retrieved October 8, 2003 from: *http://www.cnn.com/2003/LAW/06/06/florida.license.veil/index.html*

Direct Marketing Association (DMA), The (2003). FCC jumps into no-call fray: The DMA reassures consumers of compliance. Retrieved September 29, 2003 from: *http://www.the-dma.org*

EU Directive 95/46/EC (1995). Official Journal of the European Communities No. L 281/31. Retrieved on June 18, 2004 from: *http://europa.eu.int/comm/internal_market/privacy/docs/95-46-ce/dir1995-46_part1_en.pdf*

Federal Trade Commission (FTC) (2000). Privacy online: Fair information practices in the electronic marketplace. A report to Congress.

Federal Trade Commission (FTC) (2003). National do not call registry. Retrieved September 27, 2003 from: *http://www.donotcall.gov*

Flaherty, D. (1995). Cars, people and privacy: Access to personal information through the motor vehicle data base. Information and Privacy Commissioner of British Columbia, Investigation Report P95-005. Retrieved September 29, 2003 from: *http://www.oipcbc.org/investigations/reports/MVB.html*

Garfinkel, S. (2000). *Database nation: The death of privacy in the 21st century.* Sebastapol, CA: O'Reilly & Associates.

Iowa State University Office of University Counsel (ISU OUC). (2003) Public records requests. Retrieved on July 10, 2003 from: *http://www.iastate. edu/~ouc/public_records.htm*

Kelly, K. (2001). Dale Earnhardt autopsy photos to stay private. *The St. Petersburg Times*, June 14, p. A1.

LexisNexis (2003). Celebrating innovation. Retrieved September 28, 2003 from: http://www.lexisnexis.com/about

Marcano, R. (2001). Public records worth fight. *Quill Magazine*, (May), 4.

Mason, R. (1986). Four ethical issues of the information age. *Management Information Systems Quarterly*, *10*(1), 5-12.

Mollman, S. (2003). Betting on private data search. *Wired News*. Retrieved September 19, 2003 from: *http://www.wired.come/news/print/ 0,1294,57903.html*

O'Harrow, Jr., R. (1998). Are data firms getting too personal? *The Washington Post*, March 8, A1.

Packard, B. (1964). *The naked society.* New York: David McCay.

Pan, P. (1997). Halt called to Md. lawyers' mailings to at-large suspects. *The Washington Post,* December 5, D1.

Privacy Act of 1974, The (1974). Pub. L. No. 93-579, § 7, 88 Stat. 1909.

Relyea, H. (2001). E-gov: The federal overview. *The Journal of Academic Librarianship*, *27*(2), 131-148.

Scheer, D. (2003). For your eyes only: Europe's new high-tech role: Playing privacy cop to the world. *Wall Street Journal, 242*(72), p. 1, col.5.

Shutter, J. & de Graggenreid, E. (2000). *Benchmarking the eGovernment revolution: Year 2000 report on citizen and business demand.* A report by the Momentum Research Group of Cunningham Communication, Inc., commissioned by NIC, Inc. Reston, VA: NIC, Inc. Available online at: *http://www.momentumresearchgroup.com/pdf/eGov_report.pdf*

Slane, B. (1998). Bulk release of public registries: A New Zealand perspective. Address to the 20th International Conference of Data Protection Authorities. Office of the Privacy Commissioner, Auckland, NZ. Retrieved September 29, 2003 from: *http://www.privacy.org.nz/spubregf.html*

Strickland, L. (2003). Records and information management perspectives, part 2: Access to public information. *Bulletin of the American Society for Information Science, 29*(6), 7-9.

Sturdevant, C. (2003). Going the extra mile. *eWeek*, September 1, 62.

U.S. Department of Health, Education and Welfare (HEW) (1973). *Records, Computers and the Rights of Citizens: Report of the Secretary's Advisory Committee on Automated Personal Data Systems.* Retrieved June 18, 2004 from: *http://www.aspe.hhs.gov/DATACNCL/1973privacy/tocprefacemembers.htm*

U.S. Department of Justice (2002). The Privacy Act of 1974, 2002 Edition. 5 U.S.C. § 552a(n). Retrieved July 10, 2003 from: *http://www.usdoj.gov/04foia/1974ml.htm*

Warren, S.D., & Brandeis, L.D. (1890). The right of privacy. *Harvard Law Review, 4*(5), 193- 213.

Westin, A. (1967). *Privacy and Freedom.* New York: Atheneum.

Westin, A. (2002). Social and political dimensions of privacy. *Journal of Social Issues, 59*, 441-453.

Endnote

[1]   Provisions of the Health Insurance Portability and Accountability Act (HIPAA) of 1996 require health care providers to receive a patient's consent before releasing information. A consent form is usually presented to the patient for signature before medical services are provided.

Chapter VIII

Ethical Management of Consumer Information:
Solving the Problem of Information Externality Using the Coasian Approach

Christopher M. Cassidy
Marshall University, USA

Bongsug Chae
Kansas State University, USA

James F. Courtney
University of Central Florida, USA

Abstract

Society has focused on privacy solutions to problems related to consumer information, yet the problem has not gone away. Why is this? One answer is that privacy, a regulatory correction, does not fix the underlying "information externality" problem. This chapter integrates economic, ethical, and legal theories related to the issue of information management in an attempt to clarify the debate surrounding the issue of consumer information. It first explains why the debate exists by describing the basic characteristics of information. It then integrates an economic discussion of externalities with the ethical issues inherent in the problem of consumer information to suggest alternative ways to correct externalities. This chapter suggests that one way to correct the information externality is to use a Coasian approach. We apply that approach to the case study of DoubleClick, an Internet advertiser criticized for its potential yet never implemented ability to act unethically with consumer information.

Introduction

Personal information and privacy considerations are quickly becoming divisive issues in society as well as in the information systems (IS) literature (Culnan & Armstrong, 1999; Milberg, Smith, & Burke, 2000; Milne, 2000; Phelps, Nowak & Ferrell, 2000; Smith, 2001; Smith, Milberg, & Burke, 1996; Stewart & Segars, 2002). On one hand, firms can offer better, more narrowly specialized products when provided with personal information about individual consumer preferences. The marketing of those products can be narrowly targeted and distribution of those products can be made more efficient if the business has relevant customer information.

On the other hand, consumers are hesitant to divulge personal information because of the perception that some firms abuse the handling of or access to that information. This chapter first illustrates the benefits and costs associated with personal information. It then examines the characteristics, the legal treatment, and our ethical understanding of the problems associated with information. Finally, it applies theory to the real-world problem and suggests a Coasian approach to externalities for a solution.

Background

Benefits of Information

The specific benefits of free flowing information are numerous.[1] To illustrate those benefits, consider the examples of marketing and medical information. The technology exists to enable retailers to track individual purchases through the use of IDs, memberships, checking records, and credit cards. With information on individual preferences, the retailer can better satisfy consumer demands. A store owner can make specific purchases tailored to known patterns of consumption and direct consumers to those products they are most likely to desire. This is a win-win situation for both retailer and consumer. While the cost of that technology and information management is nontrivial, it may result in higher net profits and better consumer satisfaction than the alternative.

Medical information is costly and is generally produced to facilitate the diagnosis of existing symptoms. This information, contained in a person's health history, is highly useful for subsequent diagnosis and treatment. If made available, it has the potential for providing better medical service. In some cases, the accumulation and archiving of individual medical information may even permit medical service personnel to provide lifesaving treatment more rapidly. Medical ID bracelets are a low-tech solution for unconscious patients who require special attention due to allergies, diseases, or conditions. Think of the advantages of providing everyone with a digital copy of their complete medical records, perhaps contained in a chip on their driver's licenses, for use in emergencies.

Costs of Information

While the free flow of information provides tangible if not measurable benefits to society, the free flow of information has social costs to offset the potential benefits. The two examples presented above can be used to illustrate those costs. While robust amounts of information in consumer markets provide better efficiency, consumer information is a two-edged sword. That information can be used to enhance exchange for both parties, as well as to exploit exchange. Our technologically sophisticated society can compile huge amounts of information on consumers such as addresses, phone numbers, and e-mail addresses. For some companies, the low cost of mass mailings, telemarketing, and mass e-mailings is more than offset by the increases in revenues from those types of marketing. This encourages some companies to use indiscriminate methods to target huge numbers of customers at little additional cost to themselves. At the same time, a large cost is imposed on targeted consumers in the form of junk mail, obnoxious phone calls, and e-mail spam. Untargeted mass marketing and telemarketing campaigns are costly and inefficient for those subjected to them. They are costly in terms of the time wasted processing junk mail and spam, they are costly in terms of fending off zealous telemarketers, and environmentally costly in terms of wasted junk mail ending up in landfills. For these and other reasons, many consumers, businesses, and state governments have supported privacy laws to reduce untargeted marketing efforts directed into homes and businesses (Gellman, 2002; Rotenburg, 2001). The companies that have profited from untargeted marketing are highly opposed to these efforts to increase privacy.

Medical information can result in lifesaving treatment when used properly, but it can also be used to impose unnecessary costs on a patient (Schwartz, 1997).[2] Many diseases are associated with some form of prejudicial stigma. The revelation of medical information may subject the patient to social prejudice based on that association. Consider Hansen's Disease, commonly called leprosy. For several millennia, those suffering from Hansen's Disease have been treated as far more than disease sufferers; they have been treated as "morally diseased."[3] Today's equivalents of Hansen's Disease are: the traditional venereal diseases, AIDS, coronary disease, obesity, high cholesterol, old age, and alcohol and tobacco addiction. Employers, coworkers, and others may act upon or disseminate this personal medical information to harm a person's reputation or employability. The improper use of medical information can unjustly or illegally impose moral and economic costs on the individual.

These two examples illustrate the beneficial and harmful effects resulting from the use and misuse of information. These benefits and harms can be normatively assessed using economic, legal, and ethical criteria. Economic assessment generally examines the efficient use of society's scarce resources. Legal assessment considers the social institutions we can or actually use to achieve economic or ethically desirable goals. Ethical analysis generally includes an assessment of efficiency but also considers issues such as fair treatment and the concept of rights. The following sections will address our understanding of information using theory drawn from economics, law, and ethics.

Characteristics of Information[4]

Before addressing the problems highlighted above, it is necessary to review the characteristics of information. Information has two intrinsic characteristics: (1) it is non-depletable, and (2) it is nonexcludable. Both characteristics, common to public goods (e.g., parks, libraries, national defense, clean air), imply: (1)

information is not consumed through use, and (2) it is difficult to restrict the use of information to those who have purchased it. Since the initial investment in public goods is large, and the marginal cost of producing additional units is negligible, we call public goods non-depletable. The original information is not used up by the first customer and can be resold to subsequent customers. This is especially true of large-scale electronic databases where the marginal cost of duplication is essentially the cost of a CD. If information producers could be sure that all consumers would pay for the product, pricing would be based on the total cost of production and the number of expected customers. Unfortunately, the non-excludability characteristic implies that it is costly to restrict those who have not purchased the information from obtaining that information. Information, once acquired by the first customer, might be reproduced and disseminated to nonpaying demanders. The process of building structural barriers to inhibit non-payer access to information, such as Microsoft's software-tracking procedures for Windows XP or Lexis-Nexis's subscription barriers, are costly to both producer and consumer. The implication of these two characteristics is that the cost of information will always be too high and information will be produced in quantities that are too low because some demanders "free ride."

The problem of under production and high costs is addressed by society's intellectual property rights laws. These laws attempt to overcome the free rider problem by assigning patents, trademarks, and copyrights to products that incorporate information. These laws are increasingly strained by individuals and groups willing to use technological advances to circumvent intellectual property protections. Just as in the 1960s when audiocassette taping technology reduced the cost to violate music copyrights, CD and DVD technology today reduce the costs to violate copyrights on a much wider range of products. It will take a while for today's society to evolve efficient intellectual property rights protections.

Another characteristic of information pertains to its use in society and is illustrated by the two scenarios in the previous section — the problem of externalities. An externality is a type of market failure that occurs when the full costs or benefits of an action are not paid for or captured by the actor (Walters, 1993). Externalities distort markets by introducing production inefficiencies, allocative inefficiencies, and reducing the social surplus. For example, when a polluter discharges waste into the environment but fails to pay for the full cost of waste disposal, it creates a negative externality that inefficiently distorts the market by increasing the demand for goods produced from polluting processes.

This shifts either the damage or the cost of waste disposal from the polluter to society. A positive externality occurs when a marketer with many competitors advertises a product and the competitors capture some of the benefit from the advertising without paying for it. When markets fail due to externalities, prices and quantities are distorted and markets are inefficient. This market failure is both economically inefficient (Walters, 1993) and morally suspect from the perspective of distributive justice (Velasquez, 1992). Intuitively our sense of distributive justice suggests that if you create or consume value in society, you should enjoy the benefits or pay the costs (Perlman, 1963; Perlman, 1967). It seems unjust to permit someone to pollute and not pay for the cleanup. It seems unjust for a rival to free ride on the investment of an advertiser.

A more economically precise explanation of externalities demonstrates that externalities affect the supply curve (Figure 1). A positive externality forces the market supply under competition curve, $Supply_C$, up and to the left, to $Supply_{PE}$; a negative externality forces the supply curve down and to the right to $Supply_{NE}$ (Ekelund & Tollison, 1994). This alters the competitive price and quantity, P_C and Q_C, depending on whether the externality is positive or negative.

The externalities of information occur when one entity in society uses information but either fails to pay the full cost or fails to receive the full benefits of that information. Consider the examples given in the preceding section. In the case of spam, telemarketing, and mass mailings, economic benefits are gained by the advertiser while costs are imposed on marketing recipients.

Economists have catalogued a variety of methods for correcting externalities: correcting the "property rights, taxing negative externalities or subsidizing positive externalities, selling rights to create an externality, and establishing regulatory controls" (Ekelund & Tollison, 1994, p. 447). A potential tax solution to the externality of mass marketing might be for the marketer to pay for the full cost imposed on all recipients of the marketing though "Internet postage." A regulatory solution might assess the average cost to a typical consumer and force the advertiser to compensate the receiver as a precondition for receiving the advertising. While it should be obvious that both will reduce the amount of advertising, the regulatory solution that pays consumers for receiving advertising creates a perverse incentive to solicit unwanted advertising. The regulatory solution creates a system where the consumer can exploit the advertiser by requesting advertising simply for the compensation. In the case of both consumer and medical information, society has chosen to solve the externality through regulatory controls that restrict how information is to be

Figure 1. The effect of an externality on market supply

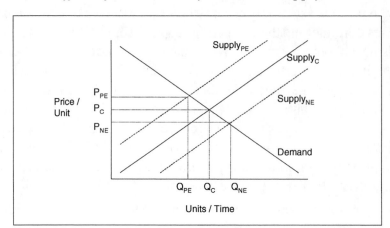

handled. It is likely that other methods could be used that would be more efficient and produce greater benefits.

Legal and Economic Assessment of the Information Externality

The externality related to consumer information exists because only business is in the position to collect, compile, and benefit from consumer information, while consumers stand to either benefit or be harmed by that activity. As of today, society has partly addressed this externality through a legal entitlement to privacy.[5] Privacy rights are very different than property rights or liability rules. A property right entitles the holder to limited control over and transfer rights to a piece of property. Generally, a holder of a property right can prohibit others from violating that right. A liability rule does not prohibit others from violating the right to property but requires them to make fair restitution if they do. A privacy right restricts one party from transferring information about another party. Privacy rights interfere with the free transfer of information and are therefore economically inefficient.

Privacy rights, while inefficient, can be justified using ethical arguments founded in justice and rights. If the free flow of information might be deemed unfair or a violation of another entitlement, then restrictions on the free flow of information are defensible. Sometimes the only way to prevent injustices and rights violations is to purchase those benefits with an efficiency trade-off.

Where feasible, the best way to correct externalities is to correct the market failure that causes them. Correcting the market failure has the advantage that, when corrected, all the market participants have the incentive to act in ways that produce the greatest value. Properly functioning markets are efficient and ethical. Government regulation of externalities, as in the case of privacy, can reduce some problems but does not correct the underlying market failure. In some cases, the market failure cannot be corrected and government regulation is the only way to solve the problem. Legislation designed to protect civil rights and prevent the sale of harmful products are examples.

Our society has implemented the right to privacy as a combination of governmentally imposed regulations, self-enforcement by groups of businesses within an industry, and voluntary restraint by individual businesses. This system of rules addresses the externality using regulatory methods without considering the interests of business (McCullagh, 2001). There is an additional problem created by using the regulatory method to solve the information externality. If there is a conflict between the financial interest of the company and a system of regulation, there will be an incentive to violate the regulations. When privacy regulations impose high costs on business, the conflicting incentives undermine compliance with the regulations.[6] The entitlement to privacy appears to be more like a system of government regulation than a property right. Moreover, it is a system of regulations to give one group an advantage over another. Further understanding of the information externality and the ethical options might suggest more efficient yet ethical alternatives.

Coase Theorem and Calabresi and Melamed's Principles Applied to Externalities

The Coase Theorem (1960) and Calabresi and Melamed's (1972) principles provide powerful insight into correcting externalities. Ronald Coase's article, "The Problem of Social Cost" (1960), argues that it does not matter to whom entitlements are assigned provided parties are free to bargain. Previous economic theory and existing legal practice emphasized that (1) only governments, by means of taxes and subsidies, could internalize externalities in economic exchange or production (Pigou, 1920), and (2) that entitlements had to be assigned to the victim. The Coase Theorem is important because it showed that society could correct the externality if it assigned an entitlement, and counterintuitively, it did not matter to which party the entitlement was assigned. Further, the entitlement could be assigned through the legal institution of liability or through the legal institution of property rights. This opened greater latitude in the assigning of entitlements. The implication is that the granting of entitlements can correct externalities and that society does not have to rely on invasive government regulation.

The granting of entitlements tends to be an efficient mechanism for correcting externalities provided the impediments to bargaining are low. These impediments, or transaction costs, increase when the parties are unknown or are large in number (Baron, 2000). Calabresi and Melamed (1972) provide guidance on situations when transaction costs are high.

Starting from the perspective of the Coase Theorem, Calabresi and Melamed (1972) consider and even expand the notion of transaction costs in the assignment of entitlement and define an entitlement as the ability of an individual to control a particular resource or to take an action, with the state protecting that control or action from infringement. The conceptual treatment of entitlements by Calabresi and Melamed opened greater latitude in the choice of entitlement mechanisms.

The nature of the protection given to entitlements is important. Calabresi and Melamed (1972) distinguish between three types of rules or mechanisms for protecting entitlements—property rules, liability rules, and inalienability rules.[7] Calabresi and Melamed caution that these three mechanisms are conceptually useful for understanding the ways society can protect entitlements but tend to overlap and leave gaps in practice.

- *Property rules:* Property rules prohibit infringement without permission of the holder of the property right (Baron, 2000). A property right provides the holder with control and transfer rights. This gives the right holder: (1) decision control — the right to decide if, when, or how to use the property; and (2) transfer control — the right to decide when, to whom, for what price to sell the property. The holder of a property right cannot legally be compelled into abandoning either control rights or transfer rights. Those rights can only be transferred to a buyer at a price deemed to be adequate by the seller.

- *Liability rules:* Liability rules protect the entitlement holder differently. Liability rules do not prevent the infringement but do require fair compensation for losses that result from the infringement. Fair compensation is determined by the market or society. For example, a home is protected from infringement by other people using a property right, but is only protected from the government by a liability rule. As Baron (2000) points out, the law of *eminent domain* allows the government to take private property for public purposes and compensate the owner for the violation.

- *Inalienability:* An example of an entitlement protected by an inalienability rule is the right to vote. In the United States, an individual's inalienable right to vote is protected by the US Constitution and cannot be given up or transferred to another person even voluntarily. While inalienability rules can be used to address the externalities of some social and legal problems, they are inflexible protections and are warranted only when individuals need extremely strong protection that cannot be efficiently provided through alternative mechanisms. Thus, inalienability rules are not considered in our discussion on the solution for information externality. Our discussion focuses on property and liability rules.

Taking the Coasian analysis of entitlement to externality, the application of either property rules or liability rules can be used to solve the information problem discussed above. In some cases, society assigns property rights to specific pieces of information that are unique and identifiable, for example, intellectual property. The total amount of information in society that is protected by property rights is relatively small. Society also makes some attempt to address the potential harms inflicted by externalities using liability rules under the law of torts (Whitman & Gergacz, 1991). Individuals who are harmed in society are entitled to some form of compensatory justice (Velasquez, 1992). For instance, if one person disseminates damaging but untrue information about another person, the second person has the right to compensation. If factual information is used improperly, for purposes of prejudicial discrimination, the victim has the right to compensation. These liability mechanisms are intended to protect individuals from inflicted harms. The next section surveys the primary ethical perspectives relevant to the information externality and potential inflicted harms.

Calabresi and Melamed's Principles

In the previous section, we discussed how to solve information externality problems using Coasian analysis, specifically through property and liability rules. The natural question is the choice between the two mechanisms and the assignment of entitlements. These issues can be addressed by a social policy choice based on economic efficiency criteria outlined by Calabresi and Melamed (1972):

1. The assignment of entitlements should favor knowledge choices between social benefits (e.g., economic efficiency) and the social costs (e.g., harm to individuals) of obtaining them.

2. In the absence of certainty as to whether a benefit is worth its costs to society, that the cost should be put on the party or activity best located to make such a cost-benefit analysis.

3. When there are alternative means of achieving social benefits (or of avoiding social costs), the costs of achieving them (or avoiding social costs from accidents) should be assigned to the party that can do so at the lowest cost.

4. In the absence of certainty as to who that party or activity is, the costs should be put on the party or activity that can, with the lowest transaction costs, act in the market to correct an error in entitlements by including the party who can avoid social costs most cheaply to do so.

5. Since markets do not work perfectly — there are transaction costs — a decision will often have to be made on whether market transactions or collective fiat is most likely to bring us closer to social efficiency (or the Pareto optimal result the "perfect" market would reach).

In general, Calabresi and Melamed's (1972) principles, following the philosophy underlying the Coase Theorem, focus on social efficiency where the overall social costs are less than the overall social benefits and address those social costs known as externalities.

> *The cost of exercising a right is always the loss which is suffered elsewhere in consequence of the exercise of that right ... It would clearly be desirable if the only actions performed were those in which what was gained was worth more than what was lost ... In devising and choosing between social arrangements we should have regard for the total effect. This is the change in approach which I am advocating. (Coase, 1960. p. 44)*

Various Ethical Perspectives

While there are a vast number of ethical theories that can be used to interpret the benefits and harms associated with information (Lewis, 1989), Velasquez (1992) suggests that most ethical situations can be analyzed using three basic principles: Utilitarianism, Justice, and Rights. These perspectives are reviewed and applied to the information externality.

In brief, the principle of Utilitarianism tells us that we should make choices that produce the greatest amount of positive net benefit and avoid choices that result in net harm. The definition of net benefit would be the total benefit minus total harm. For example, if one alternative would result in $100 of benefit but will cost $50, the alternative would provide a net gain of $50. If we have two alternatives that produce different quantities of net benefit, we should choose the alternative that produces the greatest net benefit. Cost-benefit analysis incorporates the principle of Utilitarianism. Utilitarianism argues for efficiency and value maximization. While the principle seems reasonable, it has many problems and critics (Velasquez, 1992). Utilitarianism does not care how the harm or benefit is distributed over individuals in society. This omission creates conditions that might permit unjust allocations of benefit and harm or conditions that violate individual rights.

The principle of Distributive Justice argues that the distribution of benefits and harms in society should be governed by impartial criteria. Further, it says that equals should be treated equally and unequals treated differently, but only in proportion to their difference (Perlman, 1967; Velasquez, 1992). The general principle of Justice, set forth in the previous sentence, is a meta rule and should be used to craft more specific justice principles. Three of these more specific justice principles are listed here. Those who believe in capitalist or meritocratic justice argue that people should be treated differently based on their productive output. Those who believe in socialist or Marxist justice argue that people should be treated differently based on a combination of their abilities and needs. Egalitarians argue that there are no differences between people that justify unequal treatment. Most people would agree that the principles are situation specific. For instance, people who have been brought up in the US political tradition probably believe that egalitarianism should prevail in matters of political freedom — that all people are entitled to a single vote and that each person should be entitled to equal protection under the law. The same people might be more meritocratic when it comes to economic freedom — that all people should be entitled to the output of their productive labors regardless of how much or little someone else produces. There are, of course, exceptions to both views framed from one of the other types of justice.

The ethical principle of rights derives from the notion that individuals have value that goes beyond their economic contribution to society. Rights follow from the belief that people have intrinsic self-worth that results from their humanity. Rights entitle people to specific protections or liberties that must be provided by others. These rights are designed to prevent society from violating a person's intrinsic self-worth. Rights can be classified as positive vs. negative, granted vs. claimed, and legal vs. natural. A negative right imposes the responsibility of non-interference on others. The negative right to free speech requires other members of society to refrain from censorship or obstruction. On the other hand, positive rights require others to act to provide the right. The positive right to healthcare would impose on some other entity the responsibility to provide that costly good. Some rights are claimed by self-interested individuals, but only a few are granted by society or the legal system. Legal rights are rights granted by legal authority. Natural rights are rights recognized by society independent of legal authority. The natural right for individuals to be free from torture or slavery would not change even if the government made either practice legal.

These three ethical principles seem most appropriate for analyzing ethical issues related to consumer information. It is important to note that while there is a great deal of overlap between the three ethical perspectives, each provides a unique perspective on the social problem of information externality.

Case Analysis: DoubleClick[8]

The case of DoubleClick, Inc. will serve to integrate the economic, legal, and ethical issues surrounding consumer information. DoubleClick, Inc., a large Internet ad agency, drew criticism for its November 1999 acquisition of Abacus Direct Corp. Prior to the merger, DoubleClick possessed the capability to collect extensive consumer behavior information through the use of Internet cookies. This anonymous consumer data could be sold to various retailers. At the same time, Abacus possessed marketing databases containing extensive consumer information. When DoubleClick released plans to merge both companies, privacy supporters filed suit against DoubleClick. Privacy advocates argued that the merged capabilities might violate the privacy of consumers because DoubleClick would be able to link consumers' identities with the Web sites they visit and the products they purchase. DoubleClick emphasized that consumers could opt-out of participation in a marketing campaign involving 50 million Web ads.

Each side of the issue emphasized its respective position. DoubleClick argued that advertising can be tailored to the specific needs of consumers, which would result in efficient targeted advertising and less spam. Privacy advocates argue that regardless of an advertiser's ability to target consumers with appropriate and desirable advertising, the companies could not be trusted not to use the information responsibly. They argued that the company must be prevented from compiling the information in the first place.

Solving the Information Externality:
Property and Liability Rules

According to the Coase Theorem, assignment of an entitlement would solve this information externality problem. In the case of consumer information, that right could be assigned to one of three separate entities: (1) the specific consumer described by the information, (2) the entity that loaded the information or caused the information to be loaded into a database, or (3) the archivist who compiled a particular database from existing sources. While the Coase Theorem indicates that we do not need to worry about who receives the entitlement, transaction cost analysis suggests that the assignment to one entity might be more efficient than assignment to another.

According to the prior discussion and the five principles suggested by Calabresi and Melamed (1972), we know: (1) that there are positive net benefits that justify information sharing, (2) that there are substantial harms that accrue to consumers when information is misused but that the value of those claimed harms can be inflated by opportunistic consumers, (3) that business is in the unique position to be able to determine the most efficient method of protecting consumers from information abuse, and (4) that business should shoulder the costs of protecting consumers from harm because it, as the central repository of consumer information, has the lowest transaction costs.

If society decides to solve the information problem using a property rule, it would assign control rights, much like ownership rights, to specific pieces or components of information, similar to the way it provides for patent and trademark protections. The "owner" of "consumer information" would hold exclusive rights to the use, handling, and distribution of that information. In each of these three cases, the owner would hold veto authority over the use, handling, and distribution of a consumer's information.

Because of the high transaction costs, it would be inefficient to assign property rights to individual consumers.[9] Consider the high cost of banking if individual consumers had the right to withdraw their information from databases that monitor creditworthiness. Banks would have to raise interest rates and lower credit limits on any individual who withdrew from the system in order to compensate for unforeseeable risks. It makes more sense to assign property rights to the various database archivists because of the lower transaction costs. On the other hand, unless we hold those archivists accountable for the harms they cause, they will have little incentive to minimize the harm to consumers. Consumers and/or society should have some way to monitor both data collectors and database archivists for both improper use and incorrect information.

One downside to the use of property rules is their higher costs compared to liability rules (Baron, 2000). If society decides to solve the information problem using a liability rule, it will need to assess the benefits and costs, in monetary terms, transferred from one actor to another and reallocate those costs and benefits to the specific actors that caused them. This is easier said than done.

Value estimation of the costs and benefits resulting from the use and handling of information is very difficult if not impossible. The problem is that the benefits and costs of information are in many ways intangible and user specific. The intangibility of information leads the various parties in a transaction to disagree over the costs and/or benefits. The enormous variance in the damages assigned by product safety and medical malpractice lawsuits suggests that such disagreements will be hard to overcome. The value of information is user specific since the value may change depending on the unique capabilities and efficiencies of the various parties that use the information. The more efficient user of information is likely to be able to extract more profit than another and hence value it more highly. These valuation problems greatly hinder the ability to implement an entitlement using liability rules.

To be able to assign the entitlement using liability rules, there needs to be some consensus over the value of information. Some social process must be implemented to value information. This can be done in a number of ways. Society can arbitrarily assign a value to information. Society can create a competitive market for information that will assign the value. Either of these methods will still create distributive injustices because of intangibility and user specificity.

The implementation of a liability rule would force businesses to compensate consumers for the harm caused by their actions. In the assessment of harm, society would have to distinguish between real harm and the expected distributive consequences of a market economy. For instance, consumers compete for scarce resources in many markets with price being the arbiter of who wins. The outcome of two consumers competing for loans, where one consumer uses credit responsibly and the other does not, should be that the consumer who uses credit responsibly gets more favorable terms. On the other hand, some less than responsible consumers may cry foul – "I've been harmed by the use of my credit information." Obviously, consumer claims of harm must be judged against some objective criteria if they are to be considered.

Consumers who have been prejudicially discriminated against should be entitled to compensation from the discriminator. Consumers who have been treated unfairly due to inaccurate information should be entitled to compensation from the data collector. Consumers who are burdened by untargeted advertising should be compensated by the advertiser.

From a more practical point of view, the implementation of a liability rule in the US might take the form of the existing law of torts that assess responsibility on the basis of actual or proposed standards such as absolute liability, strict liability, negligence, or privity.[10] Negligence requires that the culprit both caused damage and acted improperly. Strict liability only requires that the culprit caused damage (Whitman & Gergacz, 1991). Strict liability removes the necessity of the consumer to prove that the business was acting improperly. "The law evolved because it is often not feasible for a consumer to prove negligence" (Birnbaum, 1988, p. 142). The government needs to formalize a law of strict liability that provides organizations with basic but clear guiding principles for collecting, using, and distributing consumer information.[11] This law should be *flexible* and *minimal*[12] enough so businesses are not inordinately constrained by it. The increasing confidence by consumers stemming from such a law might actually lead to market efficiency and increased transactions, as well as ethical data management. One example of the strict liability would be Fair Information Practices Act[13] containing principles and guidelines to govern personal information.

One reason why society adopts liability rules is to increase "precaution" in a party's decision and action. A negligence rule holds the business liable for damages only if "due care" has not been taken in undertaking the collection, use, and distribution of consumer information in both electronic and physical settings. As an example, a recent case in which the court extended liability for damage caused by selling personal information[14] illustrates the application of negligence rules to consumer information. Another example might be to directly compensate the targets of mass marketing.[15] In the United States, currently without a comprehensive strict liability law, negligence rules are often applied in the court.

Overall, what is desired is neither a government regime ("a visible hand") nor a pure market-based regime ("an invisible hand"), but a "semi-visible" regime to information externality using the liability approach. This semi-visible, liability approach should correct market failure by balancing control and autonomy simultaneously. This liability rule approach is also expected to accommodate the reasonable expectations of the parties and enforces minimum levels of morality in collecting, using and distributing personal information.

Conclusions

Society has opted to use privacy regulations to control the information externality problem. We have argued that this is undesirable because it does not correct the market failure that causes the information externality. Correcting the externality would create incentives for all parties to act efficiently. The Coase Theorem suggests that the market failure can be corrected using either property rules or liability rules. We suggest that both have costs and benefits, but that liability rules are likely to be the most socially efficient.

The semi-visible, liability regime we propose in this chapter has implications for organizations. First and foremost, the private sector should be more cautious about collecting, using, and distributing consumer information. More litigation of cases (e.g., DoubleClick, DocuSearch) concerning misuse and abuse of consumer information by organizations will not only expose businesses to more risks (e.g., damage to reputation) and potentially serious financial consequences, but also increases consumers' privacy concerns, which may lead this whole discussion of information externality to the matter of privacy. This may further drive society to adopt either a European-style[16] strong government regulation or a pure market-based approach viewing consumer information as commodities. Neither approach fixes market failure nor is favorable for organizations. Then, industries and organizations should initiate the development of self-regulatory codes and norms and make public their policies and practices respectively for handling personal information. Each industry is heavily dependent upon consumer confidence and its credibility. Such industry self-regulatory codes and norms cannot substitute for strict liability rules, but instead they would be a cost-effective means to improve consumer confidence and the credibility of the industry (and its organizations). Finally, each organization needs to be cautious with the utilization of its resources for information handling. Two primary resources would be an organization's employees and its various advanced information technologies, such as customer relationship management (CRM) systems. They often become the sources of misuse and abuse of personal information, which leads the organization to face legal charges and public outcry. Therefore, establishing the internal policies and procedures for technology use and employees training should be a priority.

Information externalities (e.g., information privacy) should be viewed with not only economic but also ethical concerns. Information management needs to be done economically and ethically. The key point in this discussion is that society should charge industry with the responsibility to find the lowest cost method to correct and prevent future injuries to consumers resulting from the use of their information. Such an outcome would be both economically efficient and ethically desirable.

We note that there are still many cases where privacy regulation needs to remain in effect. The privacy regulations surrounding national security seem to be the best way to prevent the dissemination of that type of information.

References

Baron, D. P. (2000). *The environment of business* (3rd ed.). Upper Saddle River, NJ: Prentice Hall.

Barret, F. (1998). Creativity and improvisation in jazz and organizations: Implications for organizational learning. *Organization Science, 9*(5), 605-622.

Barron, J., & Staten, M. (2000). *The value of comprehensive credit reports: Lessons from the U.S. experience.* Retrieved from: *http://www.privacyaliiance.org/resources/research.shtml*

Birnbaum, N. (1988). Strict Liability and Computer Software. *Computer Law Journal*.

Calabresi, G., & Melamed, D. A. (1972). Property rules, liability rules and inalienability: One view of the cathedral. *Harvard Business Review, 85*, 1089-1128.

Coase, R. H. (1960). The problem of social cost. *Journal of Law and Economics, 3*, 1-44.

Culnan, M. J., & Armstrong, P. K. (1999). Information privacy concerns, procedural fairness, and impersonal trust: An empirical investigation. *Organization Science, 10*(1), 104-115.

Davies, S. (1997). Re-engineering the right to privacy: How privacy has been transformed from a right to a commodity. In P. Agre (Ed.), *Technology & privacy*. Cambridge, MA: MIT Press.

Ekelund, R. B., & Tollison, R. D. (1994). *Economics*. New York: Harper Collins College.

Gellman, R. (2002). *Privacy, consumers and costs*. Washington, DC: Electronic Privacy Information Center.

Hedberg, B., Nystrom, C., & Starbuck, W. (1976). Camping on seesaws: Prescriptions for a self-designing organization. *Administrative Science Quarterly, 21*, 41-65.

Kahn, C., McAndrews, J., & Roberds, W. (2000). *A theory of transactions privacy*. (Working Paper, 2000-22). Federal Reserve Bank of Atlanta.

Kaplow, L., & Shavell, S. (1996). Property rules versus liability rules. *Harvard Law Review, 109*, 713-790.

Lewis, P. V. (1989). Ethical principles for decision makers: A longitudinal survey. *Journal of Business Ethics, 8*(4), 271-278.

McCullagh, D. (2001). The economics of regulating privacy on the Internet. *The Library of Economics and Liberty*.

Melville, D. W. (1999). Liability rules, property rules, and incentives not to bargain: The effect of competitive rivalry on the protection of legal entitlements. *Seton Hall Law Review, 29*(4), 1277-1297.

Milberg, S. J., Smith, H. J., & Burke, S. J. (2000). Information privacy: Corporate management and national regulation. *Organization Science, 11*(1), 35-57.

Milne, G. R. (2000). Privacy and ethical issues in database/interactive marketing and public policy: A research framework and overview of the special case. *Journal of Public Policy and Marketing, 19*(1), 1-6.

Nott, L. (2003). *Financial privacy: An economic perspective.* Government and finance division, Congressional Research Service.

Perlman, C. (1963). *The idea of justice and the problem of argument* (J. Petrie, Trans.). New York: The Humanities Press.

Perlman, C. (1967). *Justice.* New York: Random House.

Phelps, J., Nowak, G., & Ferrell, E. (2000). Privacy concerns and consumer willingness to provide personal information. *Journal of Public Policy and Marketing, 19*(1), 27-41.

Pigou, A. C. (1920). *The economics of welfare.* London: Macmillan and Co.

Priest, W. C. (1997). *An information framework for the planning and design of information highways* (Report). Melrose, MA: Center for Information, Technology and Society.

Rotenberg, M. (2001). *Prepared witness testimony.* Subcommittee on Commerce, Trade, and Consumer Protection.

Schwartz, P. M. (1997). Privacy and the economics of personal health care information. *Texas Law Review, 73*(1).

Shiels, M. (2002). Why One Spam Could Cost $50. *BBC News,* 9 April.

Singleton, S. (1998). *Privacy as censorship: A skeptical view of proposals to regulate privacy in the private sector.* Washington, DC: Cato Policy Analysis.

Smith, H. J. (2001). Information privacy and marketing: What the US should (and shouldn't) learn from Europe. *California Management Review, 43*(2), 8-33.

Smith, H. J., Milberg, S. J., & Burke, S. J. (1996). Information privacy: Measuring individuals' concerns about organizational practices. *MIS Quarterly, 20*(2), 167-196.

Stewart, K. A., & Segars, A. H. (2002). An empirical examination of the concern for information privacy instrument. *Information Systems Research, 13*(1), 36-49.

Velasquez, M. (1992). *Business ethics* (3rd ed.). Englewood Cliffs, NJ: Prentice-Hall.

Walters, S. J. K. (1993). *Enterprise, government and the public.* New York: McGraw-Hill.

Warren, S., & Brandeis, L. (1890). The Right to Privacy. *Harvard Law Review, 4*(5).

Webster. (1980). *Webster's new collegiate dictionary.* Springfield, MA: G. & C. Merriam Company.

Whitman, D., & Gergacz, J. W. (1991). *The legal environment of business* (3rd ed.). New York: McGraw Hill.

Endnotes

1   See Barron and Staten (2000). The paper argues that the free flow of credit records benefits consumers.

2   Schwartz (1997) observes that the easy dissemination of this highly sensitive data and use of the data to predict future health risks causes significant individuals with costly medical conditions. He predicts that unless health care information receives adequate legal protection from inappropriate disclosure, private health data increasingly will be used for discriminatory purposes, such as denial of employment or health care coverage, to individuals by employers who are likely to get burdened with the costs.

3   Webster's Dictionary (1980) even gives an alternative definition for leprosy as a "morally or spiritually harmful influence."

4   See W. Curtiss Priest (1997). The article offers an extensive discussion about the characteristics of information.

5   Privacy advocates stringent regulation in privacy issues. Among the classical citations we see in the privacy literature is the *Harvard Law Review* paper by Warren and Brandeis (1890). They viewed privacy as a right "to be let alone." In this vein, Rotenburg (2001) stated that "the protection of privacy in law is central to the American legal tradition." See also Davies (1997).

6   See Kahn, McAndrews and Roberds (2001). Their paper argues there are two sources of externalities in the market for financial privacy. First, it is difficult to commit to not using information once it is acquired because, once collected, it is hard to unlearn. Second, the usefulness of the

information may be tied to sunken investments required to analyze the data, investments the financial institutions may not be able to recoup if a significant number of consumers opt out.

[7]   For further discussions about these types of property rights, see Kaplow and Shavell (1996) and Melville (1999).

[8]   For more information about this case, see United States District Court for the Southern District of New York, No. 00-CIV-0641. OBJECTION BY SETTLEMENT CLASS MEMBERS ELECTRONIC PRIVACY INFORMATION CENTER, JUNKBUSTERS. May 6, 2002. Available at: http://www.epic.org/privacy/cookies/doubleclickobjection.pdf

[9]   See Singleton (1998) and Nott (2003). Singleton points out the potentially high transaction cost of property rules for personal information by noting "if personal information such as a name is property, the implication is that the owner must give permission for every use or collection of the name, not just commerce uses."

[10]   Society has yet to embrace the concept of absolute liability and has abandoned the rule of privity. Absolute liability would hold manufacturers responsible for any injury resulting from the use a product regardless of who was at fault. It has been described as the equivalent of including a zero deductible insurance policy with every product. Absolute liability has been predicted to dramatically increase the cost of goods. Privity is a liability concept from contract law that held that only the parties to a contract could hold each other responsible for injury resulting from a product. Privity was used to shield manufacturers from consumer lawsuits provided they sold their products through middlemen. Privity probably originated as an incentive to spur rapid growth during industrialization.

[11]   Unlike the EU, the US has neither enacted comprehensive data protection legislation, nor designated an independent agency to oversee privacy issues. No federal law governs the collection use and storage of personal information by the private sector. America's Privacy Act of 1974 protects all records held by US federal government agencies and requires them to apply basic fair information practices in the collection, storage and use of personal information. Twenty states have introduced their own laws but can only enforce them within their borders. For example, no one has been prosecuted under California's four-year-old statute (Shiels, 2002). See Privacy and Human Rights 2003 available at: http://www.privacyinternational.org

[12]   From complexity theory, organizational theorists suggest that minimal structures enable both control and autonomy. For further discussion, see Hedberg, Nystrom and Starbuck (1976) and Barret (1998).

[13]   See Privacy Online: Fair Information Practices (FIPs) in the Electronic Marketplace - A Report to Congress, available at: http://www.ftc.gov/reports/privacy2000/privacy2000.pdf. Whether FIPs are flexible and minimal or not is a topic for debate, and this needs future work.

[14]   Docusearch.com is a provider of online investigation solutions. Recently, the New Hampshire Supreme Court has assigned liability for the personal information the company sold to a client over the Internet when the client used the information to trace and murder New Hampshire resident, Amy Boyer. A related court document is available at: http://www.courts.state.nh.us/supreme/opinions/2003/remsb017.htm

[15]   EarthLink wins $16 million in spam case, available at: http://www.pcworld.com/resource/printable/article/0,aid,110627,00.asp

[16]   Despite the long-standing European tradition of tightly regulating most forms of privacy, including online data collection, a recent study by Consumers International shows that European Union Web sites offer visitors quantifiably less privacy than those in the US, where Internet privacy regulations have been largely nonexistent, available at: http://www.consumersinternational.org/Newsdocs/{F3660154-6236-4980-B20D-DAEE6CA93E62}.doc

Chapter IX

Ethics of "Parasitic Computing":
Fair Use or Abuse of TCP/IP Over the Internet?

Robert N. Barger
University of Notre Dame, USA

Charles R. Crowell
University of Notre Dame, USA

Abstract

This chapter discusses the ethics of a proof-of-concept demonstration of "parasitic computing." A "parasite" computer attempts to solve a complex task by breaking it up into many small components and distributing the processing of these components to remote computers that perform this processing without the knowledge or consent of those owning the remote computing resources. This is achieved through the use of the TCP/IP Internet protocol and, in particular, the checksum function of this protocol. After a discussion of similar exploits, the ethical issues involved in this demonstration are analyzed. The authors argue that harm should be the standard for determining if parasitic computing is unethical.

They conclude that a revised notion of the rights of ownership is needed when dealing with the shared nature of the Internet. Suggestions for future research are offered.

Introduction

This chapter will examine some of the issues raised by a proof-of-concept demonstration of "parasitic computing" reported in the journal, *Nature* (Barabasi, Freeh, Jeong, & Brockman, 2001). In this type of computing, a "parasite" computer attempts to solve a complex task by breaking it up into many small components and distributing the processing related to those components over a number of separate remote computers. While the parasitic procedure represents a form of distributed computing, it differs importantly from other well-known examples such as the Search for Extraterrestrial Intelligence (SETI) Project (SETI@home, 2003). The distributed computing utilized in SETI involves volunteers from around the world who allow their local computers to be used for ongoing analysis of vast amounts of data obtained from a radio telescope constantly scanning the heavens. SETI allows anyone with a computer and Internet connection to download software that will read and analyze small portions of the accumulated data (SETI@home, 2003). In effect, SETI has created a super computer from millions of individual computers working in concert.

Like SETI, parasitic computing takes advantage of the power of distributed computing to solve complex problems, but the parasite computer induces "participating" computers, already connected to the Internet, to perform computations without the awareness or consent of their owners. By their own admission, Barabasi et al. (2001) were aware of the ethical issues involved in their demonstration of parasitic computing. On the project Web site they state: "Parasitic computing raises important questions about the ownership of the resources connected to the Internet and challenges current computing paradigms. The purpose of our work is to raise awareness of the existence of these issues, before they could be exploited" (Parasitic Computing, 2001). In this chapter, we will begin to explore these "important questions" by focusing on the type of exploitation inherent in parasitic computing and by considering some of the ethical issues to which this new form of computing gives rise.

Background

The proof-of-concept demonstration reported by Barabasi et al. (2001) involved a single "parasite" computer networked to multiple "host" Web servers by means of the Internet. The underlying communication between the parasite and hosts followed the standard TCP/IP protocol. Within this context, the parasite exercised a form of *covert exploitation* of host computing resources, *covert* because it was accomplished without knowledge or consent of host owners, and *exploitation* because the targeted resources were used for purposes of interest to the parasite, not necessarily the host owners. Covert exploitation of networked computing resources is not a new phenomenon (Smith, 2000; Velasco, 2000). In this section, we will review a few common examples of covert exploitation including some that take advantage of known vulnerabilities in the Internet communication process.

Internet Communication Protocols

The Internet evolved as a way for many smaller networks to become interconnected to form a much larger network. To facilitate this interconnection, it was necessary to establish standards of communication to insure uniformity and consistency in the ways by which a computer attached to one part of the Internet could locate and exchange information with other computers located elsewhere. These standards, known as "protocols," emerged through the influence of the Internet Society, the closest thing the Internet has to a governing authority. The de facto standard that has emerged for Internet communication is a family of protocols known as the Transmission Control Protocol/Internet Protocol (TCP/IP) suite (Stevens, 1994). This TCP/IP standard helps to insure certain levels of cooperation and trust between all parties employing the Internet.

As shown in Figure 1, the TCP/IP protocol suite usually is represented as a layered stack where the different layers correspond to separate aspects of the network communication process (Stevens, 1994). The bottommost *link* layer in the stack corresponds to the physical hardware (i.e., cables, network cards, etc.) and low-level software (i.e., device drivers) necessary to maintain network connectivity. The middle two layers represent the *network* and *transport* layers, respectively. Roughly speaking, the network layer is respon-

Figure 1. Layers of the TCP/IP protocol

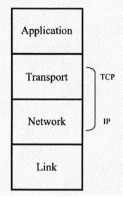

Adapted from Stevens (1994), Figure 1.1

sible for making sure that the "packets" of information being sent over the network to a remote computer are being sent to the proper destination point. Several different forms of communication are employed by this layer, but IP is the main protocol used to support packet addressing. The transport layer, just above network, uses TCP as its main protocol to insure that packets do, in fact, get where they are supposed to go. In essence, at the sending end, the TCP layer creates and numbers packets, forwarding them to the IP layer, which figures out where they should be sent. At the receiving end, the TCP layer reassembles the packets received from the IP level in the correct order and checks to see that all have arrived. If any packets are missing or corrupt, TCP at the receiving end requests TCP at the sending end to retransmit. The top layer of the stack contains *application* services users employ to initiate and manage the overall communication process, applications like file transfer (FTP), e-mail (POP and SMTP), and Web browsing (HTTP).

Worms, Viruses, and Trojan Horses

Covert exploitation of computing resources has taken many forms over the years, some more malicious than others. Perhaps the most nefarious examples are those involving what is called "malware," short for malicious software, designed to damage or disrupt a system (Wiggins, 2001). Malware often takes the form of worms, viruses, or Trojan horses, problems that have become all too common in recent years and do not need to be explored further here.

Suffice it to say that while there is some debate about the precise distinctions among these variants of malware (Cohen, 1992), it is clear that all operate covertly to insinuate themselves into computer systems for purposes of exploitation.

IP-Related Vulnerabilities

Prior to the widespread use of networks and the Internet, the spread of malware among stand-alone computers was dependent upon transfer by means of removable media like floppy disks. With the advent of networking, and the attendant increase in e-mail usage, many other methods became available for gaining unauthorized access to computing resources. While e-mail still may be the most common method used to achieve the spread of malware (Wiggins, 2001), certain forms of covert exploitation associated with vulnerabilities in the TCP/IP protocol have been known for some time (Bellovin, 1989). Space limitations preclude a detailed treatment of this matter here, but three categories of vulnerability will be mentioned: IP spoofing, denials of service, and covert channels. Each represents exploitation of the "trust" relationships Barabasi et al. (2001) describe as being inherent in the TCP/IP protocol.

IP spoofing, as described by Velasco (2000), is a method whereby a prospective intruder impersonates a "trusted" member of a network by discovering its IP address and then constructing network packets that appear to have originated from this source. Other network computers may then accept those packets with little or no question because they seem legitimate and further authentication is not mandatory under the TCP/IP protocol (i.e., trust is assumed). While the technical details of this approach are rather intricate, involving both the impersonation process itself as well as a method for disabling TCP acknowledgments sent back to the system being impersonated, intruders have used this technique to establish communications with remote computers, thereby potentially "spoofing" them into further vulnerabilities and/or unauthorized access (Velasco, 2000).

Denials of service involve malicious attempts to degrade or disrupt the access of network members to a particular host by consuming the TCP/IP resources of the host or the bandwidth of the network itself (Savage, Wetherall, Karlin, & Anderson, 2000). Like IP spoofing, denials of service usually exploit TCP/IP trust and also normally involve some effort to conceal the identity of the perpetrator. An important protocol vulnerability here is based on how the TCP layer responds to an incoming request from the network for communication. TCP trusts that such requests are legitimate and, therefore, upon receipt, it automatically reserves some of its limited resources for the expected pending communication. By flooding a host with bogus requests and withholding follow up from the presumed senders, a malicious perpetrator literally can "choke" the host's communication capacity by keeping its resources in the "pending" mode. Alternatively, by flooding the network with bogus traffic, a perpetrator can consume bandwidth, effectively preventing legitimate traffic from reaching its intended destination.

Covert channels are forms of communication hidden or disguised within what appears to be legitimate network traffic (Smith, 2000). Using such channels, intruders may be able to gain unauthorized access to networked computing resources. As Smith (2000) indicates, certain Internet protocols, like TCP/IP, are susceptible to this potential problem. For example, information directed to or from the TCP layer is marked with a unique identification "header." Generally, in the TCP/IP suite, each layer has its own distinct header. Certain spaces within these headers may be "reserved for future use," and therefore may not be checked or screened reliably. This space thus offers a vehicle by which a covert channel could be established. Data placed in this channel normally would not be subject to scrutiny within the TCP/IP protocol and therefore might be used for malicious purposes. Smith (2000) has reviewed several examples of this kind.

Other Covert Exploits

Bauer (2001) has identified several other forms of covert exploitation involving Internet protocol features. Unlike the circumstances described above, these exploits are not malicious and appear to be largely harmless, yet they represent unauthorized uses of networked computing resources. Many of Bauer's examples apply to the uppermost layer of the TCP/IP protocol, and therefore involve application services like e-mail and HTTP rather than the inner workings of TCP/IP itself. For example, one way to exploit e-mail systems as a means of temporary storage is by sending self-addressed mail through an open mail relay system and then disabling receipt until desired. For at least some period of time, the relay system thus will serve as a temporary storage unit. A similar exploit can be accomplished using a Web server that is instructed to store information of interest to the server owner within cookies on the computers of those who browse to a particular webpage hosted on the server. Assuming they will eventually return to the site, the people with the cookies on their computers are unwittingly providing temporary storage to the server owner.

Parasitic Computing

As noted above, the proof-of-concept demonstration of parasitic computing reported by Barabasi et al. (2001) essentially was an experiment in distributed computing in which a complex problem was decomposed into computational elements that each had a binary, yes or no, outcome. The parasitic computer then "out-sourced" these elements to multiple Web servers across the Internet. Each server receiving an element unwittingly performed its task and reported its binary outcome back to the parasite. The "participating" servers were induced to perform their tasks through another form of TCP/IP vulnerability. As Barbarasi et al. (2001) note, their demonstration was predicated on the fact that "the trust-based relationships between machines connected on the Internet can be exploited to use the resources of multiple servers to solve a problem of interest without authorization" (p. 895). To understand how this was done, we need to look again at the TCP/IP protocol.

TCP Checksum Function

One feature of the TCP protocol that is very important to the Barabasi et al. (2001) implementation of parasitic computing is the checksum property. Checksum is that part of TCP layer operation that is responsible for insuring integrity of packet data being sent over the Internet. Before a packet is released to the IP layer (Figure 1) of the sending computer, TCP divides the packet information into a series of 16-bit words and then creates a one's complement binary sum of these words. The resulting so-called "checksum" value is a unique representation of the totality of information in that packet. The bit-wise binary complement of this checksum is then stored in the TCP header before the packet is sent. When the packet arrives at the receiving computer, the TCP layer there performs its own binary sum of all the information in the packet including the checksum complement. If the packet was received without corruption, the resultant sum should be a 16-bit value with all bits equal to 1 since the original checksum (i.e., the total arrived at by the sending computer) and its exact complement would be added together forming a unitary value (see Barabasi et al., 2001, Figure 2, for more details). If this occurs, the packet is retained as good and is passed to the application layer for action; if not, the packet is dropped and TCP waits for a prearranged retransmission of the packet by the sending computer.

As Freeh (2002) indicates, the TCP checksum function performed by the receiving computer is, in essence, a fundamental "add-and-compare" procedure that forms the basis for any other Boolean or arithmetic operation. As a consequence, TCP can be exploited to perform computations without "invading" (i.e., hacking or cracking into) those systems induced to participate (Barabasi et al., 2001; Freeh, 2002). In this sense, then, parasitic computing is a "non-invasive" form of covert exploitation that does not penetrate beyond the TCP/IP layers of the host. This differentiates parasitic computing from the other methods described above for capitalizing on IP-related vulnerabilities.

NP-Complete Satisfiability Problem

To demonstrate how this exploitation of the TCP checksum function was possible, Barabasi et al. (2001) elected to solve an NP-complete satisfiability (SAT) problem via distributed computing. As described by these authors, the specific version of the problem was a 2-SAT variant involving a Boolean equation with 16 binary variables related by AND or XOR operators (see Barabasi et al., 2001, Figure 3, for more details). The method used to solve this problem involved parallel evaluations of each of the 2^{16} possible solutions. To accomplish these parallel evaluations, a TCP/IP Checksum Computer (TICC) was devised (see Freeh, 2002) that could construct messages containing candidate solutions to the problem that were then sent, along with a template for determining the correct solution, over the Internet to a number of target Web servers in North America, Europe, and Asia. Similar to the behavior of a biological "parasite," the TICC acted to take advantage of the targeted "hosts" by inducing them to evaluate the candidate solutions they received against the correct solution template and return for each one a binary, "yes/no" decision to the TICC.

Inducement without security compromise (i.e., invasion) was achieved by exploiting the TCP checksum function on each targeted host. The parasitic TICC constructed special message packets for each host and injected them directly into the network at the IP layer. These messages contained one of the possible 2^{16} candidate solutions encoded as packet data in two sequential 16-bit words, along with a 16-bit version of the correct solution (in complemented form) substituted in place of the normal TCP checksum value. When the packet was received by the host computer, the two 16-bit words containing the candidate solution, which were presumed by the host to be packet data, were added together with the complemented checksum (i.e., the correct solution) according to the usual operation of the TCP checksum function described above (see Barabasi et al., 2001, Figure 3, for more details). If the enclosed candidate solution was a correct one, then its one's complement binary sum would combine with the complemented correct solution, masquerading as the TCP checksum, to form a 16-bit unitary value, just as would occur if normal packet data had been transmitted without error. In response to a unitary sum, the host's TCP layer passed the packet up to the HTTP application layer, acting as if the packet were not "corrupted." However, because the packet's message was artificial and thus unintelligible to the host, it was prompted to send a response back to the parasitic TICC saying it did not understand the message. This returned response was an indication to the parasite that the candidate solution was, in fact, a correct one, a decision made automatically, but unwittingly, by the host in response to the "artificial" packet. Messages containing an incorrect solution failed the checksum test on the host and were presumed to be corrupt; therefore, no response was sent back to the parasite as per the standard behavior of TCP.

Barabasi et al. (2001) acknowledge the possibility that "false negatives" could have complicated their demonstration of parasitic computing. This complication arises from the fact that incorrect solutions were signified by no return response from the host. However, a lack of returned responses also could be caused by other means such as artificial packets that never made it to their intended hosts for evaluation, or by host responses that got lost on the way back to the parasite. So, this means that correct solutions could be erroneously categorized as incorrect if a false negative occurred. Reliability tests by the authors performed by repeatedly sending correct solutions to hosts showed that false negatives occurred no more than 1% of the time and sometimes less than one in 17,000 cases (Barabasi et al., 2001, pp. 896-897).

Ethical Issues Raised by
Parasitic Computing

As the first author of this chapter has noted elsewhere (Barger, 2001a), most ethical problems considered under the rubric of Internet Ethics are basically variants of older ethical issues (e.g., theft, copyright infringement, invasion of privacy) disguised in modern-day (i.e., electronic or digital) clothing. Parasitic computing may be unique, however, in that, on the surface, it seems to present a truly original conundrum: namely, whether or not it is ethical for a parasitic computer to generate Internet-based communications in a manner that induces remote "host" computers, freely attached to the Internet by their owners, to perform computations of interest to the parasite without the knowledge or permission of host owners. The ethical "gray area" here arises from the fact that the specific host resources targeted by the parasite already were part of the "public domain" by virtue of being attached to the Internet. Moreover, these resources were not instigated to do anything malicious or even out of the ordinary. However, the uses to which the host resources were put by the parasite clearly were not sanctioned in any explicit way by the host owners.

It is perhaps a truism to say that ethical behavior must be assessed against standards inherent within an accepted moral code. Is there an accepted "moral code" for computer ethics? In a white paper published by the Computer Ethics Institute, Barquin (1992) presented what he called the "Ten Commandments of Computer Ethics," which amounts to a list of moral imperatives to guide ethical behavior related to the use of computing and information technology resources. These guidelines have become fairly well known and have been endorsed by other professional societies (e.g., Computer Professionals for Social Responsibility, 2001). Barquin's "commandments" overlap with similar strictures contained in a statement published by the Association for Computing Machinery (ACM) entitled the "ACM Code of Ethics and Professional Conduct" (Association for Computing Machinery, 1992). For purposes of the present discussion, certain of Barquin's "commandments" appear directly relevant to the ethics of parasitic computing.

Thou Shalt Not Use a Computer to Harm Others or Interfere with their Computer Work

These imperatives, abstracted from Commandments 1 and 2, clearly position as unethical any form of "malware" or other type of covert exploitation of computer resources with harmful purpose or consequences. Benign forms of exploitation without mal-intent, like the Barabasi et al. (2001) demonstration of parasitic computing, would seem under this mandate to be an instance of "no harm, no foul." One difficulty here, however, lies with the assessment of harm. Directly harmful effects to a user as a result of someone else's covert exploitation are one thing, but indirect consequences may be quite another. How does one know for sure what might have happened had the covert exploitation not been ongoing, or what might have been precluded by its presence? In an interview with one of the parasitic project authors, reported in the September 6, 2001, issue of *Security Wire Digest*, Vincent Freeh said this about that: "It's sort of like meeting a friend and leaving one car in a shopping center parking lot. You've used the facilities in an unintended way that doesn't benefit the provider of the parking lot — most people wouldn't consider that unethical. But if you bring in a fleet of cars, impacting people who come to do business at the store, I think that's unethical" (McAlearney, 2001).

The second difficulty, alluded to in the above comment by Freeh, arises from the potential for future harm given an escalation of the exploitation. As the authors of an online dictionary, *The Word Spy*, put it in comments under their entry for "parasitic computing": "The bad news is that, although messing with a few checksums won't cause a perceptible drop in the performance of the server, hijacking millions or billions of checksum calculations would bring the machine to its digital knees. It's just one more thing to keep Web site administrators chewing their fingernails" (The Word Spy, 2001). The authors themselves acknowledge this possibility in stating that (a presumably escalated form of) parasitic computing "could delay the services the target computer normally performs, which would be similar to a denial-of-service attack, disrupting Internet service" (Barabasi et al., 2001, p. 897). But, as Freeh (2002) points out, the TICC implementation employed by these authors is not likely an effective platform for the launch of denial-of-service attacks.

In the final analysis, then, we are not convinced that the demonstration of parasitic computing reported by Barabasi et al. (2001) was harmful in any sense. However, the potential may well exist for harmful effects stemming from an elaborated or escalated form of parasitic computing.

Thou Shalt Not Use Others' Computing Resources without Authorization or Snoop in their Files

These imperatives, adapted from Barquin's Commandments 2 and 7, potentially pose the most serious ethical challenges for parasitic computing and also highlight the ethical "gray area" associated with this matter. Parasitic computing does not appear to us in any way to be a form of invasive "hacking." We thus agree with the authors' contention that "unlike 'cracking' (breaking into a computer) or computer viruses, however, parasitic computing does not compromise the security of the targeted servers..." (Barabasi et al., 2001, p. 895). Clearly, there was no "snooping," data corruption, or even residue (back doors, etc.) as a result of their implementation of parasitic computing. Moreover, it is important to emphasize that lack of "awareness" is not necessarily the same thing as lack of authorization. As the authors note, their version of parasitic computing operated "without the knowledge of the participating servers" (Barabasi et al., 2001, p. 895), but does this mean it was unauthorized?

To answer this question we must pose two related queries. One is: To what extent is this TICC version of parasitic computing just a form of normal Internet communication? Barabasi et al. (2001) contended that "parasitic computing moves computation onto what is logically the communication infrastructure of the Internet, blurring the distinction between computing and communication" (p. 897). If this is true, then parasitic computing as implemented by these authors involves nothing more than mere Internet traffic. From the viewpoint of the receiving "host" computers, this certainly was true. As noted above, the specially prepared packets sent by the parasite were reacted to in exactly the same way as all other Internet traffic and were indistinguishable from "normal" packets in terms of their consequences for the host, at least at the level of TCP. That the special packets sent by the parasite were not "normal" does not automatically imply that they exercised a form of unauthorized access.

Therefore, a second important question is: To what extent does the owner of a Web server consent implicitly to the exercise of TCP/IP functions on that machine, which happen automatically because of network traffic anyway, by virtue of the fact that it was connected to the Internet in the first place? There are different viewpoints here. On the parasitic computing Web site at Notre Dame, under a FAQ section, the authors both ask and answer the following question: "How do I reliably stop parasitic computing from occurring on my Web server? [Answer] Unplug it from the net" (Parasitic Computing, 2001). This answer certainly suggests that any computer connected to the Internet has made an implicit acknowledgment that TCP/IP functions may be exercised on that machine. Barabasi et al. (2001) state their position on this matter even more clearly by saying that parasitic computing "accesses only those parts of the servers that have been made explicitly available for Internet communication" (p. 895).

But, is connecting a computer to the Internet the same thing as giving permission for any conceivable use of TCP/IP? Server owners could argue that, even if one grants that those parts of a computer connected to the Internet are in the public domain, there is still a reasonable expectation that Internet traffic will be constituted only in conventional ways. When it is not so constituted, this could be construed as a form of protocol abuse.

However, what exactly is abusive about the exercise of TCP/IP functions on a Web server by non-standard Internet traffic? An analogous question could be posed about "non-standard" uses of any other physical sensors (e.g., motion sensors, electric eyes, etc.) located in the public domain? The most obvious answer here would focus on categorizing any exercise of public domain resources for purposes other than they were intended as being forms of abuse. By this view, electing to sleep on a picnic table in a public park or picnic on a children's merry-go-round would constitute abusive behavior, just as would asking a remote computer to help solve a problem that is of no interest to its owner. Again, however, there is not unanimous accord on this matter. Two of the parasitic computing researchers expressed a different view, as quoted in a *Nature* Science Update about parasitic computing by Whitfield (2001). In that article, Jay Brockman was quoted as saying: "The Web is a source of information. If someone can contrive a question so as to get an answer other than the one intended, I view that as clever, rather than subversive." Along the same lines, Freeh reportedly indicated, "If you have a public service, I have the ability to use it for a purpose that you didn't intend" (Whitfield, 2001).

Yet, surely, there must be some limits on unintended uses of public or private resources, some line of demarcation between acceptable and abusive. Of course, this is the very problem with "gray areas." In them, it is often very difficult to discern sought-after boundary lines. As a result, some like Mark Rash, an attorney who used to prosecute hackers, will say that parasitic computing probably qualifies as trespassing, although it was done without malice (National Public Radio, 2001). Others, like Freeh, will see it as being more like parking one's car in a shopping center's lot without going in to shop: no harm, no foul. In the end, with respect to the use of public resources, we are persuaded that harm should be the arbiter of abuse.

The principal reason for our "harm being the arbiter of abuse" position in relation to parasitic computing lies in the shared nature of the Internet as a public resource. Traditional views of ownership rights involving the idea that an owner has sole control over use and profit from personal property (Calabresi & Melamed, 1972) do not apply strictly, in our opinion, when personal and public property are juxtaposed in a dependency relationship as they are in the context of computers being connected to the Internet. Because the act of connecting to the Internet in order to receive communication services is optional and elective, such action necessarily involves an implicit consent to a form of property sharing that trumps sole propriety. This act is analogous to placing a mailbox on the public easement in front of one's house in order to receive postal service. In these instances, personal property (mailboxes or TCP/IP layers) are made explicitly available to the public so that valued communication services thereby can be obtained. The dependency of the private upon the public arises here because one's personal communications in these instances must pass through a public handling system. Of necessity, this means that one's mailbox or TCP/IP protocol is subject to public interrogation, which amounts to a kind of shared relationship between owner and public.

Of this shared relationship, at least two things can be said. First, as Barabasi et al. (2001) have noted, such actions are undertaken by an owner with a sense of trust that no harm will befall that which is made publicly accessible. In the case of a mailbox this means a trust that it will not be smashed, painted shut, locked, or stuffed so full of irrelevant material that intended mail will no longer fit. Any such circumstances would constitute a violation of this trust and therefore would harm the owner. Similarly, in making an Internet connection, a computer owner trusts that no one will attempt to invade or gain access to the computer, affect its inner workings, or attempt to deny or circumvent its access to the public communications system by means of the shared TCP/IP layer made available to the public.

Second, the nature of the implicit consent involved is limited. In the case of the mailbox, the limitation restricts public access only to the mail receptacle and does not extend it to the yard or the house. For the computer owner, consent to public access is limited to the TCP/IP layer and is not extended generally to the RAM, processor, hard drive, or other peripheral resources connected to the computer.

Philosophic Perspectives

We now briefly examine the two basic opposite world views, Idealism and Pragmatism, along with the ethical viewpoints to which these positions give rise as they relate to parasitic computing. The Idealist derives greater meaning from ideas than things. Ideas do not change, so reality is basically static and absolute. The Idealist philosopher Immanuel Kant used what he called the "Categorical Imperative" to assess the ethics of any action. The first form of his Categorical Imperative states: "Act only on that maxim by which you can at the same time will that it should become a universal law" (The Internet Encyclopedia of Philosophy, 2001). In other words, if you wish to establish (or adhere to) a particular moral or ethical standard, you must be willing to agree that it would also be right for anyone else to follow that standard. It seems, then, from an Idealist perspective, that the originally intended purposes of things (i.e., the ideas upon which they were based) would weigh heavily in ethical judgments regarding their use or abuse. Thus, using anything, even an Internet protocol, for any purpose other than its intended one would be unethical on this view.

The Pragmatist finds meaning neither in ideas nor things. Rather, it is found in experience or change. Pragmatism might therefore be regarded as a more expedient approach than Idealism. Since this philosophical view holds that everything can change, there is no permanent essence or identity. In terms of ethical behavior, this outlook implies that all moral values must be tested and proven in practice since nothing is intrinsically good or bad. If certain actions work to achieve a socially desirable end, then they are ethical and good (Barger, 2001b).

In contrast to a Kantian Idealist perspective, Barabasi et al. (2001) seem to take, if anything, a Pragmatist approach to the ethics of parasitic computing. The Pragmatist prefers to look at intent or consequences to see how it could affect the morality of an action, whereas the Idealist would concentrate on the intrinsic character of the act itself, something the Idealist believes is unaffected by intent or consequences. If a complex problem can be solved more effectively by distributing the computational load among many remote computers that are induced to perform calculations unwittingly, then such actions are acceptable, provided they represent some form of "greater good."

We must acknowledge, however, that these authors depart from full-blown Pragmatism when they note that their demonstration of parasitic computing currently is a very inefficient way to implement distributed computing. To this effect, they state: "To make the model viable, the computation-to-communication ratio must increase until the computation exported by the parasitic node is larger than the amount of cycles required by the [host] node to solve the problem itself instead of sending it to the target. However, we emphasize that these are drawbacks of the presented implementation and do not represent fundamental obstacles for parasitic computing. It remains to be seen, however, whether a high-level implementation of a parasitic computer, perhaps exploiting HTTP or encryption/decryption, could execute in an efficient manner" (Barabasi et al., 2001, p. 897). Obviously, this statement openly questions the effectiveness (i.e., the "greater good") of their method. It also illuminates the need for further research on this topic. Also, these authors are less than fully pragmatic when they express concern about the potential harm that could be caused by parasitic computing were it to be conducted with malicious intent. As we have mentioned above, Barabasi et al. (2001) explicitly acknowledge the possibility of denial-of-service-like attacks using their general approach, however inefficient such attacks might be. Such openly stated concerns by these authors once again challenge the possibility that parasitic computing may conform to the pragmatist's emphasis upon the "greater good." Regardless of one's position on the ethics of parasitic computing, the motivation behind this line of research is laudable. As stated on the parasitic computing Web page, these researchers say: "By publishing our work we wish to bring the Internet's various existing vulnerabilities to the attention of both the scientific community and the society at large, so that the ethical, legal, and scientific ramifications raised by it can be resolved" (Parasitic Computing, 2001).

Conclusions and Future Trends

The demonstration of parasitic computing by Barabasi et al. (2001) has provided us with an interesting and provocative example of how many computers can be recruited to work together in pursuit of solutions to complex problems even when the respective participants are unaware of their involvement. How is one to evaluate the ethics of parasitic computing? Even the researchers involved seem to differ among themselves on this question. Judging by their published remarks, Vincent Freeh and Jay Brockman do not find ethical problems with the covert exploitation involved in their demonstration of parasitic computing. In contrast, when asked the question "Was it ethical?" in a National Public Radio interview, Albert-Laszlo Barabasi replied: "That's a very good question. My thinking [is] that it is not. And that was one of the reasons actually why we haven't really pushed much further" (National Public Radio, 2001). Such disagreement among principals is vivid testimony to the above-noted ethical "gray area" associated with parasitic computing; an area that we think calls for ongoing examination and debate.

The question of where research on parasitic computing is headed is an interesting one from several perspectives. From an efficiency standpoint, as noted above, some attention could be focused on how the overall paradigm can be improved along the lines noted by Barabasi et al. (2001): "To make the model viable, the computation-to-communication ratio must increase until the computation exported by the parasitic node is larger than the amount of cycles required by the node to solve the problem itself instead of sending it to the target" (p. 897). One way to do this, as noted by Freeh (2002), is to increase the number of packets sent by a parasite to a single host. Such an approach also would increase the importance of dealing with the reliability problems associated with parasitic computing (i.e., false negatives and false positives). In terms of the TCP/IP vulnerability exploited by parasitic computing, Freeh (2002) has noted that more work is needed to better define and understand the viability and level of threat associated with various forms of exploitation inherent in Internet protocols. Finally, with respect to a justification for parasitic computing, Vinton Cerf, the co-inventor of the TCP/IP protocol suite, has noted that "one should also consider that compute cycles are highly perishable—if you don't use them, they evaporate. So, some justification [for parasitic computing] might be found if the arriving packets had lowest possible priority for use of the computing cycles." He would not, however, condone the use of parasitic computing on machines whose owners had not authorized such use (Personal communications, September 12 & 21, 2003). This observation suggests that a form of parasitic computing that took advantage of "cycle priority" and/or a "cycle donor pool" might be a less ethically challenging alternative.

References

Association for Computing Machinery. (1992). *ACM Code of Ethics and Professional Conduct*. Retrieved September 9, 2003 from: *http://www.acm.org/constitution/code.html*

Barabasi, A.-L., Freeh, V. W., Jeong, H., & Brockman, J. B. (2001). Parasitic computing. *Nature, 412*, 894-897.

Barger, R. N. (2001a). *Is computer ethics unique in relation to other fields of ethics?* Retrieved September 9, 2003: *http://www.nd.edu/~rbarger/ce-unique.html*

Barger, R. N. (2001b). *Philosophical belief systems*. Retrieved September 9, 2003 from: *http://www.nd.edu/~rbarger/philblfs.html*

Barquin, R. C. (1992). In pursuit of a 'ten commandments' for computer ethics. *Computer Ethics Institute*. Retrieved September 9, 2003 from: *http://www.brook.edu/its/cei/papers/Barquin_Pursuit_1992.htm*

Bauer, M. (2001). *Villian-to-victim computing and applications: Abuse of protocol features*. Retrieved September 9, 2003 from: *http://www1.informatik.uni-erlangen.de/~bauer/new/v2v.html*

Bellovin, S. M. (1989). Security problems in the TCP/IP protocol suite. *ACM Computer Communications Review, 19*(2), 32-48.

Calabresi, G., & Melamed, D. A. (1972). Property rules, liability rules and inalienability: One view of the cathedral. *Harvard Business Review, 85*, 1089-1128.

Cohen, F. (1992). A formal definition of computer worms and some related results. *IFIP-TC11 Computers and Security, 11*(7), 641-652.

Computer Professionals for Social Responsibility. (2001). *The ten commandments of computer ethics*. Retrieved September 9, 2003 from: *http://www.cpsr.org/program/ethics/cei.html*

Freeh, V.W. (2002). Anatomy of a Parasitic Computer. *Dr. Dobb's Journal*, January, 63-67.

Internet Encyclopedia of Philosophy, The (2001). *Immanuel Kant (1724-1804): Metaphysics*. Retrieved September 9, 2003 from: *http://www.utm.edu/research/iep/k/kantmeta.htm*

McAlearney, S. (2001). Parasitic computing relatively benign. *Security Wire Digest, 3(68)*. Retrieved September 9, 2003 from: *http://infosecurity mag.techtarget.com/2001/sep/digest06.shtml*

National Public Radio. (2001). *All things considered*. August 29. Retrieved September 9, 2003 from: *http://www.npr.org/ramfiles/atc/20010829. atc.14.ram*

Parasitic Computing. (2001). Retrieved September 9, 2003 from: *http:// www.nd.edu/~parasite/*

Savage, S., Wetherall, D., Karlin, A., & Anderson, T. (2000). Practical network support for IP traceback. *Proceedings of the 2000 ACM SIGCOMM Conference,* August (pp. 295-306).

SETI@home. (2003). Retrieved September 9, 2003 from: *http:// setiathome.ssl.berkeley.edu/*

Smith, J. C. (2000). Covert shells. Retrieved September 9, 2003 from: *http:/ /gray-world.net/papers/covertshells.txt*

Stevens, W. R. (1994). *TCP/IP illustrated, Volume 1*. Reading, MA: Addison-Wesley.

Velasco, V. (2000). *Introduction to IP spoofing*. Retrieved September 9, 2003 from: *http://www.giac.org/practical/gsec/Victor_Velasco_ GSEC. pdf*

Whitfield, J. (2001). Parasite corrals computer power. *Nature*, August 30. Retrieved September 9, 2003 from: *http://www.nature.com/nsu/010830/ 010830-8.html*

Wiggins, G. (2001). Living with malware. Sans Institute. Retrieved September 9, 2003 from: *http://www.sans.org/rr/paper.php?id=48*

The Word Spy. (2001). *Entry for "parasitic computing"* (posted Dec. 6, 2001). Retrieved September 9, 2003 from: *http://www.wordspy.com/ words/parasiticcomputing.asp*

SECTION IV:

PRIVACY VS. SECURITY

Chapter X

Counterterrorism and Privacy:
The Changing Landscape of Surveillance and Civil Liberties

Michael Freeman
Dartmouth College, USA

Abstract

This chapter addresses how new surveillance technologies and programs aimed at fighting terrorism affect privacy. Some of the new programs and technologies considered include the USA PATRIOT Act (Uniting and Strengthening America by Providing Appropriate Tools Required to Intercept and Obstruct Terrorism), biometrics, national ID cards, video surveillance, and the Total Information Awareness program. This chapter first evaluates the pre-9/11 status quo in terms of what techniques were used, and then examines how the new technologies and programs that have recently been implemented affect privacy constitutionally, legally, and normatively. This chapter argues that many of the recent changes do not, in fact, undermine privacy at a constitutional or legal level, but do run counter to what Americans want and expect in terms of privacy.

Introduction

New surveillance technologies and government programs are being rapidly developed and implemented to fight terrorism, but pose serious challenges to civil liberties and privacy rights. For instance, the PATRIOT Act, the Total Information Awareness program, and national ID cards have all been hotly debated as everyone from libertarians to librarians have worried over how these new programs redefine how the government conducts surveillance of suspected terrorists. At the heart of many of these programs are new technologies such as advanced data-mining software, facial recognition devices, retinal scanners, and other advances in biometrics.

The goal of this chapter is to address how these new technologies and programs can be understood in relation to privacy concerns. To do so, we first need to look at the right of privacy from several angles, specifically, how it is conceived constitutionally, legally, and normatively (by looking at public opinion). Afterwards, various surveillance methods will be divided into three broad types: communications surveillance, information surveillance, and identity surveillance. Communications surveillance looks at what people say or write over e-mail or the phone; the PATRIOT Act is the major source of change in how this information is obtained. Information surveillance looks at the records people have at various places, like banks, hospitals, libraries, etc. New database mining software, the Total Information Awareness project, and provisions in the PATRIOT Act have changed how we think about this type of surveillance. Identity surveillance tracks who you are, possibly with biometric identifiers, or where you are, with video cameras and face recognition technology. For each of these surveillance types, this chapter will evaluate the pre-9/11 status quo in terms of what techniques were used and how they impacted privacy concerns and then examine how the new technologies and programs that have recently been implemented change the pre-9/11 status quo.

Assessing Technology's Impact on Privacy

With the passage of the PATRIOT Act and technological advances in surveillance and biometrics, the future of privacy has been hotly debated. On one side, the ACLU claims, "the surveillance monster is getting bigger and stronger by the day" (Stanley & Steinhardt, 2003, preface), while others disagree, arguing that there are times "when we are justified in implementing measures that diminish privacy in the service of the common good" (Etzioni, 1999, p. 3). With so much hyperbole coming from all sides, the following analysis aims to provide a more objective framework for how we should think about privacy concerns as they are threatened by new measures to fight terrorism.

In assessing the challenges to privacy, it is useful to look at privacy from constitutional, legal, and normative perspectives. Constitutionally, while many people cite the Fourth Amendment as the guarantor of privacy, the word privacy is never actually used. The Fourth Amendment states, "The right of the people to be secure in their persons, houses, papers, and effects, against unreasonable searches and seizures, shall not be violated, and no warrants shall issue, but upon probable cause, supported by oath or affirmation, and particularly describing the place to be searched, and the persons or things to be seized." Our current understanding of how the Fourth Amendment protects privacy is based on a 1967 Supreme Court ruling in which Justice John Harlan argued that there must be "a reasonable expectation of privacy" in order to require a warrant under the Fourth Amendment (Gellman, 2001, p. 203; Regan, 1995, p. 122). In the following sections, the changes in surveillance will be evaluated in terms of the requirements of the Fourth Amendment. Specifically, do investigators still need to get warrants based on probable cause where there are reasonable expectations of privacy?

Legally, there have been several pieces of legislation passed to regulate how the government deals with privacy issues; these include the Omnibus Crime Control and Safe Streets Act (Title III) of 1968, the Foreign Intelligence Surveillance Act (FISA) of 1978, the Electronic Communication Privacy Act (ECPA) of 1986, the Privacy Act of 1974, the PATRIOT Act of 2001, and other acts legislating the disclosure of such data as motor vehicle, credit, and video rental records (Regan, 1995, pp. 6-7). The following sections will examine whether or not the new surveillance technologies and programs change how privacy has been treated by these various legislated acts.

Lastly, privacy is more than just a constitutional or legal right. The right to privacy is a fundamental, constitutive norm of American democracy; civil liberties, including the right to privacy, offer important constraints on the power of the government. People want and expect a certain right to privacy, even to an extent that is sometimes greater than what the law guarantees. As a result, some government program might not violate privacy in any legal sense, but there would still be concerns if it goes against the normative expectation of privacy.

Polling data will be used to look at how the public views the new technologies and government programs.

By looking at privacy from several dimensions, we can more fully understand how new surveillance programs affect our right to privacy. Moreover, this analytical framework can be used for analyzing new surveillance methods in the future. The goal is that this approach can offer a more objective analysis that can avoid the rhetorical grandstanding that it is so common in the debates over privacy.

Communications Surveillance

Under the auspices of the PATRIOT Act, the government's ability to monitor electronic communications has expanded. Wiretaps were previously governed by the Fourth Amendment, case law, Title III, FISA, and the ECPA. According to the Fourth Amendment, the state cannot search a person or property without first acquiring a warrant based on probable cause. Wiretapping was not always protected by the Fourth Amendment and only has been treated as a Fourth Amendment search since the 1967 Supreme Court ruling in *Katz v. United States* (Gellman, 2001, p. 203).

Following this court decision, wiretapping was divided into four categories, depending on whether or not the *content* of the communication was being monitored and whether the surveillance was directed against criminals or foreign agents (Simpson & Bravin, 2003). Title III governed wiretaps of criminals and applied to the content of the communications. Under Title III, the content of communications was protected by the Fourth Amendment and therefore required a court-ordered search warrant based on probable cause (Electronic Privacy Information Center, 2003f).

The ECPA governed the surveillance of criminals when content was not involved. The ECPA allowed the use of pen registers, which monitor outgoing phone numbers, and trap-and-trace devices, which monitor incoming phone numbers. Because the content of the messages was not monitored, these procedures did not violate the Fourth Amendment. Consequently, the investigators only needed to show that the information would be relevant to an ongoing investigation, and not that there was probable cause. Additionally, the court was required to approve the request (Electronic Privacy Information Center, 2003g).

Recognizing the differences between criminal investigations and investigations involving national security, the Supreme Court urged Congress to consider separate legislation to cover foreign intelligence gathering. To that end, Congress passed FISA in 1978, which governed both content and "non-content" aspects of communications of agents of foreign powers. While FISA was originally intended to govern foreign intelligence wiretapping, it was expanded in 1994 to include physical searches, and in 1998 to include pen register and trap-and-trace searches (Electronic Privacy Information Center, 2003c). Surveillance under FISA must be approved by the Foreign Intelligence Surveillance Court (FISC) and by the Attorney General. The application to the FISC needs to contain a statement that there is probable cause that the target is an agent of a foreign government (although not necessarily engaging in criminal activity) and that normal surveillance means are not adequate. The FISC has approved over 15,000 requests since 1979 with only a handful of rejected applications (Electronic Privacy Information Center, 2003d; Lithwick & Turner, 2003).

The PATRIOT Act has changed how surveillance can be conducted. Before 9/11, there were two types of surveillance targets: criminals (Title III and ECPA) and spies (FISA). Suspected terrorists are now a difficult third category, which the PATRIOT Act has essentially placed in the spy/FISA category. Several parts of the PATRIOT Act relax some of the FISA provisions. Specifically, Section 206 allows for roving FISA wiretaps, whereby a FISA court can issue a warrant against an intelligence target rather than a specific phone or computer. Section 218 lowers the standards required for a FISA warrant. Previously, FISA warrants were issued when the "primary purpose" of the investigation was intelligence gathering. Now, only a "significant purpose" of the search has to be intelligence gathering.

In terms of criminal surveillance, Section 216 extends the use of pen registers and trap-and-trace to the Internet. Before the PATRIOT Act, monitoring e-mail for non-content was a legal gray area; whether investigators conducted such searches depended on case-by-case decisions by the court. Section 216 makes the government's use of the Carnivore program to search the "to" and "from" lines of e-mail messages unambiguously legal. A highly contentious section of the PATRIOT Act is Section 213, the so-called Sneak-and-Peek provision that allows investigators to delay giving notice of an ongoing search. According to a Department of Justice Report, this provision had been used 248 times between September 2001 and May 2003 (Lichtblau, 4 2003). Since the 1980s, however, delayed notification had been allowed and upheld by the courts in certain cases where the notification of the warrant would have had adverse effects (Talk of the Nation, 2003). Terrorism cases already qualified as an exception, so the real change in the law is that delayed notification can now be used in almost any criminal search (Lithwick & Turner, 2003).

In sum, the PATRIOT Act has legally justified measures that had been previously approved on a case-by-case basis (such as delayed notifications and Carnivore searches), placed terrorism crimes within the framework of the FISA provisions, and loosened some of those provisions to make investigations easier. With a FISA court order, investigators can now search the content of suspected terrorists' communications as long as a significant (and no longer primary) purpose of the search is intelligence gathering and can use the information obtained from the search in court. Warrants can now be issued by the FISA court for roving wiretaps that follow individuals rather than particular phones and any non-content communication (e-mail, Internet) can be monitored with a court order.

The key question for this project is: How do these changes impact privacy? In terms of the constitutional protections of privacy, search warrants still require judicial approval as does any FISA authorized search, albeit with criteria that are easier to meet. Delayed notification of searches has been approved by the Supreme Court since 1979, when the court ruled that "covert entries are constitutional in some circumstances" (*Dalia v. United States*). These changes in the PATRIOT Act, then, do not alter the constitutional protections of privacy.

Legally, the PATRIOT Act changes many of the earlier provisions of Title III, FISA, and ECPA, but most of these changes are simple common-sense updates to wiretapping laws or merely a result of classifying suspected terrorists as the equivalent of foreign agents and consequently using the more relaxed FISA guidelines to conduct surveillance against them. Some of the common-sense updates include the use of roving wiretaps, the extension of pen register and trap-and-trace measures to e-mail and the Internet, and the use of delayed notification of searches where warranted. Fixed wiretaps may have been adequate in the age of fixed land lines, but a roving wiretap allows the police to monitor any device used by a suspect. Likewise, the ability to monitor the "non-content" of e-mail had already been approved on a case-by-case basis by the courts. Legally and constitutionally, then, none of these measures are violations of privacy. Orin Kerr, law professor at George Washington University, accordingly describes the PATRIOT Act as "primarily modifications to pre-existing law… [and] is significantly more modest than most people fear" (Talk of the Nation, 2003).

In terms of public opinion, whether or not the PATRIOT Act is an infringement on individual privacy is hard to say, largely because of the imprecision of polling questions. In some polls, the population seemed split on whether privacy was under attack. For example, in a *New York Times* poll in December 2001, 48% of respondents supported more surveillance, while 44% thought that more surveillance would violate their rights (Electronic Privacy Information Center, 2003e). In other polls, however, the majority of the respondents seem opposed to the current surveillance methods. For instance, in an April 2002 poll by the Institute for Public Policy and Social Research, 77% opposed warrantless searches of suspected terrorists and 66% opposed monitoring telephone and e-mail conversations, even though all of this was legal previous to the PA-TRIOT Act (Electronic Privacy Information Center, 2003e). Likewise, in a December, 2001 *New York Times* poll, 65% of respondents opposed the government monitoring communications in order to fight terrorism (Electronic Privacy Information Center, 2003e). And yet, other polls show that the vast majority of Americans support the PATRIOT Act. Attorney General John Ashcroft has cited a USA Today/CNN/Gallup poll from August 2003, in which 74% of respondents think that the government has either been about right or even not gone far enough in restricting civil liberties to fight terrorism. Regarding the PATRIOT Act specifically, 69% think the legislation is just right or does not go far enough in restricting liberties (Department of Justice, 2003).

Clearly, there is no overwhelming consensus among Americans on how they think about government surveillance, the PATRIOT Act, or their civil liberties. How any particular question is answered seems to depend largely on how the question is phrased. As a result, proponents of either side of the debate can offer polling data to support their claims. Perhaps the best that can be said about public opinion is that there is neither overwhelming opposition nor support for increased government surveillance of suspected terrorists.

Taken as a whole, the changes to how the government conducts communications surveillance do not violate constitutional standards, do not significantly change existing laws governing surveillance (which already allowed many of the powers contained in the PATRIOT Act, just as exceptions), and do not overwhelmingly violate any normative expectations by the population of what they can expect in terms of individual privacy.

Information and Data Surveillance

Information surveillance is another type of surveillance that is undergoing rapid changes in the name of fighting terrorism. At its extreme, information surveillance would allow the government unfettered access to any information or record of any individual, from bank records, medical charts, and credit ratings to library borrowing records and information on purchasing habits. Technologically, new data-mining software is at the forefront of these changes. On the policy side, the Total (renamed Terrorist) Information Awareness program and elements of the PATRIOT Act have caused the most controversy.

Before 9/11, if investigators wanted access to somebody's records, they could either get a court-issued search warrant, a court-ordered subpoena, or could use an administrative subpoena (under particular circumstance). If investigators wanted records from multiple sources they were constrained by the requirement that they get separate warrants or subpoenas for each database to be searched. This changed with the PATRIOT Act and the proposed Total Information Awareness program.

To make it easier to get records of suspected terrorists, Section 215 of the PATRIOT Act allows the government to go to a FISA court and subpoena any third-party record, as long as the data is needed for a terrorism investigation. There is no need for probable cause nor for the suspect to be an agent of a foreign power. This allows the FBI to demand records, for example, at libraries, book stores, doctors' offices, etc. (Lithwick & Turner, 2003). Despite the protestations of librarians, Attorney General John Ashcroft claimed that Section 215 has never been used to look at library records (Williams, 2003). While Section 215 has gotten probably the most publicity of any section of the PATRIOT Act, Section 505 actually allows for even easier access to records, but has largely escaped criticism. Section 505 allows for administrative subpoenas that require no probable cause or court oversight. They can be administered by FBI field offices to obtain phone, e-mail, and financial records in any terrorism investigation (Lithwick & Turner, 2003).

In addition to these new abilities to subpoena records, the government also flirted with the idea of creating a centralized, comprehensive database under the Total (or Terrorist) Information Awareness (TIA) program run by the Defense Advanced Research Projects Agency (DARPA). Some of the categories of information that the TIA hoped to access included education, housing, medical, travel, veterinary, transportation, and financial records. The goal was to imagine terrorist attacks and develop scenarios for how they might be planned, and then use technologically advanced data-mining programs to see if there was a pattern in the data of airline tickets, weapons purchases, equipment rentals, etc. This program was under constant criticism; the Senate banned deployment of the program in January 2003, cut off funding in July 2003, and finally shut it down in September 2003 (Clymer, 2003; Partlow, 2003).

How do these changes in information surveillance affect privacy rights? From a constitutional perspective, subpoenas do not constitute a search; the subpoenaed party can refuse to deliver the subpoenaed records and fight the subpoena order in court. Also, there is no clear expectation of privacy when records are held by third parties. For bank records, specifically, the Supreme Court ruled in *United States v. Miller* (1976), that they are not protected by the Fourth Amendment. The court wrote, "The depositor takes the risk, in revealing his affairs to another, that the information will be conveyed by that person to the Government." Allowing investigators to subpoena records for terrorism investigations changes none of this. Likewise, the implementation of the TIA would have been constitutional because the records that would have been searched would have been in the public domain or legally accessible by purchase or subpoena.

Legally, there is little to stop the government from getting access to records of individuals. The Privacy Act of 1974 banned the government from keeping information on citizens who are not the targets of investigations, but the government can get around this by either purchasing the information from private sources or using subpoenas to get it (Stanley & Steinhardt, 2003). Also, there is a legal precedent for the use of administrative subpoenas, which are already authorized for more than 300 types of investigations (Lichtblau, 2003). In the end, the use of subpoenas in terrorism investigations does not challenge privacy from legal or constitutional grounds, although administrative subpoenas, with a lack of judicial oversight, are worrying in times when abuses of power seem more likely.

In terms of public opinion, the use of subpoenas has received a great deal of criticism. Librarians have been in an uproar over the possibility that FBI agents might demand access to patrons' borrowing records. Librarians in Santa Cruz shredded sign-in sheets for computer terminals, while the Montana Library Association passed a resolution saying the PATRIOT Act is "a danger to the constitutional rights and privacy rights to library users" (Kohler, 2003). Likewise, there was so much controversy over the Total (or Terrorism) Information Awareness program, as well as the terrorism futures market, that

John Poindexter resigned from leading the program and Congress cut off funding for these programs (Graham, 2003). The access that might have been granted to TIA would have violated the normative aspect of privacy because it would have removed any relationship to criminal activity by searching for patterns of behavior rather than people or places (Electronic Privacy Information Center, 2003a; Stanley & Steinhardt, 2003). According to Timothy Edgar, a legislative counsel for the American Civil Liberties Union office in Washington, the TIA "was a hugely unpopular program with a mission far outside what most Americans would consider acceptable in our democracy" (Hulse, 2003). In a Business Week/Harris Poll, 95% of the American public "were uncomfortable with profiles that included tracking of browsing habits, identity, and other data, such as income and credit data" (Electronic Privacy Information Center, 2003e). Evaluating privacy in all of its aspects is particularly useful here, because it shows that, while the TIA may have not infringed on privacy in legal or constitutional ways, it was still vehemently criticized by the public, and this criticism affected policy decisions.

In sum, in terms of data surveillance, subpoenas of records are legal and constitutional, yet are largely unpopular and unsupported by the American populace. Likewise, sweeping searches of large databases for patterns of behavior are also technically legal, but overwhelmingly unpopular.

Identity Surveillance

Another area where technology is shaping new surveillance methods is the realm of identity surveillance. This category includes video surveillance, which aims to monitor public places, and biometric-based national ID cards that can positively identify any individual. Both types of surveillance hope to be able to help the government know who you are and where you are.

The old methods for identity surveillance were fairly simple. To monitor what was going on in public places, the police simply put officers on the street and had them look for suspicious activity. Likewise, if a business or government agency needed to know your identity, you provided a birth certificate, passport, or driver's license with a picture and probably a signature (both of which are basic biometric indicators of your identity). All of this is rapidly changing with the dramatic increase in the use of video cameras and with the technological advances being made in biometrics.

Biometrics, in general, is a fast-growing field with new identifiers offering tremendous promise and is "poised to become a common feature in the technological landscape" (Electronic Privacy Information Center, 2003b). Some biometrics, like fingerprints, have been used for decades, but even they are going through technological advances. New fingerprint scanners use light scanners, infrared beams, and silicon sensors to immediately verify your identity (Lubell, 2003). There are also new methods to make sure fingerprints come from "living human skin" (Chartrand, 2003). Iris scanning is also being developed as a tool for uniquely identifying individuals. Some airports have already run pilot programs using this technology (Austen, 2003), and a bank in England uses iris scans to identify customers (Brin, 1998).

Facial recognition technology is also rapidly improving. According to a 2003 report by the National Institute of Standards and Technology, facial recognition technology has improved substantially since 2000 and could be used in combination with "other biometric systems to verify that people are who they claim to be" (Feder, 2003). This report, though, also noted the need for continued advances, citing the fact that the best system only made a correct match 50% of the time. Since 9/11, Congress mandated that entry and exit points use biometric identifiers by the end of 2004, while the Department of Homeland Security plans to install fingerprint and facial recognition devices in airports, seaports, and border crossings (Shenon, 2003).

Facial recognition technology is also being combined with video cameras to make video surveillance of public areas potentially pervasive. While the use of video cameras in the US is still fairly limited, the future may look more like Great Britain, where there are over 1.5 million cameras (Electronic Privacy Information Center, 2003h; Parenti, 2003). Future increases in video surveillance would be both quantitative (by increasing the numbers of cameras) and qualitative (from advances in facial recognition programs and the digitization of video, which results in cheaper cameras, transmission of video, and storage) (Stanley & Steinhardt, 2003; Whitaker, 1999).

Another security exploitation of biometric technology is the proposed creation of a national ID card (Parenti, 2003, p. 84). Currently, there is no centralized, uniform national ID; instead, we prove our identity by showing passports, green cards, driver's licenses, birth certificates, etc. These forms of identification, however, are easily forged because they rely on primitive biometrics such as pictures or signatures (Kent & Millett, 2002). A national ID card based on biometrics would be incredibly more difficult to forge, while also providing centralized, standardized content that is easily shared between government agencies (Kent & Millett, 2002).

How do these new programs and technologies impact privacy? From constitutional and legal perspectives, video surveillance is not protected by the Fourth Amendment because there is no expectation of privacy in public spaces. According to legal experts, using video cameras to watch public spaces is the logical equivalent of using police officers to watch public places (Taylor, 1997). On the issue of national ID cards, being compelled to provide proof of your identity does not constitute an invasion of privacy. There are already countless of examples of times when we need to show ID, from boarding an airplane to setting up a bank account to walking into a bar (Etzioni, 1999). The real change with a national ID card would occur if citizens were compelled to carry it at all times and compelled to provide it to officials beyond the times we are already required to show identification. Just changing our ID systems from state driver's licenses to a national ID would not, however, necessitate these changes. From legal and constitutional perspectives, then, neither national ID cards nor video surveillance pose a threat to privacy.

In terms of public opinion, video surveillance is widely accepted, at least in its current form (without facial recognition attached to it). Video surveillance, according to the pro-privacy Electronic Privacy Information Center (2003h), at least "enhances people's sense of security" even though its effectiveness is debated. National ID cards, though, are viewed much differently by the public. Historically, national ID cards have always been unpopular (Eaton, 2003; Electronic Privacy Information Center, 2002). "Citizens' concern for civil liberties, their historic association of ID cards with repressive regimes, and states' rights concerns have discouraged movement toward a governmentally sanctioned nationwide identity system" (Kent & Millett, 2002, p. 7). Immediately after 9/11, national IDs became more popular, with 68% of Americans supporting the idea. In subsequent polls, however, support for a national ID dropped to 44% in November 2001 and 26% in March 2002 (Electronic Privacy Information Center, 2003e). Therefore, while national ID cards do not violate any constitutional or legal protections of privacy, they run counter to a constitutive American norm about what we see as government's appropriate role in our daily lives.

Conclusions

The issue of technology versus privacy is not new, nor will it ever go away. Advances in surveillance technology will continually redefine how we *might* fight terrorism, although not necessarily how we *should*. Hopefully, the framework provided in this chapter will help in evaluating how new technologies and programs affect privacy and, by extension, whether we *should* use various programs in our counter-terrorism effort. In this regard, this chapter is very much concerned with the ethics of how the government acquires information about US citizens in its campaign against terrorism. Much of what is argued on both sides of the current dialogue is extreme and biased, to say the least, with both sides engaging in threat inflation (whether the threat comes from terrorists or the government). By objectively looking at privacy from constitutional, legal, and normative aspects, we can better assess how, exactly, the new initiatives actually change how privacy is protected.

While each individual program or technology impacts privacy in different ways, there are several broad generalizations that come out of this study. First, technology is good. Technologies like biometrics and data-mining software are just beginning to be exploited and have numerous potential security applications. While the use of new technologies undeniably raises concerns for privacy, these technologies can also strengthen individual privacy. Biometrics, for example, when linked with a national ID card, can make identity theft (and the devastating loss of privacy that goes with it) much more difficult.

Second, oversight is good for protecting privacy. Judicial oversight is a central component of the Fourth Amendment. Also, civil rights watchdog groups like the ACLU and EPIC play a critical role in defending civil liberties and protecting privacy and other freedoms even though their arguments are at times too extreme. Likewise, Congress's insistence that the Justice Department report on its use of the PATRIOT Act should be lauded. Measures that bypass any legal or judicial oversight should be undertaken reluctantly and only if absolutely necessary.

Third, common sense is good. Many of the concerns for privacy are justified, but can be ameliorated with common-sense solutions. Most Americans, for example, are opposed to a national ID card in part because it would store various pieces of personal information that could be abused by government investigators. Yet, simple measures — like filters that would screen out unnecessary data or audit trails that could track who accessed a particular file — are common-sense solutions that would allow us to have both privacy and security (De Rosa, 2003).

In sum, privacy is a cherished value in American society and should be protected as much as possible. Before accepting the rhetoric of various groups, we need to objectively analyze how new programs and technologies exactly affect privacy. Looking at privacy from constitutional, legal, and normative perspectives is the first step in this process.

Acknowledgments

I would like to thank Adam Golodner, Beryl Howell, and Joe Onek for their assistance. I also wish to acknowledge the support of Dartmouth College's Institute for Security Technology Studies.

References

Alderman, E., & Kennedy, C. (1997). *The right to privacy*. New York: Vintage Books.

Austen, I. (2003). A scanner skips the ID card and zeroes in on the iris. *The New York Times*, May 15, p. G8.

Brin, D. (1998). *The transparent society: Will technology force us to choose between privacy and freedom?* Reading, MA: Perseus Books.

Chartrand, S. (2003). Verifying people's identities by using their hands, eyes, or voices. *The New York Times*, August 11, p. C2.

Clymer, A. (2003). Threats and responses: Surveillance; Senate rejects Pentagon plan to mine citizens' personal data for clues to terrorism. *The New York Times*, January 24, p. A12.

Dalia v. United States, 441 U.S. 238 (1979).

Department of Justice (2003). Preserving life and liberty. Retrieved September 16, 2003 from: *http://www.lifeandliberty.gov/*

De Rosa, M. (2003). Privacy in the Age of Terror. *The Washington Quarterly*, (Summer), 27.

Eaton, J. W. (2003). *The privacy card: A low cost strategy to combat terrorism.* Lanham, MD: Rowman &Littlefield.

Electronic Privacy Information Center, The (2002). National ID cards. Retrieved July 31, 2003 from: *http://www.epic.org/privacy/id_cards/*

Electronic Privacy Information Center, The (2003a). The attorney general's guidelines. Retrieved July 31, 2003 from: *http://www.epic.org/privacy/fbi/*

Electronic Privacy Information Center, The (2003b). Biometric identifiers. Retrieved July 31, 2003 from: *http://www.epic.org/privacy/biometrics/*

Electronic Privacy Information Center , The (2003c). Foreign intelligence surveillance act. Retrieved July 31, 2003 from: *http://www.epic.org/privacy/fisa/default.html*

Electronic Privacy Information Center, The (2003d). Foreign intelligence surveillance act orders 1979-2002. Retrieved July 31, 2003 from: *http://www.epic.org/privacy/wiretap/stats/fisa_stats.html*

Electronic Privacy Information Center, The (2003e). Public opinion on privacy. Retrieved July 31, 2003 from: *http://www.epic.org/privacy/survey/default.html*

Electronic Privacy Information Center, The (2003f). Title III electronic surveillance 1968-2002. Retrieved July 31, 2003 from: *http://www.epic.org/privacy/wiretap/stats/wiretap_stats.html*

Electronic Privacy Information Center, The (2003g). The USA PATRIOT Act. Retrieved July 31, 2003 from: *http://www.epic.org/privacy/terrorism/usapatriot/*

Electronic Privacy Information Center, The (2003h). Video surveillance. Retrieved July 31, 2003 from: *http://www.epic.org/privacy/surveillance/*

Etzioni, A. (1999). *The limits of privacy.* New York: Basic Books.

Feder, B. (2003). Face-recognition technology improves. *The New York Times*, March 14, C2.

Gellman, R. (2001). Does privacy law work? In P. E. Agre & M. Rotenberg (Eds.), *Technology and privacy: The new landscape* (pp. 193-218). Cambridge, MA: MIT Press.

Graham, B. (2003). Poindexter resigns but defends program; Anti-terrorism, data scanning efforts at Pentagon called victims of ignorance. *The Washington Post*, August 13, A2.

Hulse, C. (2003). Congress shuts Pentagon unit over privacy. *The New York Times*, September 26, A20.

Kent, S. T., & Millett, L. I. (Eds.) (2002). *IDs – Not that easy: Questions about nationwide identity systems.* Washington, DC: National Academy Press.

Kohler, J. (2003). Librarians across the country chafe under USA PATRIOT Act Restrictions: Groups file lawsuit. The Associated Press, July 31.

Lichtblau, E. (2003). Justice dept. lists use of new power to fight terror. *The New York Times*, May 21, A1.

Lichtblau, E. (2003). Bush seeks to expand access to private data. *The New York Times,* September 14. Retrieved September 18, 2003 from: *http://www.nytimes.com*

Lithwick D., & Turner J. (2003). A guide to the PATRIOT Act. *Slate Magazine,* September 8-12. Retrieved from: *http://slate.msn.com/id/2087984/*

Lubell, S. (2003). Gadgets that warm to the real you. *The New York Times*, April 17, G6.

Parenti, C. (2003). *The soft cage: Surveillance in America.* New York: Basic Books.

Partlow, J. (2003). Senate vows to deny funding to computer surveillance Effort. *The Washington Post*, July 19, E1.

Regan, P. M. (1995). *Legislating privacy: Technology, social values, and public policy.* Chapel Hill, NC: The University of North Carolina Press.

Shenon, P. (2003). New devices to recognize body features on U.S. entry. *The New York Times*, April 30, A16.

Simpson, G. R., & Bravin, J. (2003). New power boosts terror fight. *The Wall Street Journal*, January 21, A4.

Stanley, J., & Steinhardt, B. (2003). *Bigger monster, weaker chains: The growth of an American surveillance society.* New York: ACLU.

Talk of the Nation (2003). USA PATRIOT Act. *National Public Radio.* April 22.

Taylor, B.J. (1997). The screening of America: Crime, cops and cameras. *Reason,* (May), 45. Retrieved September 16, 2003 from: *http://reason. com/9705/col.bjtaylor.shtml*

United States v. Miller, 425 U.S. 435 (1976).

Whitaker, R. (1999). *The end of privacy: How total surveillance is becoming a reality*. New York: The New Press.

Williams, P. (2003). No library searches, Ashcroft says. September 17. Retrieved October 27, 2003 from: *http://www.msnbc.com*

Chapter XI

Balancing Individual Privacy Rights and Intelligence Needs:
Procedural-Based vs. Distributive-Based Justice Perspectives on the PATRIOT Act

Kathleen S. Hartzel
Duquesne University, USA

Patrick E. Deegan
Duquesne University, USA

Abstract

This chapter explores how individuals using different justice perspectives to evaluate the appropriateness of the USA PATRIOT Act will logically arrive at different views on the fairness of the legislation. Some pundits believe the USA PATRIOT Act creates an increased risk for the privacy rights of US citizens. Excerpts from both Department of Justice and ACLU documents concerning the USA PATRIOT Act are presented. An analysis of these excerpts suggests that the Department of Justice applies a procedural justice perspective to demonstrate the fairness of the Act in terms of the way the law will be applied. The ACLU applies an outcome-based justice perspective that focuses on the potential for the Act to disproportionately penalize specific demographic groups. Different justice perspectives lead to different fairness judgments.

Introduction

This chapter presents a social justice perspective on people's attitudes about revealing personal data in exchange for increased government sanctioned-intelligence activity. The degree of personal and corporate data that law enforcement officials and intelligence agencies need in order to provide more comprehensive protection from terrorist attacks threatens to erode individual privacy rights granted by the Constitution and defined by the legal system. Are people willing to trade their personal privacy and autonomy to protect themselves and others or to trade privacy for convenience and profit? How does a society determine whether it is just to compromise privacy rights for increased security? Finally, if an individual's privacy has been compromised, how does that person judge the fairness of this sacrifice in relation to more effective government intelligence and increased physical safety of persons and property?

Comparing the merits of decreasing the threat of terrorist action to the personal costs of a decrease in individual privacy rights is important because of the technological capabilities available today. Technology can, and should, be used to help identify behavior leading to criminal acts. However, the processing capability of information technologies, the vast number of transaction data-bases with personal identifiers, and the ability to retrieve, integrate, and create virtual alter egos is cause for alarm. Public data of a personal nature, such as deaths, births, sales, and property transfers, have been a constant in our society. However, the difficulty, time, and expense involved in retrieving the data made it difficult to integrate the data and view it as a whole. Information technologies can remove physical barriers to accessing data and can facilitate the integration of data from multiple sources. This is especially true when this data is placed on the Web and in other publicly accessible databases. The aggregation of this public personal data can be too intrusive to be deemed appropriate for a public record (Perkins, 2002).

When electronic profiles of individuals are created, they typically are built with data collected for other, often innocent, purposes — yet they can serve as the basis for initiating more invasive intelligence activity against foreign nationals and US citizens alike. Furthermore, with today's technology, the time and cost necessary to assemble profiles are negligible after the data retrieval and integration algorithms are developed and legal clearances are available. Thus "the body of evidence" necessary to cost-justify an investigation of individuals is minuscule. As a consequence, targeting of intelligence activities could be somewhat arbitrary or capricious. Unfortunately, even the innocent subjects of this type of investigation may suffer irreparable harm once their privacy has been violated. Thus, information technologies can be used to threaten the privacy of individuals, as well as to protect them from other threats.

Privacy Rights vs. Intelligence Needs

We value our privacy from a young age. As small children we decide that we can change our clothes by ourselves. As preteens, we lock our diaries because our thoughts are private. As teenagers, we lock the bedroom door so we can be alone — free from the intrusions of Mom and Dad. As adults, the details of our relationships with other people are considered private. Typically, people do not want their financial transactions, whereabouts, or medical histories publicized. Despite our intimate familiarity and desire for privacy, definitions of privacy are often nebulous or incomplete. This is because privacy is a multifaceted concept. The classic definition of privacy is the right to be left alone (Warren & Brandeis, 1890). Privacy is also considered the right to control the use of personal information about one's self (Westin, 1967). Roger Clarke (1999) defines privacy as "the interest that individuals have in sustaining a 'personal space', free from interference by other people and organizations." He further specifies four dimensions of privacy: (1) Privacy of the person, which deals with the physical body — compulsory medical tests and treatments are representative of this category; (2) Privacy of personal behavior, which deals with what we do — this includes our religious, political, and sexual activities; (3) Privacy of personal communications, which implies personal conversations are not to be recorded; (4) Privacy of personal data, which means data about ourselves should not be revealed to other parties without our consent.

Another reason for the lack of clarity in defining privacy — in addition to its being a multidimensional concept — is that privacy is not an absolute right. As members of society, certain personal information must be made available to others. For example, the privacy of an individual's health records can be and should be compromised when public health demands it. Another example is the need of potential creditors to know about an individual's credit history in order to assess the risk of nonpayment before approving a loan.

As a society, we rely on the government to protect us from foreign powers, organizations, and their agents who would chose to do us harm. But, in order to avert a threat, you must be aware of the danger. Thus we need "intelligence." The US Government's Intelligence Community (2003) defines intelligence as:

> *a body of evidence and the conclusions drawn therefrom that is acquired and furnished in response to the known or perceived requirements of consumers. It is often derived from information that is concealed or not intended to be available for use by the acquirer ... The Intelligence Community deals with both classified and unclassified information. Its analysts produce finished intelligence by analyzing, evaluating, interpreting, and integrating such information (raw intelligence) from various sources.*

The USA PATRIOT Act (**U**niting and **S**trengthening **A**merica by **P**roviding **A**ppropriate **T**ools **R**equired to **I**ntercept and **O**bstruct **T**errorism) was drafted in response to the September 11, 2001 terrorist attacks on the US, and passed October 24, 2001. The Act extends many of the same tools that law enforcement uses in the war on crime and drugs to the war on terrorism. It applies to foreign nationals and US citizens alike. The USA PATRIOT Act is designed to protect America from clear and present dangers, but it does so at a cost to our previously acquired privacy rights. The Act has been both applauded for aggressively equipping law enforcement and intelligence agencies with the access to information that they need to fulfill their missions, and also widely protested and criticized for eroding individual privacy rights.

On September 1, 2002, in an address to the Eighth Circuit Judges Conference, John Ashcroft, US Attorney General, stated that the mission of the Department of Justice had changed in focus from the prosecution of illegal acts to the prevention of terrorist acts. In other words, intelligence activity will be the focus. Ashcroft (2002) acknowledged the conundrum that increasing intelligence activity creates. He said, "I am concerned about the expansion of preventative law enforcement. That is why we have undertaken this challenge, mindful that we seek to secure liberty, not trade liberty for security." Given this change in the stated mission of the Department of Justice, an analysis of the justifying perspectives is both timely and relevant to future policy decisions.

Social Justice Perspectives

The social justice and organizational justice literatures are concerned with perceptions of fairness in the allocation of rewards and punishments within a given population. The literature reports that people essentially use two evaluation heuristics to judge the fairness of a given situation; these heuristics are called distributive justice and procedural justice. Distributive justice is focused on the outcome of the allocation; it is rooted in equity theory and posits that each party should be rewarded based upon his or her relative contribution. The greater one's contributions, the greater his or her reward should be. The tenets of this line of reasoning have expanded to include the needs of the constituents, particularly in the social and political realms. One prominent area where distributive heuristics have been applied to demonstrate the unjust allocation of outcomes is in gender and racial representations in society. For example, if a particular demographic group is 20% of the general population, do its members hold 20% of the higher paying, more desirable jobs? Conversely, do members of this group comprise more than 20% of the prison population or of those unemployed? If a specific group does not receive a proportionate share of society's rewards (i.e., a good job) or receives a disproportional share of negative outcomes (i.e., prison sentences), there might be distributive injustice.

On the other hand, procedural justice is concerned with the process or rules used to determine the allocation of rewards or punishments. This line of reasoning emanated from the legal setting, where studies have confirmed that defendants viewed both positive and negative outcomes more fairly if they believed the process by which the outcome was determined was fair (Walker, Lind, & Thibaut, 1979). Investigation into this phenomenon revealed that a major factor in the perception of a process as fair was whether or not a participant felt he or she was treated with respect and had a chance to be heard. Having a chance to present one's case is called having a "voice." When participants have a voice in the process, they tend to judge the process as more fair, irrespective of the outcome, because they feel that they have had some control over the process (Van den Bos, 1999).

Rasinski (1987) summarized the differences in people's social justice views in this way: "People who believed that proportionality should be the basis on which benefits are distributed in society emphasized procedures in their judgments of what is fair in society, whereas those who endorsed egalitarianism stressed the fairness of the outcome" (p. 209). He further noted that this tendency increased with higher levels of education. However, other research does not view the choice as ideological, but rather as a more base response. Greenberg (1987) suggested that when people's own outcomes are favorable, they tend to rate outcomes as fair regardless of the fairness of the procedures. But when they receive low-level outcomes, procedures become very important. Whether an individual will apply a procedural justice heuristic, distributive justice heuristic, or a combination of both heuristics to judge the fairness of any given situation is often situational.

It stands to reason that if a distributive justice paradigm is to be used to evaluate outcomes, the individual must not only have knowledge of his or her own outcomes and inputs, but must also know about the outcomes of others and their contributions to the system (Van den Bos, Lind, Vermunt, & Wilke, 1997; Van den Bos, Wilke, Lind, & Vermunt, 1998). Social comparison is a critical factor in evaluating the justness of one's own outcomes relative to the outcomes of those competing for the same or similar resources (Messick & Sentis, 1983). When the knowledge of the outcomes others receive is absent, the individual must look at the fairness of the procedures as a proxy (Van den Bos, Wilke, Lind, & Vermunt, 1998).

Judicial proceedings, employee compensation, employee hiring, immigrant entitlement, affirmative action, landlord-tenant relations, retail exchange, social welfare, and presidential policies are representative of the domains where the body of work in justice theories has been tested and applied.

Privacy and Justice

It is clear that if all electronically processed information were made available and then integrated, most people would feel vulnerable and some would be harmed through the misuse of personal information. However, the typical citizen is not in a position to directly impact information privacy policy and its laws and regulations. As individual citizens, we cannot decide for society as a whole what information about individuals should be private (medical history), what information should be public (phone numbers, marriage licenses), what information becomes corporate property (purchase history, customer profiles), what information must be available for government use (tax information, criminal history), and what information should be available for intelligence activity. Although private citizens do not individually determine public policy, collectively individuals do form public opinion, and public opinion drives the decisions of officials and other public servants. Thus, the citizens' perceptions of the fairness of data access policies are important, both pragmatically and ethically.

Generally, the literature on the privacy implications of data integration and secondary data use weighs individual privacy rights against corporate financial motives. However, when we discuss unfettered access of intelligence agencies to personal data, we are weighing our individual privacy rights against the government's ability to protect not only our property, but also our lives. Creating public policy and the corresponding laws and regulations that dictate intelligence agency power and its limitations would be easy if individuals all had the same political ideology, social standing, knowledge, health consideration, and backgrounds. However, what makes us individuals also makes us different in terms of what we value and what we fear. The strong and diverse reaction to the USA PATRIOT Act is a prime example of the lack of consensus in our society as far as what is a fair and just response to terrorist threats.

The procedural and distributive justice dichotomy can be used to partially explain the variation in the public's reaction to initiatives such as the USA PATRIOT Act. But using these theories to assess the fairness of this legislation is more difficult than applying them to more traditional problems, such as hiring and promotion decision, because of the timing and the availability of information. If you are interviewing candidates for a job opening, you know that there is a position available, you know the job requirements, and you have the candidate's resume. After the decision is made, the outcome is known. The procedural rules for candidate selection may or may not be known. However, if there was no diversity in the people chosen for positions or if candidates with better qualification were dismissed, the heuristics used to determine the "fairness" of the outcome may negatively affect perceptions of the distributive and procedural justice.

It is interesting to point out that the US Government and the American Civil Liberties Union (ACLU) use procedural and distributive heuristics to argue and convince others concerning the USA PATRIOT Act. As is shown in the example below, the ACLU uses a distributive tone in explaining its arguments against the PATRIOT Act and the U.S. Government relies on a procedural tone to argue for support of the PATRIOT Act. A brief example of this can be seen by comparing a part of President Bush's State of the Union Address dealing with the PATRIOT Act (The White House, 2004) to language found on the ACLU's PATRIOT Act Web site (ACLU, 2004). The relevant language is underlined and in italics.

State of the Union Address, January 20, 2004 (Procedural Defense)

> *Inside the United States, where the war began, we must continue to give our homeland security and law enforcement personnel every tool they need to defend us.* **And one of those essential tools is the** PATRIOT **Act, which allows federal law enforcement to better share information, to track terrorists, to disrupt their cells, and to seize their assets. For years, we have used similar provisions to catch embezzlers and drug traffickers. If these methods are good for hunting criminals, they are even more important for hunting terrorists.**

President Bush is using a procedural heuristic to show that the PATRIOT Act is very similar to other accepted practices regarding the capture of common criminals. The message here is clear. The government only wishes to do that which it has been doing to "catch embezzlers and drug traffickers." The same procedures that are used and have been tested and approved for the capture of everyday criminals should be applied to the capture of terrorists.

From ACLU Web Page on the USA PATRIOT Act (Distributive Attack)

> *Just 45 days after the September 11 attacks, with virtually no debate, Congress passed the USA PATRIOT Act. Many parts of*

*this sweeping legislation take away checks on law enforcement and threaten the very rights and freedoms that we are struggling to protect. **For example, without a warrant and without probable cause, the FBI now has the power to access your most private medical records, your library records, and your student records... and can prevent anyone from telling you it was done.***

The Department of Justice is expected to introduce a sequel, dubbed PATRIOT II, that would further erode key freedoms and liberties of every American.

The ACLU uses a distributive heuristic to show how arbitrary the use of the PATRIOT Act could possibly be. They seem to be conveying the message that the rules and procedures will not protect you, and the allocation of justice has no relation to whether an individual is a terrorist. This excerpt also uses the distributive heuristic to ask why should innocent Americans have their "key freedoms and liberties" further eroded? The use of the particular language plays on the fears of American citizens who are concerned that their privacy will be infringed upon despite little or no connection to a terrorist plot.

Department of Justice (DOJ) and ACLU Arguments on the PATRIOT Act

One of the more controversial parts of the PATRIOT Act is Section 215. Section 215 amends the Foreign Intelligence Surveillance Act of 1978 to allow for access to "business records" and sets up congressional oversight. The Department of Justice and the ACLU have very different views on what Section 215 allows the government to access. Soon after the passage of the PATRIOT Act, the Justice Department created a Web site (www.lifeandliberty.gov) to provide support for the Act. On August 20, 2003, the ACLU released a report refuting the claims made by the Justice Department's Web site. Both groups state that their own position is "Reality" and the other group's is a "Myth." These documents provide an excellent opportunity to look further at how organizations will use social justice perspectives to sell their ideas concerning privacy rights. In the following examples, the relevant language is underlined and in italics.

ACLU and Justice Department Language Dealing with Library Records

From Government Web site (http://www.lifeandliberty.gov/subs/u_myths.htm) (*Procedural Defense*)

- **Myth:** The ACLU has claimed that "Many [people] are unaware that their library habits could become the target of government surveillance. In a free society, such monitoring is odious and unnecessary... The secrecy that surrounds Section 215 leads us to a society where the 'thought police' can target us for what we choose to read or what Web sites we visit." (ACLU, July 22, 2003)

- **Reality:** The PATRIOT Act specifically protects Americans' First Amendment rights, and terrorism investigators have no interest in the library habits of ordinary Americans.

Historically, terrorists and spies have used libraries to plan and carry out activities that threaten our national security. If terrorists or spies use libraries, we should not allow them to become safe havens for their terrorist or clandestine activities. The PATRIOT Act ensures that business records — whether from a library or any other business — can be obtained in national security investigations with the permission of a federal judge.

The phrase "business records — whether from a library or any other business — can be obtained in national security investigations with the permission of a federal judge," shows a procedural justification as it appeals to our sense of fairness that before any step is taken, the proper legal procedures will be followed because a judge will properly scrutinize the government action.

From ACLU (2003) report (Distributive Attack)

- **Myth:** Congress states Section 215 "specifically protects Americans' First Amendment rights."

- **Reality:** Section 215 specifically authorizes the FBI to investigate Americans based in part on their First Amendment activity, and to investigate others based *solely* on their First Amendment activity.

*The only thing that Section 215 says about First Amendment rights is that United States citizens and permanent residents can't be investigated under the provision based "solely" on their exercise of those rights. What this means in practice is that, if you're a United States citizen, the FBI can't obtain your library records or your medical records or your genetic information simply because you wrote a letter to the editor criticizing the war in Iraq. If the FBI wants to investigate you, they need to base the investigation on something else as well — something unrelated to the First Amendment. **This doesn't mean that the FBI has to have probable cause, or that they need to have any evidence at all that you're engaged in criminal activity. The "something else" could be that you were born in the Middle East, or that you took a trip to Pakistan last year. In fact, the "something else" might even be what one or your friends or associates did, if the FBI thinks that records about you will shed light on that person's activities. As long as the "something else" isn't related to First Amendment activity, it can count as a basis for the investigation.** Those who aren't United States citizens or permanent residents don't get even this minimal protection. For example, Canadians in the US on NAFTA visas can be investigated solely because of the books they borrowed from the library, the websites they visited, or the fact that they belong to the Federalist Society or ACLU.*

This is an example of applying distributive rationale to judge the Act because it clearly states that privacy rights can be intruded upon due to factors outside of direct terrorism action. This places a heavy burden on those groups that have questionable reputations despite little evidence to label them terrorists.

ACLU and Justice Department Language Dealing with Business Records

---

From Government Web site (http://www.lifeandliberty.gov/subs/u_myths.htm)

(Procedural Defense)

Examining business records often provides the key that investigators are looking for to solve a wide range of crimes.

Investigators might seek select records from hardware stores or chemical plants, for example, to find out who bought materials to make a bomb, or bank records to see who's sending money to terrorists. Law enforcement authorities have always been able to obtain business records in criminal cases through grand jury subpoenas, and continue to do so in national security cases where appropriate. In a recent domestic terrorism case, for example, a grand jury served a subpoena on a bookseller to obtain records showing that a suspect had purchased a book giving instructions on how to build a particularly unusual detonator that had been used in several bombings. This was important evidence identifying the suspect as the bomber.

This example of language reviews a specific event that shows how the procedure works. The Justice Department again relies on a procedural tone to show how the law will not infringe on an individual's privacy. The argument used is that the system, including that of a grand jury, will keep the infringement on privacy to a minimum while yielding positive results.

From ACLU (2003) report (Distributive Defense)

- **Myth:** Congress states Section 215 of the Act can only be used to obtain "business records."

- **Reality:** Section 215 is not limited to business records.

The DOJ's Web site states that Section 215 of the PATRIOT Act "[a]llows federal agents to ask a court for an order to obtain business records in national security terrorism cases." The site suggests again and again that Section 215 concerns only "business records." ***In fact, Section 215 authorizes the FBI to order any organization to turn "any tangible thing" over to the government. The provision is much broader than the DOJ now admits. The FBI could use Section 215 to demand:***

- *personal belongings, such as books, letters, journals, or computers*

- *a list of people who have visited a particular Web site*

- *medical records, including psychiatric records*

- *a list of people who have borrowed a particular book from a public library*
- *a membership list from an advocacy organization like Greenpeace, the Federalist Society, or the ACLU*
- *a list of people who worship at a particular church, mosque, temple, or synagogue*
- *a list of people who subscribe to a particular periodical*

In fact, at a June 2003 hearing before the House Judiciary Committee, the Attorney General himself boasted that the FBI could use the law even to obtain genetic information. The DOJ misleads the public by repeatedly referring to the law as a "business records" provision.

Language as used in this ACLU passage applies distributive heuristics to appeal to the reader's sense that — despite any procedural promises on the part of the government — the outcome of any particular case is not sure to be equitable or just. Instead, the ACLU argues against the PATRIOT Act by listing specific intrusions that may infringe upon our privacy. This passage also shows a disproportionate risk in relation to the reward. If you happen to be a member of a group that is suspect, your privacy may be violated even if your group has little connection to terrorism.

Applying a distributive justice heuristic to determine whether or not outcomes would be fair requires speculation and a tolerance for a high degree of ambiguity, given the outcomes are not known. Additionally, wealth, birth country, and political ideology are all among the factors that can make you more or less visible to the system, and thus more or less at risk.

Clearly, neither heuristic is sufficient to predict how the privacy-security exchange could be judged as fair across the population, a priori. It is more likely that the heuristics provide for speculative and post-hoc justification and criticism of policies. In other words, the justice paradigm applied, and its rationale and conclusions are more likely presented in support of one's ideological stance than as a product of the judgment process.

It is the government's responsibility to address the terrorist threat. Often in executing this duty, the government adopts another set of procedures and policies that are aimed at better protecting us. Of course, it is easier to implement procedures than to guarantee results. Therefore, parties responsible for outcomes have an incentive to adopt a procedural justice position. On the other hand, it is easy to select isolated cases where the outcomes were exceptionally favorable or exceptionally unfavorable and present these extreme cases as either representative or in the "this could happen to you" vein. This characterization is a speculative or post-hoc construction of a distributive justice perceptive.

Conclusions

It would be comforting to believe that people make judgments about the fairness of policies and their effects using some rationale heuristic. Unfortunately, that is not a universal truth. In fact, it may be the exception. Although we as humans want to see things as they are, our biases, ideological stances, and fears are self-sustaining. Psychologically, we tend to give those aspects of a situation that support our predisposition a lot of salience, and under weigh those aspects that are counter to our beliefs.

For those who value individual privacy rights highly and do not believe that they should be compromised at any cost, the potential cost of allowing unprecedented access to private information can not be justified. For those who believe increased security outweighs the rights of any individual to keep secrets, "fair procedures" must be put in play and followed. To influence those who can see both points, or who do not have an opinion, explaining procedures and posing hypothetical outcomes can be effective techniques to engender support. The privacy advocates present hypothetical outcomes effectively by using worst case scenarios to elicit fear. On the other hand, the government has to deal with the fear factor stemming from the events of 9/11. However, we believe those responsible for implementation of policies that change the status quo must present a realistic set of potential outcomes. They should emphasize the most likely outcomes and also acknowledge the extreme outcomes to be credible.

References

American Civil Liberties Union (ACLU) (2003). *Seeking truth from justice: PATRIOT propaganda: The Justice Department's campaign to mislead the public about the USA PATRIOT Act.* Washington, DC: ACLU. Retrieved May 25, 2004 from: *http://www.aclu.org/Files/getFile.cfm? id=13098*

American Civil Liberties Union (ACLU) (2004). USA PATRIOT Act. Retrieved May 25, 2004 from: *http://www.aclu.org/SafeandFree/ SafeandFree.cfm?ID=12126&c=207*

Ashcroft, J. (2000). National security: Justice department's new mission. *Vital Speeches of the Day.* September 1, LXVIII(22), 706-708.

Clarke, R. (1999). Introduction to dataveillance and information privacy, and definition of terms. Retrieved September 29, 2003 from: *http://www.anu. edu.au/people/Roger.Clarke/DV/Intro.html*

Greenberg, J. (1987) Reactions to procedural injustice in payment distributions: Do the means justify to ends? *Journal of Applied Psychology, 72*(1), 55-61.

Messick, D.M. & Sentis, K. (1983). Fairness, preference, and fairness biases. In D.M. Messick & K.S. Cook (Eds.), *Equity theory: Psychological and sociological perspectives* (pp. 61-94). New York: Praeger.

Perkins, R. (2002). Can public data be too public? *Target Marketing*, March, *25*(3), 51, 54.

Rasinski, K.A. (1987). What's fair is fair — Or is it? Value differences underlying public views about social justice. *Journal of Personality and Social Psychology, 52*(1), 201-211.

US Intelligence Community. (2003). Retrieved October 1, 2003 from: *http://www.intelligence.gov/2-character.shtml*

Van den Bos, K. (1999). What are we talking about when we talk about no-voice procedures? On the psychology of the fair outcome effect. *Journal of Experimental Social Psychology, 35*, 560-577.

Van den Bos, K. (2001). Uncertainty management: The influence of uncertainty salience on reactions to perceived procedural fairness. *Journal of Personality and Social Psychology, 80*(6), 931-941.

Van den Bos, K., Lind, E.A., Vermunt, R., & Wilke, H.A.M. (1997). How do I judge my outcome when I do not know the outcome of others? The psychology of the fair process effect. *Journal of Personality and Social Psychology, 72*(5), 1034-1046.

Van den Bos, K., Wilke, H.A.M., Lind, E.A., & Vermunt, R. (1998). Evaluating outcomes by means of the fair process effect: Evidence for different processes in fairness and satisfaction judgments. *Journal of Personality and Social Psychology, 74*(6), 1493-1503.

Walker, L., Lind, E.A., & Thibaut, J. (1979). The relationship between procedural and distributive justice. *Virginia Law Review, 65*(8), 1401-1420.

Warren, S., & Brandeis, L. (1890). The right to privacy. *Harvard Law Review, 4*(5), 193-220.

Westin, A. (1967). *Privacy and freedom*. London: Bodley Head.

The White House (2004). George W. Bush's State of the Union Address, January '02. News release. Retrieved May 25, 2004 from: *http://www. whitehouse.gov/news/releases/2004/01/20040120-7.html*

SECTION V:

THE HEALTHCARE INDUSTRY

Chapter XII

Information Imbalance in Medical Decision Making:
Upsetting the Balance

Jimmie L. Joseph
The University of Texas at El Paso, USA

David P. Cook
Old Dominion University, USA

Abstract

This chapter explores the ethical implications of a reduction in information asymmetry between health care providers and their patients. In many human interactions, asymmetry of information and experience typically raises ethical dilemmas for the party with the greater degree of information. This chapter illustrates that it is the reduction in information asymmetry that is raising ethical dilemmas in dealing with medical issues. Understanding this phenomenon may assist in identifying and managing future ethical quandaries that may occur as Internet resources provide broad access to information previously distributed only to a subset of the population.

Introduction

Information asymmetry is an imbalance in the information available to the parties in an interaction. This situation is not atypical and can be considered the basis for many of our most meaningful conversations. Human interactions would be far less interesting if everyone knew and "shared" the same thoughts, feelings, and discoveries at all times. While information asymmetry makes questions such as "How is the weather?" and "How was your day?" at least superficially interesting, in numerous human interactions, asymmetry of information and experience can raise ethical dilemmas for the party with the greater degree of information.

Significant academic research exists in the area of information asymmetry (e.g., finance and economics). The presumption of much of this research is that market efficiency can be increased by reducing the degree of asymmetry (Akerlof, 1970; Milgrom & Roberts, 2001; Payne, 2003). Furthermore, it is commonly held that information parity (or information access that moves the parties towards this point) can be the linchpin for the elimination of the ethical quandaries introduced by information asymmetry (Akerlof, 1970; Diamond, 1984; Hellwig, 2001).

In the field of medicine, for example, it is clear that the physician has historically possessed more information than the traditional patient. This disparity has created a peculiar set of ethical issues for medical providers, based on their fiduciary responsibility to their patients. As with many relationships, the relationship between caregiver and patient changes, however, as information asymmetry diminishes. Relaxing the assumption that there is a significant difference in the information available to the physician and patient causes a new set of ethical issues to arise. In the extreme case, information inversion exists: the patient knows more about his or her condition than the attending medical personnel. The anecdotes about doctors making poor patients approach the status of urban myth (Porter, 1992). This chapter focuses on these very issues: how do the physician-patient relationship and the resultant ethical issues change as the patient's information disadvantage decreases.

This chapter examines the effects of changes in technology and societal norms on the ethical posture of practitioners in the medical profession. Ethical, social, technical, and regulatory issues associated with consumers' increased access to medical information are explored. It is posited that situations exist where a reduction in information asymmetry does not lead to fewer, or less severe, ethical dilemmas — it leads to more severe ethical quandaries. This chapter illustrates a counterintuitive example to the presumption that increased information parity enhances market efficiency and diminishes the number of ethical quandaries in the provision of medical care. While the chapter seeks to illustrate a counterintuitive example and the ethical dilemmas it raises, it does not purport to provide a solution to these still evolving ethical issues.

Information Asymmetry and Its Costs

Problems resulting from information asymmetry are generally classified as either moral hazard or adverse selection (Akerlof, 1970; Diamond, 1984; Payne, 2003). Moral hazard problems are related to the buyer's inability to observe the actions taken by the seller (Holmstrom, 1985). Adverse selection problems are related to the buyer's inability to observe either pertinent seller characteristics or the contingencies under which the seller operates (Nayyar, 1990). Adverse selection can occur in the medical environment due to the patient's inability to determine on an *ex ante* basis the competence of the physician, the value of the service, or its quality.

Given the existence of such problems, and that they arise as a result of information asymmetries, numerous strategies have arisen to attempt to remedy or mitigate the effect of these asymmetries. Several potential remedies (e.g., contingent contracts, certification, monitoring, and reputation) exist for information asymmetries (Holmstrom, 1985; Nayyar, 1990). Each of the mentioned remedies has its shortcomings. In contingent contracts, for example, the capability must exist to identify all relevant contingencies prior to the enforcement of the contract.

Certifications only indicate an entity has met some minimum standard of performance or knowledge (as established by the certifying authority). For certification to be of benefit, it is necessary for the party with the information paucity in a transaction to understand the nature or quality of the certification or certifying agency (Diamond, 1984; Hellwig, 2001). Further, some certifying authorities may not make their criteria for certification public knowledge (Diamond, 1984; Hellwig, 2001).

Monitoring introduces additional information asymmetries between the monitor and the entity being monitored. An agency problem can arise if the party depending on the monitoring organization has no way of ascertaining the diligence of the monitoring (Diamond, 1984; Hellwig, 2001). This is especially problematic in self-monitoring organizations such as bar association monitoring boards composed of lawyers and state medical boards composed of doctors (Davies & Beach, 2000; Fournier & McInnes, 1997; Marks & Cathcart, 1974). While each of these mechanisms may have been fomented with good intentions, each is fraught with difficulty.

Another mechanism to mitigate or eliminate information asymmetry is greater informational transparency and availability. The Internet is a good example of a vehicle that can facilitate these goals. The Internet presents a medium through which unprecedented volumes of data can be made available to anyone with access and interest. However, just as other forms of asymmetry mediation have unique shortcomings, the Internet may pose its own issues.

Examples of Information Asymmetry

Many of our interactions are predicated on an asymmetry in the information possessed by the parties involved. Though numerous examples of information asymmetry in interactions could be presented, along with their associated effects and resultant moral dilemmas, two situations involving information asymmetry (the sale of automobiles with known defects and insider trading) are briefly examined here. Information asymmetry involving parties to medical interactions will be examined more closely in the ensuing sections of this chapter, and so will not be discussed here.

Automobile Sales

In used car purchases, the prospective purchaser knows exactly how much she can spend on the vehicle, but the seller has no such information. Conversely, the seller may be privy to details of a vehicle's defects, accident history, and undisclosed repairs to which a prospective buyer is not (Akerlof, 1970). For the seller, knowledge of defects creates an ethical dilemma in that he must decide whether to disclose the existence of the defects and possibly nullify the interest of a prospective buyer (Akerlof, 1970).

To help address the issue of seller information advantage, governments (both Federal and state) have developed and imposed "Lemon" laws and other statutes for consumer protection (Akerlof, 1970). The intention of such laws is to facilitate commerce and to protect consumers from the problems created by information asymmetry. These laws also reduce the moral dilemma faced by the seller: it now makes moral and legal sense to disclose all known problems with the automobile (Akerlof, 1970).

Insider Trading

When a person with access to information not available to the general public wishes to trade stock, he or she is faced with a different ethical problem. Insider trading is the result of trading stock on the basis of privileged information (Anonymous, 1998, 2003b). Such trading continues because of the tremendous potential for profit that can accrue from buying or selling ahead of the disclosure of the information to the public (Anonymous, 1998, 2003b). Few would argue that trading stock on the basis of privileged information is a fair practice; as a consequence, laws exist that disallow such activities (Anonymous, 2003b). The purpose of such laws is to level the playing field so that parties without access to privileged information are not disadvantaged on that basis.

Why Medicine is Different

There is an exception to the generally accepted proportional relationship between information asymmetry and ethical concerns: the relationship between medical providers and patients. This chapter posits that as patients achieve a reduction in information asymmetry (RIA) vis-à-vis their medical care providers, the ethical dilemmas of the formerly better informed medical professionals increase in number and/or patient impact, thus inverting the generally accepted relationship between information parity and ethical dilemmas. This trend is of concern as increasing portions of the population have Internet access at work, and high-speed Internet access at home. Omnipresent Internet access allows the general public to view information available only to medical professionals or medical researchers in prior decades.

Medical Information Access

Two characteristics of medical information that have traditionally affected its dissemination are availability and readability (Majno, 1975; Marti-Ibanez, 1962). Availability is defined here as the ability of a person to discover that information about a topic exists, and then to acquire that information. Readability entails the possession of sufficient domain knowledge (assumed to be present in the target audience when writing the information) to understand and utilize available information (Aguolu, 1997).

Prior to the invention of the Guttenberg printing press in 1436, books were hand-crafted and, consequently, too expensive for (unavailable to) the average citizen (Borgman, 2000). Magazines (journals) had not even been conceptualized at that time. Most persons did not know how to read (since it was of little practical value to their daily lives), and books were unlikely to come into their possession. Even most medical practitioners could not read, and medical knowledge was typically passed from generation to generation via an apprentice-like system of medical education (Borgman, 2000; Majno, 1975; Marti-Ibanez, 1958, 1962).

A History of Medical Interactions

The practice of medicine has largely been a dyadic one between the patient and the care provider (doctor and/or nurse, midwife, witch doctor, tribal shaman, acupuncturist, etc.) (Digby, 1997; Majno, 1975; Marti-Ibanez, 1958; Summers, 1997). In the traditional doctor-patient relationship, doctors diagnosed and prescribed a course of treatment, and patients underwent treatment as directed (Majno, 1975). News of treatments available on other continents, in other nations, or in distant regions of their own land may not have reached residents of a locale until long after the discovery (Magner, 1992; Majno, 1975; Marti-Ibanez, 1962; Robinson, 1931).

Given the lack of a formal dissemination mechanism such as "continuing education" (through which medical providers could be fully trained in new techniques and procedures), even if new medical treatment ideas arrived, there was no guarantee that the local medical caregiver would understand how to implement the new regimen. While Marco Polo may have returned with information concerning the existence of acupuncture as a treatment for headaches and other ailments, this did not provide the training necessary for European doctors to perform the procedures (Majno, 1975; Marti-Ibanez, 1958).

Since there were few books prior to the widespread distribution of the printing press, availability of information was the primary limiting factor in medical innovation dissemination (Marti-Ibanez, 1962). The availability of relatively inexpensive books brought about a renaissance in reading, and public education brought reading to the masses. This change, however, did not alter the readability issue of medical texts.

In the 19th century, and through the late 20th century, the primary means of disseminating information regarding the effectiveness of various forms of medical treatment was medical journals. Current and archived volumes of these journals were available at medical libraries and hospitals. Medical professionals could also subscribe to pertinent journals, often at substantial discounts from the retail price, through their medical associations (Majno, 1975).

However, for a citizen who was not a professional in the medical field, the journals presented two familiar hurdles: availability and readability. Unless an individual lived near a medical library, the availability of medical journals was usually limited. Medical journals were (and are) prohibitively expensive for the average citizen. Along with the cost of a current subscription, there is the cost of purchasing past issues to track streams of research. Given the large number of medical journals that are/have been published and the high cost of each journal, local libraries carry a very small selection of what may be seen by the funding community to be a highly specialized item.

If the journals are available, their readability is still problematic for most nonmedical professionals. As with most publications, medical journals are targeted to a particular audience. The target audience does not typically enjoy having to wade through the same introductory and historical information for each successive article in a stream of research. It is also a waste of publication space to use excessive verbiage when there are specific terms, phrases, and acronyms widely used in the field of specialty that convey the intended meaning quickly, succinctly, and with far greater alacrity. In medical writing, authors can assume their target audience has a college education, years of medical school, and for many medical journals, specialized training in a medical sub-field. Readability for the target audience is usually not considered a problem; readability for nonmedical professionals is not a priority.

The issue of providing information concerning new treatments or medical techniques was presumed to be the purview of the medical professional. Thus, until the latter decades of the 20th century, the dissemination of medical treatments and advances had not changed significantly from the dissemination methodologies of the middle ages (Majno, 1975; Osler, 1921; Robinson, 1931). The general forms of the traditional ethical issues facing the medical profession included:

- **Traditional Dilemma 1:** How much time to spend on learning new medical techniques (since this was time that could otherwise be spent with patients); and

- **Traditional Dilemma 2:** Whether or not to discuss a medical innovation with a patient if the medical professional was not proficient with that innovation, or if that technology or innovation was not available locally.

Traditional Medical Information Access

The primary conduit of medical information to the public is the medical practitioner (Majno, 1975). From the earliest medical discoveries of tree bark for soothing aches and pains to using leeches to remove "bad humors," medical practitioners have been the repositories of knowledge on the most effective means of treating injury, regaining health, and reducing pain (Majno, 1975; Marti-Ibanez, 1961, 1962). Once medical books and journals became practical, doctors became the local repository of medical knowledge. The size of a medical provider's private medical library could dictate the breadth and depth of treatment available in a locale (Majno, 1975). New discoveries were made known to the local medical practitioner, who dispensed this information to the general populace, if needed. Otherwise, the medical practitioner simply performed the procedures as recommended.

In the 19th and 20th centuries, continuing education, conferences, seminars, and medical journals provided doctors and nurses with information on approved, state-of-the-art medical treatments (Felch & Scanlon, 1997). Information was also made available by medical device and pharmaceutical manufacturers concerning the specific implementation and formulations of their new medical treatment technologies and techniques. Patients with questions concerning the best treatments for their conditions simply queried their medical practitioners; the answers were rarely questioned (Majno, 1975).

Modern Medical Information Dissemination

Television and the Late 20th Century

Mass media discussions of medical issues, techniques, and technologies added potential ethical concerns for the medical professional. These media made it feasible for patients to at least hear of new techniques and technologies through channels that were not under the control of the medical professional. However, in-depth discussion of the conditions under which a particular technique or innovation was optimal, side effects, interaction effects with other treatments or medications, and conditions that would eliminate a patient from being a candidate for the treatment were still left to the physician (Friedman, Furberg, & DeMets, 1998; Spilker & Cramer, 1992). Additionally, government control or licensing of mass media outlets meant that techniques, technologies, medications, and innovations that had not been approved by a particular nation's medical establishment or government regulatory body were unlikely to gain significant airtime for discussion in that country's media.

The proliferation of cable television channels dedicated to news, science, and medicine in the late 1980s began to change the dynamic of medical information dissemination. Shows could dedicate more time to discussing medical problems, symptoms, and treatments. Consequently, patients could ask more probing questions concerning treatment options in consultations with their physicians. The practical effect of such channels of information dissemination was to reduce the frequency of the occurrence of Traditional Dilemma 2. Interested patients of this era were rapidly reducing the information gap between patient and medical provider. Traditional Dilemma 2 became less problematic as physicians were increasingly bombarded with questions from patients referring to research studies and treatment regimens seen on television shows.

The question for physicians was not whether to broach the subject of certain treatment options, but rather, how to respond effectively to patient queries. A companion effect was that physicians were also forced to keep abreast of the types of studies and medical treatment options about which patients were asking questions, if for no other reason than to be able to adequately respond to patient inquiries (Felch & Scanlon, 1997; Pennachio, 2003; Shaneyfelt, 2001).

The Internet and the World Wide Web

The 1990s witnessed a significant change to the patient/provider dyad: widespread access to the Internet. The Internet solved the availability problem for patients by providing global access to medical information. Patients could access information on innovations without having the information limited by finances (personal or regional) or filtered by their medical provider, a media censor, or their national government.

Patients with Internet access were potentially one degree of freedom closer to the source of new medical innovations. Individuals could decide which innovations interested them and seek additional information. Individuals still faced the task of comprehending the information that they uncovered. The Internet, however, made it possible for interested parties to seek out multiple presentations of the same material with relative ease. This increased the potential for the dedicated information seeker to find a presentation of the material that was comprehendible, in accordance with the individual's level of subject and domain knowledge.

Medical Information Without Borders

Information available online is not limited by geopolitical boundaries. Patients can find information on treatments, pharmaceuticals, technologies, and innovations that have not been vetted or approved by their medical establishment or national government. E-mail, chat and PC-based video conferencing potentially allow direct access to medical professionals in other countries. These practitioners may provide an in-depth analysis of a particular medical treatment that is not available to the patient from traditional local information sources (e.g., television or radio shows). Medical providers face patients well versed in the efficacy, side effects, and potential benefits of a wide range of treatment options that may not be legally available in a particular locale, or about which the medical provider may have little knowledge or expertise.

Internet access has provided patients participating in medical experiments with an economical means to find and communicate with other experiment participants. While such actions may seem farfetched, consider the motivation many patients with serious ailments have to seek out information and develop a support network. These individuals are often in pain, scared, and desperate to find a cure for their illness. The ease with which USENET news groups (or threads within an existing group) can be created, combined with the ease of setting up IRC chats or Web-based chat rooms, makes contacting others in real time (or near real time) relatively simple.

Individuals participating in an experiment for a new drug, technique, or technology can now discuss their treatment and its results directly with other subjects in the experiment. This allows individuals to potentially discern if they are receiving the same benefit as others in an experiment. Participating patients who find that a different treatment is providing better results can go to their physicians or the experimenter and demand that other treatment. Information on experimental treatments and clinical trials is readily available. Patients interested in an experimental treatment can access CenterWatch at www.centerwatch.com, which provides access to information related to the clinical testing of drugs and recent FDA-approved drug therapies.

Doctor's Dilemma

Direct, and near global, access to medical information allows patients to petition their medical practitioners for pain-reducing or lifesaving treatments approved in other countries but not approved in their country of residence. Patients may now share and review information concerning treatment availability and costs from around the world. A doctor's local patients can compare their progress with that of patients in other nations taking different treatments or who are involved in medical experiments. Patients can compare symptoms and try to determine if their situation is the same as (or relatively close to) that of another sufferer.

Widespread information access on the part of patients has created ethical dilemmas for medical practitioners based on the fact that:

1.   there may be a better (more effective or less painful) treatment available than the medical professional is currently offering;

2.   regardless of the efficacy of the treatment identified by a patient, the medical professional may be prohibited from prescribing it to, and possibly even from discussing it with, her patient;

3.   there may be no clinical trials on which a medical professional can base an opinion as to the efficacy of the treatment the patient is seeking;

4.   there may be no means for patients to avail themselves of the treatment they are seeking, even if the medical professional confirms that it is a better treatment than that which is currently available locally; and

5.   patients involved in experiments may discover that they are receiving the placebo treatment, while ferreting out data indicating that the experimental treatment is providing relief to other participants.

The issues arising from a reduction in information asymmetry (RIA) can be generally categorized into the following ethical dilemmas for the health care provider:

•   **RIA Dilemma 1:** Whether to address the patient's question;

•   **RIA Dilemma 2:** Whether to provide the treatment, in possible violation of the law;

•   **RIA Dilemma 3:** Whether to place the patient in contact with a medical practitioner or source for the treatment being sought;

•   **RIA Dilemma 4:** Whether to petition the experimenters to provide the patient with access to the experimental treatment once the patient has made an explicit request.

Locally Unapproved Medical Treatments

National laws and approval bodies guide the approval of medical treatments, and medical practitioners are generally not permitted to prescribe treatment regimens or drug therapies that have not been approved by their governing bodies. This restriction, in part, helps to ensure that medical professionals are properly trained in the use, effects, and side effects of a particular treatment. It also helps to assure that the treatment regimens and drugs are efficacious and reasonably free of undesirable or unintended side effects.

In *RIA Dilemma 1*, the medical professional must decide if he or she will address a patient's concern. Should the medical professional address the patient's questions concerning unapproved medical treatments, the dyad may be venturing into territory proscribed by law. Refusing to answer the question leaves the patient without the knowledge to decide for him/herself whether to investigate the matter further. Indeed, not addressing the question may discourage the patient from pursuing a course of treatment that may provide him or her with relief or a cure. If the patient has the resources, he or she may travel to where the treatment is provided. If consultation with a medical professional after arrival contraindicates the sought after treatment, the patient would have wasted time and money that could have been better spent on the current treatment.

Providing an unapproved treatment to the patient may result in the medical professional being subject to censure, jail, or loss of medical license. In some rural areas, the loss of a single medical professional would deprive one or more communities of access to critical medical services (Hassinger, 1982). Thus, the medical provider is faced with the dilemma of helping one patient and possibly depriving a community of needed medical care.

Providing a patient with a treatment that is less efficacious than the best available may violate the Hippocratic philosophy of "First Do No Harm" (Majno, 1975; Marti-Ibanez, 1962; Osler, 1921). The physician's deliberations on whether to provide patients access to locally unapproved treatment options necessarily revolve around this oath. Knowingly denying a patient possible access to a treatment believed to be efficacious may constitute a violation of the Hippocratic Oath. On the other hand, governing medical bodies and governments have created protocols and procedures with the intention of protecting the populace from "snake oil" remedies (Anonymous, 2003a), with attendant penalties for willful violation. If the physician chooses to prescribe an unapproved drug therapy, for example, he or she may be unwittingly placing a patient at risk for serious medical complications while concurrently placing his or her medical license in jeopardy.

Locally Unavailable Medical Treatments

Medical treatments may be approved for distribution in a nation or region but may not necessarily be made widely available to a specific locale, leading to *RIA Dilemma 2*. This may be for commercial reasons, or it may be the result of government rationing (Morgan, 2003; Schwartz, Morrison, & Sullivan, 1999). In countries with nationalized healthcare, it may not be economically feasible or politically desirable to provide all treatments in all locations (Morgan, 2003). Thus, a treatment that is nationally approved may not be accessible in a given region (Schwartz et al., 1999).

Direct access to medical information from other regions and countries allows patients to petition for approved pain-reducing or lifesaving treatments that are not available in their area. Patients may now share and review information concerning treatments in other regions, and become aware of treatments being denied them on the basis of geography (Morgan, 2003; Schwartz et al., 1999).

Should the medical professional address the patient's questions, he or she may be venturing into territory proscribed by law, especially in the case of nationalized healthcare (Schwartz et al., 1999). To not answer the question is to leave the patient without the knowledge to decide for herself whether to investigate the matter further. Indeed, not addressing the question may discourage the patient from pursuing a course of treatment that may provide her with relief or a cure.

A patient may seek a recommendation from his or her local practitioner for a contact in another locale for a consultation, resulting in the practitioner facing *RIA Dilemma 3*. This can also have legal ramifications. Medical personnel may be prohibited from recommending persons not approved in their country to perform medical treatments.

Locally More Expensive Treatments

If a less expensive but still efficacious treatment is available, the medical practitioner is likely to inform the patient, as long as the treatment is governmentally authorized. If the less expensive alternative is not authorized for local patients, the medical practitioner is not likely to volunteer information on that treatment. However, should the patient raise the issue of the treatment, the medical provider is forced into a position of discussing an unauthorized treatment or leaving the patient in ignorance.

Prior to patient access to transnational information on treatment pricing, treatment cost differentials were not a major ethical issue for medical practitioners, since the patient was unlikely to be knowledgeable enough to broach the topic. If a less expensive alternative to the current treatment was not available in his or her country, the medical professional was under no obligation to mention the treatment, so *RIA Dilemma 1* was not an issue. With direct access to information concerning pricing worldwide, patients can now request information concerning specific alternatives to their current treatment. Patients may be able to find pricing information, but they may still have questions on efficacy, side effects, or interactions with current treatments.

An example illustrates this point. The presence of pharmaceuticals in Canada that are less expensive than their US counterparts is not an unheard of occurrence. In some cases, pharmaceuticals formulations used in Canada are identical to their US equivalents and are manufactured in the US. Doctors and pharmacists are placed in the position of having to decide whether to respond to their patients' or customers' inquiries about the ability to purchase the same items for less via the Internet or by traveling to Canada. For patients with fixed retirement incomes facing rapidly increasing prescription drug prices on multiple prescriptions, this may be a life-or-death decision. The practitioner is faced with the same problems found in the situation of locally unavailable treatments: he or she could be subject to disciplinary action or potential loss of medical license, if he or she is found to be recommending locally unapproved pharmaceuticals.

Unaffordable Medical Treatments

Cost is a concern for many medical providers and hospitals and is often a determinant of the medical treatment made available to patients. Cost containment is an issue common to both nationalized and privatized healthcare systems (Barry & Raworth, 2002). Some countries and medical establishments simply cannot afford to provide very expensive treatments (Barry & Raworth, 2002).

The dilemma for medical practitioners is whether to inform the patient of treatments that cannot be afforded or leave the patient in ignorance (Barry & Raworth, 2002; Gert, 2002). The former option provides the patient with the information on an alternative treatment, but also the pyrrhic knowledge that his or her suffering may be in vain because it could be alleviated—if the nation or healthcare facility could afford the treatment or technology (Barry & Raworth, 2002). The latter option denies the patient the opportunity to travel to a locale where the treatment is provided, if personal resources permit (Gert, 2002).

Medical Experiments: Request for a Specific Treatment

The final situation that we will discuss concerns medical experiments and *RIA Dilemma 4*, and has been alluded to already. Traditionally, scientifically valid experiments require a control group that received a placebo (e.g., the classic "sugar pill") treatment, and an experimental group that received the treatment to be tested (Matthews, 2000; Spilker & Cramer, 1992). There may also have been a third group that received the current treatment, although in situations where removing a patient from, or denying him access to, the traditional treatment may be deemed too detrimental to the patient, the placebo is often the currently approved treatment (Barber, 1980; Cowles, 1976; Matthews, 2000; Spilker & Cramer, 1992).

Medical practitioners treating patients with a particular condition were recruited to invite their affected patients to participate in the experiment. To ensure that medical practitioners did not inadvertently influence the patient, participating medical practitioners were usually not informed whether their patient was a member of the control group or the experimental group (Barber, 1980; Cowles, 1976; Matthews, 2000; Spilker & Cramer, 1992).

Access to the Internet and chat rooms has altered this equation. Patients now have the potential to discover that an experiment is underway or planned and request that their practitioner volunteer them for the experiment. The medical practitioner must then seek out the experimenter(s) to request permission for his or her patient to be included in the experiment. This could have the effect of excluding a patient who would be a better candidate for the experiment, but who did not know to request inclusion (Barber, 1980; Spilker & Cramer, 1992).

Internet access can also provide patients with a forum to discuss their participation in experiments. Thus, it is now possible for patients to talk among themselves, compare treatment results, and determine the success of treatments using resources such as www.spinalcord.org. By comparing results, it is possible for patients to deduce whether they are in the control group and, possibly, the efficacy of the experimental treatment.

If the experimental treatment appears successful, patients in the control group can ask their physicians for the new treatment. The medical provider is placed in the position of asking the experimenter to provide the new treatment. As a consequence, the experimenter is thrust into the position of denying the experimental treatment to a subject who knows he or she is receiving the placebo. The subject who deduces that he or she is in the placebo group is no longer valid for data analysis, because the placebo effect is destroyed; continuing with the ruse serves no useful scientific purpose.

If the experimental treatment is not helping the experimental group, patients in that group may request that their medical practitioners remove them from the experiment, and return them to the existing treatments (Friedman et al., 1998; Spilker & Cramer, 1992). Since informed consent is the cornerstone of all enlightened medical research, and since that consent can be rescinded at any time, once the physician reports the patient's feelings to the experimenter, the experimenter must release him or her from the experiment (Barber, 1980; Cowles, 1976). Thus, new medical discoveries could be imperiled.

Future Trends

An ethics discussion of the factors affecting medical professionals frees us from the constraint common to economic discussions of the topic: the need for equilibrium. As noted by Milgrom and Roberts (2001), "Almost all of economic theory is equilibrium analysis...predictions arise only once equilibrium behavior is assumed." The ethical dilemmas facing medical professionals increase as patients gain access to information, not simply once they reach information parity with their medical practitioners. Indeed, the ethical dilemmas for the medical provider continue, and may in fact increase, if a patient should surpass his or her knowledge of a specific topic, disease or treatment.

For most dyadic interactions, a reduction in the imbalance of information between parties will reduce the ethical dilemmas related to the interaction. The increasing availability and readability of information concerning new medical advances has produced the opposite effect. For medical professionals, the decrease in the traditional information imbalance between patients and medical providers has increased the number and nature of ethical dilemmas faced.

Serious illness or chronic pain provides intense motivation to pursue information on a particular affliction or condition with single-minded dedication. While a medical professional may need to track the symptoms and diseases of dozens or hundreds of patients, a particular patient can concentrate on a specific problem. Thus, a patient may be more knowledgeable about the current discoveries and findings regarding a specific problem than the medical practitioner. With the Internet providing an efficient conduit for researching a problem, a patient may be motivated to explore all available information concerning his or her affliction. Since the Internet is borderless, this research can uncover the most current medical findings worldwide.

This chapter focuses on moral dilemmas brought about through the continued spread of information access. While other chapters in this book focus on threats to privacy and intellectual property, it is important to note that there can be ethical threats engendered in the very availability of the information itself. As ever-greater volumes of information migrate online, it is possible, even likely, that other arenas of human interaction may face similar quandaries. An examination of the current issues may help prepare for a discussion of these future imbroglios.

Concomitant with such developments, the world's citizens should be prepared to deal with their governments' attempts to mitigate the effects of the ethical quandaries for which this expanded information availability is the genesis. Existing laws governing medical devices, treatments, and technologies (e.g., regulation of locally unapproved drugs) suggest that governments will likely take steps to deal with perceived problems arising from greater information flow. There is every reason to expect that regulations will be developed to counter the problems governments perceive in other arenas as well. A lively ethical debate can facilitate the development of well-reasoned laws and regulations.

Chapter Summary

National laws are based on geography: the physical limitations of jurisdiction. As with other laws in the Internet age, laws regarding the actions of medical professionals within national borders are facing the reality of borderless information access. The Internet purchase of less expensive prescription drugs in Canada by citizens in the United States is but one example of physical laws not keeping pace with the telecommunications revolution.

This chapter is designed to illuminate the issues surrounding an interesting problem with information parity vs. asymmetry in Medicine. The changing dynamics between patient and caregiver are intricate and complex, especially with the omnipresent impact of laws governing medical treatment. The impact of RIA, combined with the presence of information sources beyond the control of a single national government, complicates the ethical decisions for medical practitioners geometrically. No easy solutions are possible to this problem, and this chapter does not purport to resolve such complex issues. As desirable as a solution to these problems is, a workable solution is not practical at this juncture due to the interplay among technology, law, and ethics.

A technological solution is not tenable since it is the technology that leads to many of the ethical dilemmas facing medical practitioners: new technology may in fact introduce additional complexity in medical relationships. A legal solution is equally fraught with difficulty. National laws currently exist in many countries that are intended to address medical issues. However, the borderless society created by modern information technologies may require an international solution that addresses the realities of physician responsibility and modern data interchange. It may be impossible, however, to un-ring the bell of borderless medical information flow. The reality is that the caregiver is ultimately responsible for the ethical quandaries posed, but that researchers, politicians, and ethicists can assist by fostering an open discussion of the moral calculus.

Finally, this inverse relationship between information parity and ethical dilemmas is of concern because it may not be a singular exception to the generally held belief that information parity decreases ethical dilemmas. As high-speed Internet access becomes more pervasive in society, other situations may develop in which information that becomes available to the general public generates an increase in ethical quandaries. Future research should explore the social impact of unfiltered information becoming available in other knowledge domains. Without awareness of this possibility, ethical training and legal debate may be unprepared to confront a potent, counterintuitive, social phenomenon. It is the nature of such issues that they do not lend themselves to formulaic solutions, but require deliberations and debate to find workable options. It is our goal to begin to foster such debate with this chapter.

References

Aguolu, I. E. (1997). Accessibility of information: A myth for developing countries? *New Library World, 98*(1132), 25.

Akerlof, G. A. (1970). The market for "lemons": Quality uncertainty and the market mechanism. *Quarterly Journal of Economics, 84*(3), 788-500.

Anonymous. (1998). What is "insider trading"? U.S. Securities and Exchange Commission [Web page]. Modified: 09/01/1998. Retrieved October 13, 2003 from: *http://www.sec.gov/divisions/enforce/insider.htm*

Anonymous. (2003a). Approvals of FDA-regulated products. US Food and Drug Administration. [Web page]. Retrieved March 30, 2004 from: *http://www.fda.gov/opacom/7approvl.html*

Anonymous. (2003b). The laws that govern the securities industry. [Web Page]. U. S. Securities and Exchange Commission. [Web Page]. Modified: 06/27/2003. Retrieved from: *http://www.sec.gov/about/laws.shtml*

Barber, B. (1980). *Informed consent in medical therapy and research*. New Brunswick, NJ: Rutgers University Press.

Barry, C., & Raworth, K. (2002). Access to medicines and the rhetoric of responsibility. *Ethics & International Affairs, 16*(2), 57(15).

Borgman, C. L. (2000). *From Guttenberg to the global information infrastructure: Access to information in the networked world*. Cambridge, MA: MIT Press.

Cowles, J. (1976). *Informed consent*. New York: Coward, McCann & Geoghegan, Inc.

Davies, C., & Beach, A. (2000). *Interpreting professional self-regulation*. London: Routledge Taylor & Francis Group.

Diamond, D. W. (1984). Financial intermediation and delegated monitoring. *The Review of Economic Studies, 51*(3), 393-414.

Digby, A. (1997). The patient's view. In I. Loudon (Ed.), *Western medicine* (pp. 291-305). Oxford, UK: Oxford University Press.

Felch, W. C., & Scanlon, D. M. (1997). Bridging the gap between research and practice: The role of continuing medical education. *JAMA, 277*(2), 155(152).

Fournier, G. M., & McInnes, M. M. (1997). Medical board regulation of physician licensure: Is excessive malpractice sanctioned? *Journal of Regulatory Economics, 12*(2), 113-126.

Friedman, L. M., Furberg, C. D., & DeMets, D. L. (1998). *Fundamentals of clinical trials* (3rd ed.). New York: Springer-Verlag.

Gert, H. J. (2002). Avoiding surprises: A model for informing patients. *The Hastings Center Report, 32*(5), 23(11).

Hassinger, E. W. (1982). *Rural health organization*. Ames, IA: Iowa State University Press.

Hellwig, M. F. (2001). Risk aversion and incentive compatibility with *ex post* information asymmetry. *Economic Theory, 18*, 415-438.

Holmstrom, B. R. (1985). The provision of services in a market economy. In R. P. Inman (Ed.), *Managing the service economy: Prospects and problems*. Cambridge, UK: Cambridge University Press.

Magner, L. N. (1992). *A history of medicine*. New York: Marcel Dekker.

Majno, G. (1975). *The healing hand: Man and wound in the ancient world*. Cambridge, MA: Harvard University Press.

Marks, F. R., & Cathcart, D. (1974). Discipline within the legal profession: Is it self-regulation? *University of Illinois Law Review, 193*(Spring), 236.

Marti-Ibanez, F. (1958). *Centaur: Essays on the history of medical ideas.* New York: MD Publications.

Marti-Ibanez, F. (1961). *A prelude to medical history.* New York: MD Publications.

Marti-Ibanez, F. (1962). *The epic of medicine.* New York: Clarkson N. Potter.

Matthews, J. N. S. (2000). *An introduction to randomized controlled clinical trials.* London: Arnold, A member of the Hodder Headline Group.

Milgrom, P., & Roberts, J. (2001). Informational asymmetries, strategic behavior, and industrial organization. *Game Theory and Industrial Organization, 77*(2), 184-193.

Morgan, J. M. (2003). New device indications: Practice and cost implications in Europe. *Cardiac Electrophysiology Review, 7*(1), 49-53.

Nayyar, P. R. (1990, November/December). Information asymmetries: A source of competitive advantage for diversified service firms. *Strategic Management Journal, 11,* 513-819.

Osler, S. W. (1921). *The evolution of modern medicine.* New Haven, CT: Yale University Press.

Payne, R. (2003). Informed trade in spot foreign exchange markets: An empirical investigation. *Journal of International Economics, 61,* 307-329.

Pennachio, D. L. (2003). CME: How to get yours? Requirements are multiplying, but so are the opportunities to meet them. *Medical Economics, 80*(16), 21(23).

Porter, R. (1992). The patient in England, c. 1660-c. 1800. In A. Wear (Ed.), *Medicine in society.* Cambridge, UK: Cambridge University Press.

Robinson, V. (1931). *The story of medicine.* New York: Tudor Publishing Co.

Schwartz, L., Morrison, J., & Sullivan, F. (1999). Rationing decisions: From diversity to consensus. *Healthcare Analysis, 7*(2), 195-205.

Shaneyfelt, T. M. (2001). Building bridges to quality. *JAMA, 286*(20), 2600(2602).

Spilker, B., & Cramer, H. A. (1992). *Patient recruitment in clinical trials.* New York: Raven Press.

Summers, A. (1997). Nurses and ancillaries in the Christian era. In I. Loudon (Ed.), *Western medicine* (pp. 192-205). Oxford, UK: Oxford University Press.

Chapter XIII

HIPAA:
Privacy and Security in Health Care Networks

Pooja Deshmukh
Washington State University, USA

David Croasdell
University of Nevada, Reno, USA

Abstract

This chapter explores privacy and security issues in health care. It describes the difference between privacy and security in the context of health care, identifies sources of concern for individuals who use information technologies for health-related purposes, and presents technology-based solutions for privacy and security in health care networks. The purpose of the chapter is to provide an investigation of the sources of concern for regulations and technologies in the health care industry. The discussion is based on the Health Insurance Portability and Accountability Act (HIPAA) and its eight guiding principles. The chapter explores the implications of legal and regulatory environments driving HIPAA regulations, the need for privacy and security in health care networks, and information technologies used in the health care industry. Related ethical issues, current technologies for providing secure solutions that comply with the regulations, and products emerging in the market are also examined.

Introduction

Data communication infrastructures are changing how health information and health care is provided and received. People using tools such as the Internet for health-related purposes — patients, health care professionals, administrators, and researchers, those creating or selling health products and services, and other stakeholders — must join together to create a safe environment and enhance the value of the Internet for meeting health care needs. Because health information, products, and services have the potential to both improve health and do harm, organizations and individuals that provide health information via the Internet have obligations to be trustworthy, provide high quality content, protect users' privacy, and adhere to standards of best practices for services in health care. People using telecommunications infrastructures in health care share a responsibility to help assure the value and integrity of the information by exercising judgment in using health care sites, products, and services. Internet Health Coalition (2000)

The Health Insurance Portability and Accountability Act (HIPAA) has brought about significant changes in the procedures and practices within the health care industry. As newer information technologies are implemented in health care organizations, the challenge becomes to increase network connectivity and enable access to key information without compromising its confidentiality, integrity, or availability. With the advent of HIPAA regulations, health care organizations are required by law to have procedures in place to protect the privacy of patient information. This chapter addresses issues related to privacy and security of patient information in health care networks. It provides a background on HIPAA regulations, drivers for the need for privacy and security in health care organizations, the role of technology-based solutions, and the products available to the industry. The chapter includes a discussion of the ethical issues driving the design and implementation of information in support of HIPAA guidelines. The increased use of information technology in health care promises greater functionality and decreasing costs. While these factors point towards continued development of more robust applications, careful selection and implementation is necessary to ensure the security and privacy of patient information.

The evolution of networking technologies has enabled businesses to provide enhanced services, greater access to information, and higher levels of availability for both the service providers and the customers. While many industries have easily adopted internetworking technologies, others have been unable to do so because of the inherent complexities of their specific businesses. The health care industry is a prime example. Health care is a document-intensive industry that has faced significant challenges in migrating to the near "paperless" environments that many industries strive to achieve utilizing networking technologies (Cisco Systems, 2002). Furthermore, health care organizations work with highly sensitive data such as patients' personal health information. As such, health care organizations must be keenly aware of the privacy concerns and security risks of converting to electronic infrastructures.

Background

Anyone seeking health-related information, products, or services has a right to expect that organizations and individuals who provide such information follow a set of guiding principles. If confidences are not kept, individuals will be less forthcoming with information, which in turn may impact the care they receive. Health information includes information for staying in good physical condition as well as for preventing and managing disease. It may also include information for making decisions about health products and health services and may be in the form of data, text, audio, and/or video. In addition, enhanced health information may be available through programming and interactivity (Internet Health Coalition, 2000). Managing health information in a technological world implies the persistent storage and potential dissemination of health-related data using data communication networks. Such environments have the potential to compromise both the security and privacy of the records maintained on these networks.

Although privacy and security are terms that are often used interchangeably, there is an inherent difference between the two concepts. The Merriam-Webster online dictionary (2003) defines *security* as:

> *The quality or state of being secure: as **a**: freedom from danger: **SAFETY b**: freedom from fear or anxiety **PROTECTION** (1): measures taken to guard against espionage or sabotage, crime, attack, or escape.*

Whereas *privacy* is defined as:

> *The quality or state of being apart from company or observation: SECLUSION b: freedom from unauthorized intrusion <one's right to privacy>.*

By combining the two terms, one can gain a complete picture of protecting information in context of the health care industry. Both security and privacy must be considered in order to adequately address the issue of safeguarding patient information (Fleisher, 2001). The Health Insurance Portability and Accountability Act (HIPAA), effective as of April 14, 2000, attempts to address privacy and security issues in the context of health-related activities. Accordingly, HIPAA defines *security* as:

> *The regulations which address the protection of data resident on provider computers or networks, as well as the protection of data while it is being transmitted to third parties. Primarily, security addresses the technical components related to the collection, protection, and dissemination of data. (HIPAA Standard164.530)*

Whereas *privacy* is defined as:

> *The regulations, which address the protection of patient information in any format and by any user. Privacy necessitates providing an individual's health related information and*

disclosure of how and where that information is being used.
(HIPAA standard 142.308) (Fleisher, 2001)

More simply stated, the security regulations address technical components of health care information, which are monitored by a Security Officer. Privacy regulations are more operational in nature and are managed by a Privacy Officer (Wilson, 2002).

Organizations are becoming increasingly dependent on data communication networks for their daily business communications, database information retrieval, and distributed data processing. The rise of the Internet and wireless communications has provided opportunities to connect to computers anywhere in the world. However, this capability has also increased the potential vulnerability of organizational assets. As a result, not only do organizations need to prevent their assets from threats such as fraud and theft but they also need to be concerned with the potential loss of consumer confidence from a publicly known security break-in. Other security concerns include potential losses from disruption of an application or natural disasters (Fitzgerald & Dennis, 2000).

Security Issues in the Health Care Industry

In today's uncertain political and economic environment, many factors are driving the need for secure networks in the health care industry. A significant business challenge is to increase network connectivity and to enable access to key information assets without compromising the confidentiality, integrity, or availability of those assets. Some believe that using new technologies can assist with the process of securing patient information. According to Oracle Corporation, incorporating technology in hospitals will make the process of providing access to patient information more secure since all the data will be stored in one place (Couzin, 2001). This will reduce the risk associated with patient information "floating" around the hospital where it could potentially be accessed by multiple doctors, nurses, technicians, and administrators. In some of the solutions implemented by Oracle, doctors no longer need to spend valuable time filling out forms, tracking patient charts, or waiting to pick up X-ray or MRI results as these tasks are now automated through the use of technology (Couzin, 2001). While this has greatly increased the ease of use, it has also increased the vulnerability and security of the underlying content.

Conversely, the health care industry's steady move towards the computer-based patient record and the overall trend of delivering health care information using information technology in lieu of paper has raised anxiety regarding the security of that information. Issues related to the security of an enterprise network could create fear and uncertainty for health care executives. Securely sharing patient information over distributed regional networks that link multiple hospitals, clinics, and doctors' offices has become an issue of key importance in health care organizations (KBeta Security Web, 2001). For an organization to begin building a highly secure network, it must first understand the issue of security and why it has become such a priority in health care today.

To this end, network security has never been more important. For example, e-vandalism is occurring unnoticed in many of today's information-centric companies. Clandestine hackers and vandals not only steal a company's confidential information, but also damage its reputation in the process. The loyalty that companies have worked so hard to build could disappear if customers and business partners believe that their personal data is at risk (McMillan, 2002). The concern is thus magnified for health care enterprises trying to deploy network solutions.

Another factor driving the need for greater attention to security concerns is the move to sharing information with remote physicians. With the growth of outpatient care sites health care providers can no longer be content with just one local area network. In the past, doctors did not consider having the capacity to receive patient data in their homes. The ability of physicians to practice medicine remotely is becoming a competitive differentiation in the marketplace (Sarasohn-Kane, 2003). This practice is beneficial not only to the doctor in terms of flexibility and convenience, but also to patients who could be diagnosed and receive treatment virtually across time and physical space. Health systems and plans want to attract and retain the best physicians in the community by touting the ability to provide information anywhere and anytime a doctor needs it. The confidentiality of such information becomes paramount in the ability to conduct business.

These issues have also gained impetus as network intrusions by computer viruses have become more prevalent in recent years. The threat of new and more virulent computer worms and viruses has heightened the level of consumer awareness and concern about the use or misuse of personal health records. An IBM survey conducted in 1999 revealed that 33% of Americans would trust banks to handle their personal information properly, but only 23% placed the same faith in health care providers (Sarasohn-Kane, 2003). In a September 2000 Gallup poll, 77% of the respondents said the privacy of their personal health information was very important. Eighty-four percent were concerned that this information might be made available to others without their consent. Only 7% of the respondents said they were willing to store or transmit personal health information on the Internet and only 8% felt a Web site could be trusted with such information (Hunt, 1999).

Confidence in security measures is even more important given the push towards consumer-driven health care. Consumers' desire to access information about their own health has resulted in increased use of interactive medical networks such as the Internet and intranets. In part, the changes are due to the improving technological capability along with managed care organizations' desire for patient empowerment by asking patients to assume more self-management. Consumers' use of these networks has initiated the development of personal health information management software that may be a precursor to an electronic medical record owned by the patient. As a result, health care information is becoming more portable. Previously, the hospital literally owned patient records. In contrast today, multiple owners outside the hospital may be contending for it. The implementation of technical solutions has provided greater portability and convenience in the health care arena. At the same time, the demand for security is becoming even more imperative (Sarasohn-Kane, 2003). Copies of electronic files containing vast amounts of confidential information can easily be sent electronically over a network connection without any indication that the information was stolen.

Consumers want to control where their health information goes. Part of the enterprise's risk management analysis is to realize that we live in a litigious society. As such, it is prudent on the part of businesses to take every reasonable step to ensure the confidentiality of health care information. More trust in the health care system will help ensure better health outcomes through the use of technology.

Privacy Issues in the
Health Care Industry

Health care providers maintain and share a vast amount of sensitive patient information for a variety of reasons. Such records are kept and shared for diagnosis and treatment of the patients, payment of health care services rendered, public health reporting, research, and even for marketing and use by media. While traditional paper-based systems have vulnerabilities, they also place some natural limits on the ability of information collectors to share and disseminate information. It is sometimes a challenge to locate paper records. In order to disseminate the information, someone must physically remove the records from the premises either by carrying, copying, mailing, or faxing the documents. These limitations create a double-edged sword. Although such systems may protect information from being disseminated for improper reasons, they may also obstruct the flow of information being shared for legitimate, health care-related purposes (Choy, Hudson, Pritts, & Goldman, 2001).

Health information can be easily located, collected, and organized with the migration of the health care industry toward electronic data collection, storage, and transmission. One major drawback is that sensitive and personal patient information can be sent to any number of places thousands of miles away with the click of a mouse button. Thus, some consumers may be afraid to take advantage of the technology because of privacy and confidentiality concerns. According to the Ethics Survey of Consumer Attitudes conducted by the Cyber Dialogue and the Institute for the Future for the California Health Care Foundation and the Internet Health Care Coalition in January 2000, more than 75% of the people surveyed are concerned about Web sites sharing information without their consent, thus impacting their willingness to use the Internet for health-related services (Goldman & Hudson, 1999).

Consumers are increasingly worried about the loss of their privacy, and have heightened concerns when it comes to their health information (Brewin, 2003). They worry that their health information may be used or disclosed inappropriately and leave them vulnerable to unwanted exposure, stigma, and discrimination, possibly leading to economic losses. Patients fear that their personal information will be used to deny them health insurance, employment, credit, and housing. With the increase in the use of technology and the ease with which information can be transmitted, there has undoubtedly been a considerable increase in the access of health care information. People who access such data without appropriate authorization are motivated either by profit or at times just plain curiosity (Goldman & Hudson, 1999). As a result, consumers sometimes take drastic steps to keep their health information private. According to one survey, almost one out of six U.S. adults has taken extreme steps to maintain the privacy of his or her medical information. Patients withhold information from their doctors, provide inaccurate or incomplete information, and doctor-hop to avoid a consolidated medical record. They go as far as paying out-of-pocket for care that is covered by their insurance, or even avoiding care altogether (Goldman & Hudson, 1999).

Such privacy-protection behavior, which consumers/patients do both offline and online, can result in a significant cost to their health. A study released by the Pew Internet and American Life Project found that 89% of Internet users who seek health information online are worried that others will find out about their activities and are worried that the Internet companies will give this information away. Eighty-five percent fear that insurance companies might change their coverage after finding out what online information consumers had accessed (Choy et al., 2001). By concealing information, patients risk undetected and untreated conditions. At the same time, the doctor's ability to diagnose and treat patients is jeopardized without access to complete and accurate information. Further, future treatment may be compromised if the doctor misrepresents patient information so as to encourage disclosure. This in turn can have a detrimental effect on the community, as without full patient participation upfront, the information collected will be unreliable for users downstream. Ultimately, health care initiatives that depend on complete and accurate information may be undermined (Goldman & Hudson, 1999).

Legal and Regulatory Environment

Regulatory factors are driving the current trend toward security and privacy standards in the transmission of health care information over enterprise networks. State and federal legislation, professional and standards organizations, and internal organizational risk management departments are driving the need for security measures. Many states, for example, regulate the use of electronic signatures and medical records. The Joint Commission on Accreditation of Healthcare Organizations (JCAHO) addresses security and confidentiality issues in the Information Management section of its accreditation manual.

Overlaying all these factors, however, is the greatest of all regulatory drivers: a recent federal law called HIPAA.

The Health Insurance Portability and Accountability Act, signed into law in the United States in August 1996, mandates the adoption of national uniform standards for the electronic transmission of health and patient information. The intent of HIPAA is "administrative simplification" and protection of patient privacy. HIPAA requires that the health care industry promote a national, uniform security standard for the secure electronic transmission of patient-identifiable information.

HIPAA is a turning point for the health care industry because it requires that the industry develop a set of national standards that will help bring the much-needed data-standard unity to health care transactions and provide assurance that confidential patient information will be safe or safer than paper-based patient records.

Although HIPAA does not mandate the collection or electronic transmission of health information, it requires that standards be adopted for any electronic transmission of specified transactions. To ensure protection of privacy, the law provides for confidentiality protections for information processed in accordance with the new standards. It requires organizations to focus on *Electronic Data Interchange (EDI) transactions for health plan enrollment, eligibility, claims payment, premium payment, coordination of benefits, and referral/authorization.* HIPAA also mandates p*rotecting confidentiality of individually identifiable patient information in an automated system.* It requires organizations to be able to demonstrate sound practices that protect patient confidentiality and security.

HIPAA security requirements are broad, covering any organization that generates or otherwise handles electronic patient records and other e-medical data. HIPAA requires the health care organizations to implement encryption, user authentication, and other security measures to safeguard the integrity, confidentiality, and availability of electronic data by mid-2003. Entities affected by this law include virtually all private and government hospitals, outpatient centers, nursing centers, Health Maintenance Organizations (HMO), Preferred Provider Organizations (PPO), insurance companies, firms providing clinical information systems for medical labs, providers of pathology, radiology, patient billing, and pharmacy records, medical software application providers, and even related Web portal companies (Yozons Technology, 2003).

Penalties for noncompliance to the law can be severe. The civil penalty for violating transaction standards is up to $100 per person per violation and up to

$25,000 per person per violation of a single standard for a calendar year. The penalty for knowing misuse of individually identifiable health information can reach $250,000 and/or imprisonment for up to ten years. HIPAA has hit the nation's $1.3 trillion health care industry quickly by becoming the de facto security guideline for federal privacy standards regarding health care information. The privacy standards, which govern electronically Protected Health Information (PHI), went into effect as of April 14, 2003 and could create a legal nightmare for the health care industry, requiring a massive training effort and costing millions of dollars. There is also concern that litigation over a failure to adhere to HIPAA security standards may dampen the use of technologies such as wireless LAN systems in hospitals (Brewin, 2003).

Given the mandated HIPAA compliance, many organizations have been working overtime to ensure their organizations are aligned correctly. In order to examine the implications of HIPAA in the workplace, interviews were conducted with professionals responsible for information systems and telecommunication services in regional medical centers. The combination of HIPAA and the hospitals' endeavor to become HIPAA compliant has resulted in additional responsibilities for individuals such as the Privacy and Security Officers for their respective medical centers. On the whole, these professionals consider HIPAA to be a double-edged sword. In their opinion, to a large degree most hospitals and health care organizations have always been very sensitive to privacy and confidentiality of patient information. HIPAA has simply formalized some of those issues and ensured that the standards are being applied equally. The primary gap in the protection of patient information was seen at pharmacies as they previously shared patient information with various vendors. If a patient were to buy prescription drugs at the pharmacy, he or she might receive advertisements with information on drugs related to their condition. With the advent of HIPAA, pharmacies need to be monitored and are not allowed to share patient information with vendors without the consent of the patient. In addition, the electronic transaction of transmitting patient information to bill insurance companies needs to be supported by software that is HIPAA compliant.

Implications of HIPAA Implementation

Overall HIPAA is believed to be a very positive thing, as patients find comfort in knowing that there are standards in place to safeguard their personal health information. Still, some patients have negative perceptions regarding how HIPAA affects the privacy and security of personal information. Most hospitals are very explicit when stating what happens with patient information and with whom such information is shared. However, such an expression, alluding to a more open process, has raised concerns among some patients who have only recently become aware of such standard practices of health care organizations. They believe that HIPAA has allowed health care organizations to share more information than they previously could. In effect, HIPAA has heightened peoples' awareness of issues related to information privacy and security. For many, these concern are issues that were previously unknown or of little interest. As such, efforts are being made to educate such individuals in order to make them feel more comfortable about the privacy of their information.

The security piece of the regulation mandates the implementation of security measures within health care organizations. These security measures were previously hard to implement because there was not much return on investment. With HIPAA, it has become easier to justify these requirements from a business standpoint. The security measures may contain a layered approach to securing the network. A plan needs to be in place to ensure that every single layer of the network has been "hardened" to make it secure. In addition, some medical centers have assigned different access capacities to their various staff members depending either on their location in the hospital or the privileges assigned to them. Further constraints have been implemented in order to manage and protect the IT resources. For instance, users may need to follow a specific format for their passwords in order to ensure that they are not easily decipherable. For systems containing clinical information used to make emergency decisions, some hospitals have implemented a "break the glass" procedure, in which, for example, if a password is not working in emergency situations, physicians are still able to get to the information. Extra audits and alerts are put in place so that if someone "breaks the glass," network administrators are automatically notified and upper management can be apprised of the related circumstances.

The processes associated with accessing records have also undergone changes as illustrated in the following scenario. If a physician examines one patient and consults with another physician on the case, the second physician may be unable to access the patient's records since he or she is not the "physician of record." In such a situation, the second physician could override the access blocks by agreeing to have their name appear in the audit report. If the second physician agrees, administrators can monitor records for inappropriate activities and follow-up with the physician to address access issues as needed.

There are obvious cost implications on the implementation of HIPAA. Organizations now need to maintain a fair-sized HIPAA contingency budget every year. There are costs such as traveling to understand more about HIPAA, man-hours, and employee education.

Solutions

Health care services and professionals are working toward providing environments that safeguard health-related information. In part, actions have been encouraged and set in motion as a result of HIPAA compliance efforts. Some solutions are enabled by information and communication technologies while others rely on standards of practice that have been advanced by the health care community. The eHealth code of Ethics, initiated in 2000, helps ensure that people understand the potential risks of managing their own health care and the health of those in their care. The eight guiding principles of the code work to ensure candor, honesty, quality, professionalism, responsible partnering, accountability, informed consent, and privacy of patient information (Internet Health Coalition, 2000) (Table 1).

Table 1. Eight guiding principles of eHealth code of ethics (Internet Health Coalition, 2000)

e-Health Code of Ethics: 8 Guiding Principles	
Candor	<ul><li>Disclose vested financial interests</li><li>Disclose key information for consumer decisions</li></ul>
Honesty	<ul><li>Present information truthfully</li><li>No misleading claims</li></ul>
Quality	<ul><li>Accurate, clear, current, evidence-based</li><li>Readable, culturally competent, accessible</li><li>Citations, links, editorial board and policies</li></ul>
Informed Consent	<ul><li>Privacy policy and risks</li><li>Data collection and sharing</li><li>Consequences of refusal to consent</li></ul>
Privacy	<ul><li>Prevent unauthorized access or personal identification of aggregate data</li><li>Let users review and update personal data</li></ul>
Professionalism	<ul><li>Abide by professional codes of ethics</li><li>Disclose potential conflicts of interest</li><li>Obey applicable laws and regulations</li><li>Point out limits of online practice</li></ul>
Responsible partnering	<ul><li>Choose trustworthy partners, affiliates, and links</li><li>Maintain editorial independence from sponsors</li><li>Tell users when they are leaving the site</li></ul>
Accountability	<ul><li>Provide management contact info</li><li>Encourage user feedback</li><li>Respond promptly and fairly to complaint</li></ul>

In a similar vein, the Health on the Net (HON) Foundation (2002) Code of Conduct for medical and health Web sites addresses the reliability and credibility of information on the Internet. Specifically, it addresses the authority of the information provided, data confidentiality and privacy, proper attribution of sources, transparency of financial sponsorship, and the importance of clearly separating advertising from editorial content (Health on the Net Foundation, 2002).

Role of Technology-Based Solutions

In addition to guiding principles for behavior, health care enterprises are faced with a number of technical and operational challenges. Among these are the needs to operate more efficiently, to expand the scope of the enterprise, to provide greater access to information from a variety of locations and platforms including mobile/wireless, and to greatly improve the security and privacy of information. These challenges can, at times, seem contradictory. The responses to these challenges necessitate many different initiatives, including security planning, creation of wide area networks, and adoption of wireless/mobile platforms. In addition, the health care industry's ongoing, massive consolidation has resulted in the emergence of so-called Integrated Delivery Systems (IDS). These systems are designed for large, regional providers that need to share clinical and other information among numerous hospitals, clinics, home-care agencies, and other facilities. With the advent of multiple clinics and hospitals sharing data, a health care organization must contend with factors such as leased telecommunications lines and external circuits and services, rather than local services inside a building (KBeta Security Web, 2001).

From unauthorized users to disgruntled employees to cyber-terrorists, the threat to health care information systems cannot be taken lightly. Poorly written software, the demand for convenience over security, and overworked, undertrained IT health care professionals present substantial information systems vulnerabilities (Beaver, 2003). The HIPAA security rule is about information security best practices. Technology for secure networks includes tools such as firewalls, encryption, user authentication, and software that detects and reports network vulnerabilities and unauthorized activity (KBeta Security Web, 2001).

Management Issues

It is imperative to realize that technology is not the silver bullet that people have come to believe in and rely on. Simply relying on the technical solutions is not sufficient to ensure the security of the information. While cutting-edge network technology might be available to make networks secure, technology is only an enabler (KBeta Security Web, 2001). Other issues that need to be considered include ongoing information risk assessment, information security audits, disaster recovery, and business continuity plans (Beaver, 2003). Information security is a business issue as well. Organizational and cultural issues are paramount in making the technology fulfill its potential. The key is to impart a *culture of security and confidentiality* to an organization. As a corporate cultural issue, security and confidentiality integrate through diverse areas of technology, organization, and regulation. Security is an integrated approach in which an organization needs to have its entire management team involved in the decision-making processes. These processes should include key decision makers from multiple and varied departments such as legal, human resources, and operations.

Given the intersecting technical, organizational, and regulatory factors, it should be understood that security of enterprise networks is both an ethical as well as a cultural issue, requiring constant, iterative education and awareness. In order for information security initiatives to be effective, it is critical to not forget the end user. In fact, the human factor can be the weakest link in an information security program (Beaver, 2003). Organizations must reinforce employee awareness through an ongoing program of education, reward, and recognition. Individual user accountability is a critical component of network security. A system cannot allow, for example, several providers to use the same terminal simply by using the same password and logon for the sake of convenience.

Mobile computing applications and the use of wireless technologies in health care has seen a great deal of growth and expansion capabilities. From a security standpoint, the social changes are probably the hardest to implement. It is easy to have the firewalls and technologies in place, but it is harder as well as more important to manage the social aspect of such a change. If people leave their PC screen on and the others walking by can see the information displayed on it, then security doesn't mean anything. Similarly, if people stick their pass-words on post-it notes on their screens, then the security measures become meaningless. Maybe security will change with biotechnology, and people won't have to remember multiple passwords while they simply remember to bring their thumb to work.

The information owners must determine security risks, impact, and the severity of a potential compromise. Additionally, the information owners should be responsible for determining a balance between the costs and benefits of security for their particular organization. Organizational risk is an aggregate factor and must be determined collectively by all of the information owners within and throughout the organization. Securing an organization's information assets is ultimately an upper management responsibility and must be managed from the top down from a business perspective. Health care managers must understand the business impact of information risks and the implications involved if systems are not secured. To protect themselves from legal liabilities, health care organizations need to show due diligence in attempting to implement best practices in this regard.

Implications and Conclusions

In the end, it is necessary to understand that there is no such thing as 100% security. However, it is vital that reasonable measures be in place to reduce the chances of unauthorized access of confidential information. With HIPAA privacy regulation compliance mandatory since April 14, 2003, health care providers need to ensure that their systems meet the federal health privacy policies. Although the law allows for incidental disclosures of information, providers covered by the rule are expected to put reasonable safeguards in place to protect their patients' information. This means that sign-in sheets may be used in a doctor's reception areas but patients should no longer be asked to write down their conditions because other patients could see the sheet. In an emergency room, the large white boards listing patient names and conditions should be moved to areas out of public view. In hospitals, patient charts should be turned to face the wall so people walking by cannot read them. New computer software allows doctors' offices to identify patients by full name or just by initials, just in case others might catch a glance of a PC screen. Most hospitals have new policies regarding the release of information regarding a patient's condition. Such information was once routinely provided to family, friends, clergy, and reporters who called. Under the new rules, hospitals must give patients a chance to opt out of any hospital directory. No information, even that a person is a patient in the hospital, may be released without the patient's consent. Even if a patient agrees to being included on a general patient listing, hospitals may release only limited information without specific patient authorization and only if a caller asks about a patient by name (Meckler, 2003).

Technologically, the continued growth and acceptance of the Internet, widespread growth of wireless devices with greater functionality and decreasing costs of technology solutions all point towards continued development of more robust software applications. These developments may improve adoption of technology, but careful selection and implementation are necessary to ensure the security and privacy of patient information. Eventually, organizational policies, technical solutions, and regulatory guidance should improve the acceptance of e-technology and increase its value to the health care organizations. With greater security of patient information, health care organizations can build patient trust by protecting confidential patient information. This trust between the patient and the provider in turn will lead to improvement in the overall quality of health care.

References

Beaver, K. (2003). Information security issues that healthcare management must understand. *Journal of Healthcare Information Management,* April, *17*(1), 46-49.

Brewin, R. (2003,). New HIPAA security rules could open door to litigation. *Computerworld,* February 20. Retrieved April 23, 2003 from: *http:// www.computerworld.com/governmenttopics/government/policy/ story/0,10801,78684,00.html*

Choy, A., Hudson, Z., Pritts, J., & Goldman, J. (2001). Exposed online: Why the new federal health privacy regulation doesn't offer much protection to Internet users. Report of the Pew Internet & American Life Project. Health Privacy Project, Institute for Health Care Research and Policy, Georgetown University, Washington, DC. Retrieved April 30, 2003 from: *http://www.healthprivacy.org/usr_doc/PIP_HPP_Health Priv_report.pdf*

Cisco Systems (2002). Network security solutions for health care: Making HIPAA SAFE. August 21. Retrieved May 17, 2003 from: *http:// www.cisco.com/warp/public/cc/so/neso/sqso/hipaa_wp.htm*

Couzin, J. (2001, March 26). A Hospital for the Digital Age. *IDG.net.* March 26. Retrieved April 10, 2003 from: *http://www.idg.net/go.cgi?id= 477347*

Fitzgerald, J,. & Dennis, A. (2000). *Business data communication and networking* (6th ed.). New York: John Wiley & Sons.

Fleisher, S.M. (2001). Health care data security: HIPAA draft security rules and California law. *California Health Care Symposium 2001.* May 10. Retrieved April 09, 2003 from: *http://www.ehcca.com/presentations/ casymposium/fleisher.pdf*

Goldman, J., & Hudson, Z. (1999). Health privacy 101 exposed: A health privacy primer for consumers. Retrieved April 23, 2003 from: *http:// www.healthprivacy.org/info-url_nocat2302/ info-url_nocat.htm*

Health On the Net (HON) Foundation (2002). HON code of conduct (HONcode) for medical and health Web sites. Retrieved January 15, 2004 from: *http://www.hon.ch/HONcode/*

Hunt, K. (1999). Confidentiality of medical records: National survey . The Princeton Survey Research Associates for the California HealthCare Foundation. Retrieved April 23, 2003 from: *http://www.chcf.org/ press/view.cfm?itemID=12267 - 41k*

Internet Health Coalition (2000). eHealth code of conduct. Retrieved January 15, 2004 from: *http://www.ihealthcoalition.org/ethics/ehcode.html*

KBeta Security Web (2001). White Paper: Security and Health Care Enterprise Networks: Balancing Technology and Culture. Retrieved April 25, 2003 from: *http://www.kbeta.com/SecurityTips/hipaa/CiscoHipaa WhitePaperori.htm*

McMillan, M.H. (2002). Cognitive security management: Meeting the challenges of eHealth, *2002* Annual HIMSS Conference and Exhibition: Session 48.

Meckler, L. (2003). New patient privacy rules to take effect: Health data handling facing adjustments. Associated Press. Retrieved June 22, 2003 from: *http://www.boston.com/dailyglobe2/104/nation/*

Merriam-Webster Online (2003). The language center. Retrieved April 19, 2003 from: *http://www.m-w.com/cgi-bin/dictionary*

Sarasohn-Kahn, J. (2003). Public perceptions and health care privacy. *CSO Magazine* [online]. Retrieved April 28, 2003 from: *http://www.cio.com/ sponsors/041502cisco/public.html*

Wilson, M., (2002). Security and privacy— Two sides of the same coin. *HIMSS Proceedings: Educational Sessions.*

Yozons Technology (2003). Healthcare, biotech and pharmaceuticals. Retrieved April 23, 2003 from: *http://www.yozons.com/pub/uses/medical.jsp*

SECTION VI:

CODES OF ETHICS

Chapter XIV

Limitations of Having Diversity in Codes of Information Ethics:
A Professional and Corporate Perspective

Mary Brabston
The University of Manitoba, Canada

Jennifer Dahl
BestBuy, Canada

Abstract

In this chapter, we examine three frameworks or models that could be used in developing codes of information ethics and then review two codes of information ethics for IST professionals and three codes of ethics or conduct for corporations based on their fit with these three frameworks. Based on our review, we make recommendations that call for a unified code of information ethics based on standardized language and for the possible certification of these codes by professional associations. We also call for stronger language regarding penalties for violations of codes of information ethics.

Introduction

Information is a source of power in society, but unlike money and weapons, information is not tangible. Because information is intangible, unique issues and ethical dilemmas emerge from the information environment. Accordingly, individuals who use information systems and technology (IST) in their work environment are faced with distinctive ethical dilemmas about the use of their power and access to information.

What is meant by the notion of an ethical issue? An ethical issue may be defined as any situation where a party pursuing its objectives engages in behavior that materially affects the ability of another party to pursue its own goals (Mason, 1995). When ethics is applied to IST, it refers to a set of rules or principles used for moral decision making regarding computer technology and computer use (Pierce & Henry, 1996). These sets of rules or principles for guiding conduct are codes of ethics. Many IST professional organizations have ethics codes for their members to follow. Most corporations have general corporate codes of ethics. Some IST issues may be addressed in corporate codes of ethics or conduct, but we question whether corporations address IST ethical issues sufficiently and effectively.

This chapter reviews several professional and corporate codes of information ethics using three different frameworks of information ethics. These frameworks include the entity to whom the ethical obligation is owed and the types of ethical issues that should be included in these codes. This chapter explores the importance of information technology ethics codes in IST professional organizations and in corporations. Unfortunately, the diversity we found in these codes presents limitations, which we then explore. Finally, we propose the adoption of a unified code of ethics for both IST professionals and corporations and possible certification of these codes.

Importance of Codes of Information Ethics

Codes of information ethics in corporations and professional organizations are important for many reasons. Codes of information ethics for an IST professional organization help to establish the IST industry as a profession by regulating the membership in the organization. In other words, members must obey the ethics code in order to be part of the recognized organization. A code of information ethics establishes a minimum standard for the profession. Information ethics codes provide benefits that are equally significant to a corporation or professional organization.

First, a code holds the IST professional and other corporate users accountable to the corporation and/or the public to maintain the standards set out by the code, which encourages responsible behavior. Second, a code of information ethics serves as a form of public relations, ensuring the public that there are rules in place to protect society. This may be especially important because research has shown that the public is wary of how IST is used (Pierce & Henry, 2000). An ethics code may mitigate negative perceptions by communicating that what the public fears will not happen.

Third, codes of information ethics can aid individual IST professionals in decision making when they face their own ethical dilemmas. Guidelines are especially important in an IST environment because the nature of technology depersonalizes relationships and provides anonymity (Pierce & Henry 2000). Fourth, a sound code of information ethics may provide some legal protection for the IST professional and the employer.

Fifth, a code allows an organization to enforce compliance because members are aware of what is expected of them and the consequences they may face if the code is violated. Finally, an ethics code may save an organization money in the long run. Unethical acts and the penalties that may follow cost organizations a significant amount of money and employee time. In addition, ethics scandals can lead to unfavorable public images. An ethics code that has established disciplinary procedures and penalties may help to mitigate or avoid these situations. Undoubtedly, a code of information ethics is an important document for professional organizations and corporations.

Role of Personal, Informal, and Formal Codes of Information Ethics

An individual facing an IST ethical dilemma may reference three types of codes of ethics. First, most individuals have their own personal code of ethics based on their own personal values and experience. Second, many organizations have an informal code of ethics. This would be the expectations co-workers or other members of a professional organization have about their actions. An informal code is the way ethical decisions are made in an organization. It is an unwritten code that is influenced by peer pressure from colleagues.

The third type of code is formal and is the subject of this chapter. These codes are official written policies that an organization expects its members to follow. An example would be the Code of Conduct that Canadian Information Processing Society members are to follow, or the corporate code of conduct with which a company, such as Nortel Networks, expects its employees to comply.

Which of these codes of information ethics do IST professionals use in what circumstances? The presence of a formal organizational code shifts perceived importance to formal codes of conduct. In later studies, Pierce and Henry (2000) found that individuals in organizations with formal codes rate organizational disapproval of questionable ethical behavior much higher than individuals who work in organizations without a formal code. Their research also showed that individuals in organizations with formal codes showed more personal disapproval of questionable ethical behavior in select situations than individuals in organizations without formal codes. Pearson, Crosby, and Shim (1997) found that older and higher ranking IST professionals appear to place more value on the formal codes of professional associations than younger and less senior IST professionals.

Although it appears that IST professionals do not always place as much emphasis on formal ethics codes as organizations would like, the argument for formal codes is still very strong. Pierce and Henry (2000) found that employees of companies that have formal ethics codes feel that formal codes are more important in decision making than employees who work for organizations that do not have any formal code. Therefore, simply having an ethics code in an organization makes employees feel more strongly about using codes to aid in making ethical decisions. Behavior appears to be especially influenced when an individual internalizes the code as accepted normative behavior and believes that the employer will enforce the code (Pierce & Henry, 2000). Therefore, if a code is well communicated, has consequences that are enforced by the employer, and becomes a norm within the company, it should be effective in supporting ethical behavior.

Pierce and Henry (2000) concluded that a formal corporate code of ethics does influence employee decision making. Kreie and Cronan (2000) also found that an established code of ethics can affect employee decisions in ethical situations. In addition, more senior IST professionals appear to have a better understanding of ethical behavior than less experienced IST professionals. Ethics codes may help less experienced IST professionals understand appropriate ethical behavior (Pearson, Crosby, & Shim, 1997). Thus, evidence suggests that formal ethics codes do influence individual decision making and that corporations should have a formal code of ethics in place. This is the focus of our chapter.

IST Ethical Issues and Frameworks

First, we review the three generally accepted frameworks for codes of information ethics. We hypothesize that the codes we then review will address the issues found in one or more of these models. The first framework or model for information ethics was developed by Mason (1986), who segmented ethical dilemmas into four ethical issues of the Information Age.

The first ethical issue proposed by Mason is privacy. Large numbers of employees have personal information about customers at their fingertips. How can we be sure that personal information is kept private? Mason's second ethical issue is accuracy. Accuracy in recording and entering data is extremely important. Mistakes can affect people's lives. For example, misinformation on a person's credit history can affect his or her ability to purchase a car or home. Inaccurate data can affect the survival of a firm. The third ethical issue is property. Who owns the information? How does copyright apply to computing programs or material available on the World Wide Web? The fourth and final issue is accessibility. Who should have access to personal information and confidential company information?

In 1992, Oz proposed that codes of information ethics can be examined along the lines of one's obligation to various stakeholders or entities. According to Oz (1992), an IST professional owes an obligation to society, his or her employer, clients, colleagues, the professional organization, and the profession itself. A comprehensive code should recognize all of these obligations. In addition, Oz outlined specific responsibilities of an IST professional to each of these stakeholders. For example, for the obligation to society, these responsibilities are: educate the public about IST, protect privacy and confidentiality of information, avoid misrepresentation of qualifications, avoid misrepresentation of IST, obey laws, and avoid taking credit for the achievements of others.

Because Oz's work was based on his examination of IST professional associations' codes of information ethics, it is to be expected, of course, that a review of these organizations' current codes will reflect the obligations and responsibilities that Oz elucidated. While to a certain extent this is circular logic, these obligations and responsibilities that Oz observed are prescriptive as well as descriptive as a framework for what should be in all codes of information ethics and should also apply to codes not studied by Oz.

In 1995, Mason, Mason, and Culnan (1995) expanded Mason's (1986) original conceptualization of the ethical issues facing the IST profession. They identified six major issues in information management. The first issue is who owns the intellectual output created by IST? Second, how private is personal information, and who is entitled to it? Third, how are information accuracy and quality safeguarded? Fourth, to whom and under what conditions is information accessible? Fifth, who should control the flow and content of information? Finally, what are appropriate applications of technology? These issues illustrate the complexity and significance of the ethical use of IST. These are the types of concerns that information ethics codes need to address.

We have presented three fairly consistent frameworks with which to compare various codes of information ethics (or those portions of corporate codes that pertain to information ethics). These are represented in Table 1.

The following sections describe specific IST professional and corporate codes of information ethics, analyzing them from the preceding more generic discussion about codes of information ethics. We also compare these codes and make recommendations based on our analysis.

Table 1. Factors elicited in frameworks about information ethics issues and codes

Mason	Oz	Mason, Mason, and Culnan
Privacy	Society	Ownership of intellectual property
Accuracy	Employer	Privacy
Property	Fellow employees	Accuracy and quality
Access	Company	Access
	Profession	Control
	Professional association	Appropriate applications

IST Professional Codes of Ethics

In this section, we review codes of information ethics for two IST professional organizations: the Canadian Information Processing Society (CIPS) and the Association for Computing Machinery (ACM). Both of these codes were reviewed by Oz (1993) but have been subject to review since then. CIPS and ACM are two of the oldest IST professional organizations in Canada and the US and should be representative of the ethics focus of mature IST professional associations.

CIPS Code of Ethics and Standards of Conduct

Founded in 1958, the Canadian Information Processing Society (CIPS) has evolved into Canada's largest association of computer professionals, with more than 8,000 members. CIPS started the Information Systems Professional of Canada (ISP) certification program in 1989. CIPS also offers accreditation programs to management information systems and computer science programs at Canadian colleges and universities (Canadian Information Processing Society, 2004). These certification programs strive to standardize the education of IST professionals and maintain a high profile and level of credibility for the profession.

The ethics code that CIPS members are to follow is the Code of Ethics and Standards of Conduct, an eight-page document available on CIPS' Web site (Canadian Information Processing Society, 2004). The code clearly outlines the obligations that an IST professional owes to various parties, as described by Oz (1993). CIPS members have an obligation to the public to protect the public interest at all times. The code goes further to say that IST professionals will not withhold information pertinent to public issues relating to IST.

A CIPS member also has an obligation to his or her employer and clients to give "conscientious service" to further the employer's and/or client's "legitimate best interests through management's direction" (Canadian Information Processing Society, 2004). To colleagues, IST professionals have an obligation to treat them with integrity and to respect their right to succeed. The code combines the obligation to the profession with an obligation to one's self, to guard competence and effectiveness as a valuable possession. The obligation owed to the professional organization, CIPS itself, is implied.

By becoming a member of CIPS, an individual agrees to abide by the rules and conduct set forth as an obligation to the professional organization. The CIPS code adds that IST professionals have an obligation to their students to provide a scholarly education in a supportive and helpful manner. The code also requires employees to observe their obligation to uphold the code of ethics of the professional societies to which they belong. CIPS' code addresses three of Mason's (1986) four ethical issues. The code also does not address the last two of Mason, Mason, and Culnan's (1995) questions related to access and control.

CIPS policy does not detail how to contact CIPS if a member faces an ethical dilemma and wishes to obtain advice. The CIPS code has a detailed, three-and-a-half page section outlining "enforcement procedures" for violation of the specified standards, including an appeals process. Finally, after all proceedings have been exhausted and the time allowed to initiate an appeal has lapsed, the ruling and punishment are published in the appropriate CIPS publication. CIPS appears to have a fair process for code violation that results in a tangible reprimand, which may deter unethical behavior.

ACM Code of Ethics and Professional Conduct

The Association for Computing Machinery (ACM) is an international professional association based in the United States. Founded in 1947, it is the oldest and largest educational and scientific computing society in the world. ACM has 80,000 members, both professionals and students, in over 100 countries (Association for Computing Machinery, 1992). ACM has a Technical Standards Committee that represents the organization in industry standard-related activities but does not offer a certification program. The Technical Standards Committee also seeks to disseminate as much information as possible to ACM members on industry standards.

The ethical regulations with which ACM members are expected to comply is the ACM Code of Ethics and Professional Conduct. This code has a section that instructs members to contribute to society and human well being. It prompts IST professionals to "minimize negative consequences of computing systems" (Association for Computing Machinery, 1992). Members are to avoid doing harm to their employers. Members are also instructed to honor their contracts, agreements, and assigned responsibilities, which would include those with employers. There is no section on obligations to clients, but a duty to clients is implied as members are instructed to avoid harm to others, respect the privacy of others, and honor confidentiality.

The ACM code includes employees as a group to which IST professionals have an obligation. Employees are one of the parties that ACM members are to avoid harming. The ACM code also states that members are to "manage personnel and resources to design and build information systems that enhance the quality of working life" and "articulate and support policies that protect the dignity of users and others affected by a computing system" (Association for Computing Machinery, 1992).

The ACM code requires members to "improve public understanding of computing and its consequences" (Association for Computing Machinery, 1992). The issue of protecting privacy and confidentiality of information is contained in several sections. Members are to "respect privacy of others" and "honor confidentiality" (Association for Computing Machinery, 1992). The concept of not misrepresenting IST is implied when the ACM code states, "give comprehensive and thorough evaluations of computer systems and their impacts, including analysis of possible risks" (Association for Computing Machinery, 1992). This suggests that IST professionals should be realistic and communicate accurately about IST systems and solutions. ACM members are told to "know and respect existing laws pertaining to professional work," including "local, state, province, national, and international laws unless there is a compelling ethical basis not to do so" (Association for Computing Machinery, 1992). The ACM codes does not discuss the obligations an IST professional has to colleagues, but this duty is implied as well. Members are to "give proper credit for intellectual property" (Association for Computing Machinery, 1992), which would mean that members are to respect and give credit to one another. ACM instructs members directly to "not take credit for other's ideas or work, even in cases where the work has not been explicitly protected by copyright, patent, etc." (Association for Computing Machinery, 1992).

An IST professional's obligation to the profession and to ACM itself is not specifically mentioned but is implied in the code. If a member abides by the code, he or she is fulfilling an obligation to the profession and ACM. One aspect in which the ACM code contrasts with the CIPS code is that there is a specific imperative to "be fair and take action not to discriminate" (Association for Computing Machinery, 1992) on the basis of race, sex, religion, age, disability, or national origin. The idea of accepting diversity is present throughout the ACM code. Again, access and control are not mentioned in the ACM code, meaning that the Mason (1986) and Mason, Mason, and Culnan (1995) frameworks are not entirely covered in these two IST professional codes.

Like the CIPS Code, the ACM Code does not include contact information in case a member faces an ethical dilemma and wishes to obtain advice on a situation. The code does not include a section on enforcement procedures. The only mention of punishment for violation of the code is "if a member does not follow this code by engaging in gross misconduct, membership in ACM may be terminated" (Association for Computing Machinery, 1992). While the threat of revoking membership may be a tangible threat, the process by which a violation would be investigated is not covered, so it is difficult to judge whether violations are dealt with fairly and efficiently. In addition, the value of the ACM membership in terms of advancing an IST professional's career is relatively negligible, so any penalties would probably not have serious consequences.

Corporate Codes of Ethics

As we have shown, North American IST professional organizations typically provide comprehensive codes of information ethics for their members. Many members of CIPS and ACM are also employees of large corporations. Do most corporations have comprehensive codes of ethics that cover IST issues? Ten Canadian corporations were contacted to determine if they had a separate code of information ethics. None of them had an ethics code specifically pertaining to IST. This chapter examines corporate codes of general corporate conduct or ethics to see if corporations are sufficiently addressing information ethics issues.

Because information and IST have become so critical to organizations and so pervasive, ethical dilemmas regarding information and IST can have significant, even devastating, consequences when handled unethically. For this reason, we feel it is appropriate to examine corporate codes of ethics to determine how corporations deal with these issues. While it could be argued that corporations should then have sections in their ethics codes about accounting practices, contracting practices, and so forth, we argue that, since computers and the use of information have become so pervasive in organizations, corporations need to incorporate a section on information ethics in their more general codes of ethics or conduct.

In the following sections, we review the codes of conduct of three Canada-based major corporations of various sizes in various industries. We feel that these codes are representative of mature North American corporations. We chose large corporations to ensure that these issues had been addressed because we felt that smaller companies might not have developed a code of conduct due to constraints such as resources and expertise. The frameworks used to examine the professional ethics codes will be utilized to analyze the corporate codes, even though corporate codes will most likely not have exactly the same objectives as the codes of professional organizations. For example, a corporate code of ethics might not include Mason, Mason, and Culnan's (1995) question about control of information or Oz' (1992) responsibility to educate the public about IST. Because IST professionals are required to adhere to both corporate and professional policies, they should ideally be relatively consistent.

BC Hydro Director and Employee Code of Conduct

The first corporate code we review is that of BC Hydro, the electric utility in British Columbia. In 2001, the company had revenues of $7.9 billion CDN. The corporation's general corporate code of ethics is the Director and Employee Code of Conduct. The BC Hydro policy does not delineate the parties to whom their employees owe an obligation. Throughout the document, though, there are several mentions of the parties included in the Oz (1993) framework. Employees are to treat each other with respect and avoid practicing discrimination or harassment. Society is not specifically included, but the protection of the environment is emphasized. The code's regulations have a comprehensive section regarding BC Hydro staff belonging to a recognized profession. There are three expectations of employees who are members of a recognized profession. First, they are "to keep abreast of professional developments in their field;" second, they are "to perform their duties in accordance with the recognized standards of that profession;" third, they are "to abide by any code of ethics adopted by their professional association" (BC Hydro, 2004). This is a very progressive requirement because it supports the work of professional organizations such as CIPS.

The BC Hydro code covers the importance of protecting confidentiality of information, by stating that employees "should at all times maintain the confidentiality of all confidential information and all records of BC Hydro" (BC

Hydro, 2004). BC Hydro's code does compel employees to obey the law. All employees "shall comply with all applicable provisions of laws and regulations of the countries in which BC Hydro operates" (BC Hydro, 2004). The code fails to advise staff to avoid taking credit for the achievements of others. The BC Hydro code includes penalties by stating, "an employee's failure to adhere to these standards could lead to disciplinary action, and the policies and procedures currently in place at BC Hydro respecting disciplinary action will apply" (BC Hydro, 2004).

The BC Hydro code also has a section titled "Procedure for Disclosure to the Code of Conduct Advisor" (BC Hydro, 2004). The Code of Conduct Advisor is an independent contractor, appointed by the company's board of directors. This procedure is followed when a suspected breach of the code takes place and is reported. The first step is for the Code of Conduct Advisor to determine if the violation has the potential to cause serious harm to the public, the company, or its employees. If the reporting party does not wish to tell management about the violation and it is not expected to inflict serious harm, the Advisor records the issue, and it is kept confidential. If the party reporting the violation wishes to tell company management or if the violation may inflict serious harm, the violation is publicized within the company. At that point, there will be an investigation into the circumstances, and the person accused of the breach will be able to respond to the allegations. If appropriate, the person accused of the violation will also be able to contribute to the discussion on how the breach can be remedied. Disciplinary action for the party in violation of the code will then be decided. The code makes reference to the Code of Conduct Advisor as the person to be contacted if an employee faces an ethical dilemma and requires advice or if an employee wishes to report suspected unethical behavior.

Standard Aero Limited Code of Conduct

The second corporation whose code we reviewed is Standard Aero Limited, based in Manitoba, Canada. Standard Aero is a gas turbine engine and accessory repair and overhaul facility. It is a privately held company, so revenues are not available. The company employs 4,000 worldwide in more than six countries. Standard Aero's general corporate code of ethics is the Code of Conduct. This code does not outline to whom the employees owe an obligation in any form. The policy does include confidentiality by stating that employees should not obtain material they are not authorized to access. In addition, Standard Aero staff "may only have access to and use information and documents that are obtained in accordance with standard industry practice" (Standard Aero Limited, 2004). The notion of avoiding the misrepresentation of qualifications and IST are related to the statement, "no misleading, deceptive, or untrue statements may be made in relation to Standard Aero" (Standard Aero Limited, 2004). This does not completely address the substance Oz (1993) intended, but it does discourage misrepresenting the company. The code's regulations do not address the issue of avoiding taking credit for others' achievements.

Employees are to obey "laws of the area in which a Standard Aero facility is located, in which a customer is located, and any laws which, if not observed, may result in Standard Aero losing a contract" (Standard Aero Limited, 2004). The section covering law states that a breach of law may result in disciplinary action, dismissal, and any legal repercussions, including fines, imprisonment, civil damages, and legal costs. Penalties for violating the code are outlined in the document. Violations may result in discipline, dismissal, and consequences of the law. The code also states that any person who retaliates against a person who has reported unethical behavior will be dismissed. To encourage people to report questionable behavior, the code states, "by reporting suspected activities, it is less likely that you would be viewed as participating in that activity" (Standard Aero Limited, 2004). The policy provides a contact e-mail and address for the company ethics officer, so that employees who face an ethical dilemma can obtain assistance. The officer can also be contacted to report suspected unethical behavior.

Nortel Networks' Guide to Ethical Business Practices

The third company whose code we reviewed is Nortel Networks, a communication network technology company based in Ontario, Canada. Revenues in 2001 were US$17.5 billion. Nortel has operations in approximately 150 countries. Nortel's general corporate code of ethics is called Guide to Ethical Business Practices (Nortel, 2004). The Nortel code states that employees have an obligation "to each other, to shareholders, customers, suppliers, and the communities in which we do business." This is fairly parallel to the Oz (1993) framework that states that an IST professional owes an obligation to society, his or her employer, clients, and colleagues. Nortel's corporate code does include employees owing an obligation to their profession because it is a general business code and employees will come from different professions, e.g., engineering and accounting.

Nortel's code stresses the importance of protecting privacy and confidentiality of information several times. It specifically mentions that employees are expected to keep employee, customer, and corporate information confidential. The document does not specifically mention avoiding misrepresentation of employee qualifications or of IST itself, but it does stress it is important not to make promises to customers "unless we are reasonably confident that we will be able to keep them." This means that employees are not to misrepresent what Nortel and its agents are capable of producing and completing. Wherever Nortel operates, employees are expected to abide by "all national and local laws." The policy does not mention the issue of avoiding taking credit for the achievements of others.

The Nortel code does not specify penalties for violation of the code, except in the case of selling or taking illegal drugs on company property, which may be grounds for dismissal. The code provides a contact e-mail and confidential phone number for the corporate ethics function at Nortel, so that employees who face an ethical dilemma may obtain assistance. This function can also be used to report unethical behavior.

Recommendations for Revisions to Corporate Ethics Codes

Up to this point, we have simply described the current state of codes of information ethics in North America. Now, we will propose our ideas to improve these codes to make them more effective.

The general corporate ethics codes that we examined do not comprehensively cover all of the issues that are considered to be important for IST professionals. Generally, the corporate codes do not do a good job of delineating to whom IST professionals owe an obligation. It should be considered important for all employees of an organization, including IST professionals, to know to whom they have an obligation and in what order those obligations are owed. It is reasonable that the corporations do not ask their employees to educate the public about IST, but there are other responsibilities of an IST professional that are neglected. With the exception of Nortel Networks, the companies did not cover the importance of privacy and confidentiality of information sufficiently, nor did the companies thoroughly discuss avoiding misrepresentations about qualifications and IST. It makes sense that all employees should be aware of this issue, not just IST professionals. It is bad business practice to exaggerate skills and capabilities in order to win contracts and business.

All of the corporations described the need to obey laws effectively. None of the firms instructed their employees to avoid taking credit for the achievements of others. This is another concept that should be included.

Codes of information ethics should have penalties attached for violation of the codes. A written policy should be in place that explains the process that occurs when there is a suspected violation of the code. The process may include an investigation, a hearing, or a decision from a committee, but it must be clearly documented so that all situations are treated equally. A code should also outline what the consequences are for violating it, so that professionals and employees realize the seriousness of any infractions. The penalties may include ejection from the professional organization or suspension or dismissal from employment. Whatever the cost to the professional, there must be a tangible punishment for offenses outlined in the code.

The corporate codes also failed to clearly explain processes and penalties in the event the code is violated. Nortel did not discuss penalties to any extent. Standard Aero outlines extensive consequences to violation of its code, but it does not explain any sort of fair process to determine if a violation has been committed. BC Hydro provides a process for which suspected code violations are investigated. BC Hydro's penalties are detailed in an internal document that was not available for this chapter but is available for its employees who are expected to adhere to the code. All of the corporate codes examined could be improved by looking at CIPS' code's enforcement procedures.

Because corporate codes of general business ethics are missing elements that are important to IST, revisions to these codes are recommended. One possible solution would be for corporations to adopt a unified code for information ethics. This code could be a section within their current general corporate codes. A code of information ethics should not be strictly for the IST department because many jobs utilize information and IST. Thus, a code of information ethics must be understood and followed by the whole organization, not just the IST department.

There are several benefits to having a sound, unified information ethics code that an entire corporation can follow. First, a unified code would utilize a standardized language that all members of the organization could understand. Standardized language would also prevent varying interpretations of code sections. Second, it is far less expensive for a corporation to adopt an existing code than to design its own with attorney consultation. Third, there is less risk of litigation if a company has a comprehensive ethics code. Fourth, a unified code could have provisions to provide independent advice in cases of moral complexity and ethical dilemma. Fifth, a unified code would enhance the public's confidence in the IST profession and in the corporations that adopt the code. Thus, a unified ethics code produced by an independent source or IST professional organization would be a positive step for corporations.

Another solution would be for IST professional organizations, such as CIPS, to provide a certification process to corporations. CIPS already has extensive experience in certification with its ISP program and the accreditation of MIS and computer science programs at colleges and universities. A corporate certification program could work in a similar fashion to the CIPS accreditation program. A professional IST organization, such as CIPS, would set up an independent committee to administer its certification program. Corporations wishing to obtain certification could contact that committee. The corporation would submit a detailed questionnaire on its internal ethics code, and policies, procedures, and practices used to ensure the proper conduct of information ethics within the organization. If the initial questionnaire screening process is satisfied, a site visit by committee members could be planned.

A virtual site inspection, using ample documentation from the corporation, would look for a comprehensive code of ethics, employee awareness and practice of the code, and a penalty process in place that is well communicated to employees. The code could be one designed by the corporation or an adaptation of a unified code if one is available. If committee members are satisfied by the virtual inspection, certification is granted. CIPS currently charges universities $3,500 for the accreditation process, but corporations could be charged a sum that completely covered all of the expenses incurred by such a process. The certification could be awarded for several years, at which point the code of information ethics would be re-examined. A certification program such as this would assure the public, customers, businesses that deal with the organization, and investors that the corporation practices sound information ethics.

Limitations and Future Research

Certainly, a review of a small number of codes from one continent is subject to the biases associated with the use of a small sample and local culture. As a result the findings may not be universally generalizable.

Future research should examine whether the issues and obligations covered in the frameworks used in this chapter are universal — that is, future studies should examine codes of information ethics of IST professionals and corporations located outside of North America as well as examining additional North American codes. Where these codes have been violated, it would be useful to review the consequences of these violations.

Conclusions

While our discussion has only focused on two professional and three Canadian corporate codes of information ethics or professional conduct, we feel the results are generalizable to at least the North American population. Further study should prove both the ability to generalize and the need for improvements in codes of information ethics throughout North America.

Although many IST professional organizations provide their members with a comprehensive code of conduct to follow, most corporations fail to give employees a complete IST code of ethics to follow. Codes of information ethics must define to whom IST professionals owe an obligation and also clearly describe their responsibilities as professionals. In addition, codes of information ethics must identify a process for investigating suspected unethical behavior and set forth the penalties for those in violation of the policies.

To aid corporations in effectively addressing IST ethical issues, we recommend that a unified code of information ethics for corporations be created by an independent organization and be adopted by companies. Alternatively, a certification process could be created that is administered by an independent professional organization to declare that the company practices sound information ethics.

References

Association for Computing Machinery (1992). *ACM code of ethics and professional conduct.* Retrieved February 7, 2004 from: *http://www.acm.org/constitution/code.html*

BC Hydro. (2004). *Director and employee code of conduct.* Retrieved February 7, 2004 from: *http://www.bchydro.com/rx_files/policies/policies1425.pdf*

Canadian Information Processing Society (2004). *Code of Ethics and Standard of Conduct.* Retrieved February 7, 2004 from: *http://www.cips.ca/about/ethics/english/ethics.pdf*

Kreie, J., & Cronan, T.P. (2000). Making ethical decisions. *Communications of the ACM, 43*(12), 66-71.

Mason, R.O. (1986). Four ethical issues of the information age. *MIS Quarterly, 10*(1), 5-12.

Mason, R.O., Mason, F., & Culnan, M. (1995). *Ethics for information management.* London: Sage.

Nortel Networks Limited. (2004). *Guide to ethical business practices.* Retrieved February 7, 2004 from: *http://www.nortelnetworks.com/corporate/community/ethics/guide.html*

Oz, E. (1992). Ethical standards for information systems professionals: A case for a unified code. *MIS Quarterly, 16*(4), 1-12.

Oz, E. (1993). Ethical standards for computer professionals: A comparative analysis of four major codes. *Journal of Business Ethics, 12*(9), 1-24.

Pearson, M., Crosby, L., & Shim, J.P. (1997). Measuring the importance of ethical behavior criteria. *Communications of the ACM, 40*(9), 94-100.

Pierce, M.A., & Henry, J.W. (1996). Computer ethics: The role of personal, informal, and formal codes. *Journal of Business Ethics, 15*(4), 1-15.

Pierce, M.A., & Henry, J.W. (2000). Judgments about computer ethics: Do individual, co-worker, and company judgments differ? Do company codes make a difference? *Journal of Business Ethics, 28*(4), 1-15.

Standard Aero Limited. (2002). Code of conduct. Retrieved February 7, 2004 from: *http://www.standardaero.com/code_of_conduct.asp*

Glossary of Terms

Access: the availability of computers and computing resources to individuals, often used in terms of access to the Internet

Accessibility: the extent to which individuals can access information across a variety of systems and technologies, including the security of these systems

Accuracy: the extent to which the information contained within databases and transmitted via computers is correct

Authentication: the process of verifying who you are to a computer or network

Biometrics: an authentication technique utilizing physical or biological features of humans such as fingerprints, iris or retina scans, facial recognition, and voice recognition

Business Software Alliance (BSA): an international organization representing the software industry

Checksum: the part of the TCP layer operation (see TCP/IP protocol) that is responsible for insuring integrity of packet data being sent over the Internet

Coase theorem: an economic theory stating that society can correct an externality if it is assigned an entitlement, and counterintuitively, it does not matter to which party the entitlement is assigned

Code of conduct: official written policies regarding all aspects of the work environment that an organization expects its members to follow

Code of ethics: personal rules for handling ethical dilemmas based on individual values and experiences

Computer-mediated communication: communication methods/techniques that utilize a computer, i.e., e-mail, online discussions, and chats (a subset of Technology-mediated communication)

Computer ethics: see Information ethics

Consequentialism: see Utilitarianism

Covert channels: forms of communication hidden or disguised within what appears to be legitimate network traffic

Covert exploitation: the use of targeted resources for purposes of interest to the parasite, not necessarily the host owners, accomplished without knowledge or consent of the host owners

Cracking: breaking into someone else's computer system, often on a network; bypassing passwords or licenses in computer programs; or in other ways intentionally breaching computer security

Decision-support system (DSS): a specific type of computer application designed to support individual decision making for quantitative or qualitative problems and situations

Denial of service: malicious attempt to degrade or disrupt the access of network members to a particular host by consuming the TCP/IP resources of the host or the bandwidth of the network itself

Denial of service attack: see Denial of service

Deontological: a worldview that states an act is morally right if and only if the agent of the act can consistently will that the generalized form of the maxim of the act be a law of nature

Distributive justice: a worldview that argues the distribution of benefits and harms in society should be governed by impartial criteria, and that equals should be treated equally and unequals treated differently, but only in proportion to their differences

e-Government: the availability and access to vast amounts of governmental information, forms, and services via electronic media (most often the Internet)

e-Healthcare: the availability and access to vast amounts of medical information, diagnoses, and tools via electronic media (most often the Internet)

Electronic Data Interchange (EDI): a specific form of secure electronic data transmission characterized by proprietary networks between two or more organizations

Electronic patient record: a digitally stored medical record

Encryption: a security method for data transmission whereby the data is encoded, or encrypted, by an algorithm prior to transmission and then decrypted by the recipient using the same algorithm in reverse

Ethical theories: a collection of perspectives, worldviews, and theories used to interpret the benefits and harms associated with information

Externality: a type of economic market failure that occurs when the full costs or benefits of an action are not paid for or captured by the actor

Flaming: a situation where an individual makes derogatory or off-color comments via e-mail or in a chat room that very likely would not be made in a comparable face-to-face situation

Hacker: one who engages in hacking and is known for counterculture attitudes, disdain of authority, and technical skill

Hacking: technically, a clever programmer, though commonly associated with cracking (see Cracking) – illegal uses of computers often associated with computer crime, identity fraud, identity theft, denial of service attacks, political statements, and ecommerce disruptions

HIPAA: the Health Insurance Portability and Accountability Act, effective April 14, 2000, which addresses privacy and security issues in the context of health-related activities and patient information

Idealism: a worldview that derives greater meaning from ideas than things

Immaterial property rights: see Intellectual property rights

Individual property rights: see Property

Information age: the modern times in which computer use has become the norm in businesses, the Internet has become mainstream for businesses and individuals, and systems and databases are connected around the world

Information asymmetry: an imbalance in the information available to the parties in an interaction

Information ethics: variants of older ethical issues (e.g., theft, copyright infringement, invasion of privacy) disguised in modern-day (i.e., electronic or digital) clothing

Information externality: an externality specifically applied to information (see Externality)

Information privacy: the right of an individual to control what personal information is made public and when

Intellectual property rights: the rights granted to the creator of intellectual property to exploit that property for financial gain, if he or she so wishes

International Federation of the Phonographic Industry (IFPI): an international organization representing the recording industry

Internet ethics: see Information ethics

IP spoofing: a method whereby a prospective intruder impersonates a "trusted" member of a network by discovering its IP address and then constructing network packets that appear to have originated from this trusted source

IS ethics: see Information ethics

Justified hacking: a specific type of hack (see Hacking) where the intent of the hack is not to exploit software vulnerabilities, steal proprietary data, or shut down Web sites, but rather to bring about social justice where the ends justify the means

Liberalism: a worldview in which the value of work is considered to be the factor that gives one a right to ownership of what one has worked upon

Malware: short for "malicious software" or software that is created to intentionally inflict harm on another system

Moral dilemma: a conflict between two ethical standards, both of which are right

Open source software: a form of software development and distribution where the source code of the application is made freely available to others for testing, manipulation, and feedback

Parasitic computing: a situation where a "parasite" computer attempts to solve a complex task by breaking up the task into many small components and distributing the processing related to those components over a number of separate remote computers without the knowledge of the remote computers' owners

Patriot Act: see USA PATRIOT Act

Perceived behavioral control: an individual's belief that he or she can complete an action

Piracy: the illegal act whereby an individual knowingly or unknowingly copies a piece of software in violation of the copyright agreement associated with that software

Pirating: see Piracy

Pragmatism: a worldview that finds meaning neither in ideas nor things; rather, it is found in experience or change

Privacy: the right of an individual to control what personal information is made public and when

Procedural justice: a worldview in which processes or rules are used to determine the fair allocation of rewards or punishments

Property: the right of an individual to control what personal information belongs to himself/herself and to gain benefits from said information

Property rights: see Property

Softlifting: the illegal act of copying a software package in violation of the licensing agreement for personal use (see Piracy)

Software and Information Industry Association (SIIA): an international organization representing the software industry

Software piracy: see Piracy

Spamming: the practice of sending unsolicited e-mail to large quantities of recipients at once

TCP/IP protocol: the de facto standard that has emerged for Internet communication – a family of protocols known as the Transmission Control Protocol/Internet Protocol

TCP/IP suite: helps to ensure certain levels of cooperation and trust between all parties employing the Internet and usually represented as a layered stack where the different layers correspond to separate aspects of the network communication process

Technology-mediated communication: communication methods/techniques that utilize technology (rather than face-to-face), i.e., telephone, fax, and computer-mediated communication

Theory of Planned Behavior (TPB): a theory stating that behavior is determined by intent which, in turn, is determined by attitude, subjective norms, and perceived behavioral control

Theory of Reasoned Action (TRA): a theory stating that behavior is determined by intent which, in turn, is determined by attitude and subjective norms

Total Information Awareness (TIA): a planned, but never deployed, program of the U.S. Government to create a comprehensive, centralized database of education, housing, medical, travel, veterinary, transportation, and financial records; technologically advanced data-mining programs would then be used on this database to see if there were any patterns in the data, for example, of airline ticket purchases, weapons purchases, equipment rentals, etc.

USA PATRIOT Act (Uniting and Strengthening America by Providing Appropriate Tools Required to Intercept and Obstruct Terrorism Act): a 2001 act of Congress expanding the U.S. Government's ability to monitor electronic communications under the auspices of detecting and deterring terrorist activities

Utilitarianism: a worldview that tells us that we should make choices that produce the greatest amount of positive net benefit and avoid choices that result in net harm

About the Authors

Lee A. Freeman is an assistant professor of MIS and Director of Distance Learning and Teaching in the School of Management at the University of Michigan–Dearborn (USA). He has a BA from the University of Chicago and he received both his MBA and PhD in Information Systems from Indiana University. His teaching interests include systems analysis and design, end-user computing, and human-computer interaction. His primary research interests include the conceptualization and use of information systems knowledge, systems analysis and design, information ethics, and information security. He has published in *MIS Quarterly*, the *Communications of the ACM*, *Information Systems Frontiers*, the *Journal of IS Education*, and *Communications of the AIS*, among others.

A. Graham Peace is an associate professor of MIS at the College of Business and Economics, West Virginia University (USA). He received his PhD in management information systems from the University of Pittsburgh (1995). His teaching interests include systems analysis and design, e-Business, and database management systems. He is also active in executive education and study abroad programs. Dr. Peace's research interests include the ethical issues of software piracy, privacy, censorship and freedom of speech. He has had research articles published in several journals in the field. Prior to entering academia, Dr. Peace worked as a systems engineer with IBM.

*   *   *

Robert N. Barger is an associate professor in the Computer Applications Program at the University of Notre Dame (USA), where he currently teaches courses in computer ethics, and in the HTML, JavaScript, and Java programming languages. He is also a professor emeritus at Eastern Illinois University, where he taught and served as university director of affirmative action. Additionally, he has taught at Indiana University, the National University of Ireland, and the University of Illinois. He has earned five academic degrees in the fields of education, history, philosophy, and theology and has published more than 100 books, chapters, and articles.

Mary Brabston is tenured assistant professor of management information systems with the Department of Accounting and Finance at the University of Manitoba, Canada. Prior to coming to Winnipeg in 1997, Dr. Brabston taught for four years at the University of Tennessee at Chattanooga. Before that, Mary managed information resources in the arenas of banking, political campaigns, fund raising, and academic administration. Her teaching and research interests involve strategic planning and applications of information systems and information resource management, as well as electronic commerce and information ethics. Her work has appeared in such publications as the *Journal of Computing and Information Technology*, the *Journal of Computer Information Systems*, the *Journal of Information Systems Education*, *Human Relations*, and the *Journal of Data and Industrial Management,* and various books.

Christopher M. Cassidy is an assistant professor at Marshall University (USA). He holds a PhD in management from Texas A&M University. He does research in the area of strategic management and business ethics. His theoretical interests are in agency theory, economics, and the resource-based view. His research interests focus on corporate governance, executive compensation, business ethics, the management of knowledge, and other value-creating activities. His research has appeared in *Advances in Strategic Management* and been presented at national and international conferences.

Bongsug Chae is an assistant professor of management information systems at Kansas State University (USA). He holds a PhD in management information systems from Texas A&M University. His current research interests are in the area of large-scale information system and information infrastructure, knowledge management, technology adaptation, decision-support systems, and ethics and social theories for IS research. His work also appears in *Decision Support Systems, OMEGA: The International Journal of Management Science, Electronic Journal of Information Systems for Developing Countries, Information Resource Management Journal, International Journal of Information Technology and Decision Making*, and *Journal of KMCI*.

David P. Cook is an associate professor with the Department of Information Systems and Decisions Sciences in the College of Business and Public Administration at Old Dominion University (USA). He graduated from the University of Kentucky with a PhD in production and operations management. Dr. Cook has published in such journals as *Production and Inventory Management, APICS - The Performance Advantage, Human Systems Management,* the *Journal of Computer Information Systems, Production and Operations Management,* and *e-Service Journal.* His research interests include quality management, service operations, and electronic commerce.

James F. Courtney is professor of management information systems at the University of Central Florida in Orlando (USA). He formerly was Tenneco professor of business administration with the Information and Operations Management Department at Texas A&M University. He received his PhD in business administration (management science) from the University of Texas at Austin (1974). His papers have appeared in several journals, including *Management Science, MIS Quarterly, Communications of the ACM, IEEE Transactions on Systems, Man and Cybernetics, Decision Sciences, Decision Support Systems,* the *Journal of Management Information Systems, Database, Interfaces,* the *Journal of Applied Systems Analysis,* and the *Journal of Experiential Learning and Simulation.* His present research interests are knowledge-based decision-support systems, ethical decision making, knowledge management, inquiring (learning) organizations, and sustainable economic systems.

David Croasdell is an assistant professor of management information systems in the Department of Accounting and Information Systems at the University of Nevada (USA). He received his PhD in information and operations management from Texas A&M University. He has also earned a MS in business computing science from Texas A&M University and BS in zoology from the

University of Idaho. Dr. Croasdell's primary areas of research are organizational memory, knowledge management, and inquiring organizations. He serves as the cluster chair for knowledge management, organizational memory and organizational learning at the Hawaii International Conference on Systems Science.

Charles R. Crowell is an associate professor of psychology and director of the Computer Applications Program at the University of Notre Dame (USA). Besides his work on basic mechanisms of learning and motivation, he has been involved in applied research on learning, productivity, and performance improvement in organizations and has investigated how technology can influence personal behavior and performance. He has published and lectured on topics including performance diagnosis, behavioral methods to increase organizational success, and the use of technology to facilitate learning and work effectiveness.

Jennifer Dahl completed a Bachelors of Commerce, specializing in marketing, at the Sauder School of Business at the University of British Columbia (1996). In 2002, she graduated from the I.H. Asper School of Business at the University of Manitoba with a Master of Business Administration, specializing in management. Jennifer currently resides in Vancouver, British Columbia, and works for Best Buy Canada in supply chain, as the national senior inventory manager for entertainment.

Bruno de Vuyst is associate professor of law, Vesalius College, Vrije Universiteit Brussel (Belgium); senior researcher at the Institute for European Studies, Vrije Universiteit Brussel; advisor, industrial policy, Vrije Universiteit Brussel; secretary-general, BI3 Fund, Vrije Universiteit Brussel; and Of Counsel, Lawfort, Brussels. Bruno de Vuyst has degrees from Antwerp and Columbia Law School and was formerly an executive with the World Bank, the UN, and Citibank.

Patrick E. Deegan is an assistant professor of law and technology in the Schools of Business at Duquesne University (USA). He earned his law degree from Widener University School of Law and received his MBA and MS from Duquesne University. His professional experience includes the practice of law and several entrepreneurial ventures. Classroom interests vary, but have been primarily involved business law and introduction to computers classes. Research interests include distance learning, constitutional law, and law of business organization.

Pooja Deshmukh recently graduated from Washington State University (USA) with a master's degree in business administration. Her area of emphasis was management information systems. Pooja is currently working as a technology and security risk consultant with a global professional services firm.

Asim El-Sheikh is head of the Department of Information Systems at the Arab Academy for Banking and Financial Sciences, Amman, Jordan. He received his PhD in economics and political science from the University of London (1987). Dr. El-Sheikh's research interests include software piracy, software outsourcing, simulation modeling, and software engineering. He is the author of two books and many articles in the field. Dr. El-Sheikh has extensive business experience, having worked as a computer programmer, consultant, and manager with various organizations in the Sudan. He also spent seven years as an assistant professor in the Department of Econometrics at the University of Khartoum.

Alea M. Fairchild is assistant professor of Business and Technology at Vesalius College, Vrije Universiteit Brussel (Belgium), as well as a postdoctoral researcher in the Department of Information Management, Tilburg University. Dr. Fairchild received her Doctorate in Applied Economics from Limburgs Universitair Centrum in Belgium, in the area of banking and technology. She has a master's degree in international management from Boston University/ Vrije Universiteit Brussel, Brussels, Belgium, and a bachelor's degree in business management and marketing from Cornell University, Ithaca, New York.

Michael Freeman is a research fellow at Dartmouth College's Institute for Security Technology Studies (USA). His current research focuses on the relationship between terrorism and democracy, specifically how fighting terrorism affects democratic states and their civil liberties as well as how spreading democracy impacts the occurrence of terrorism. He is the author of *Freedom or Security: The Consequences for Democracies Using Emergency Powers to Fight Terror* (2003). His broader research interests include counterterrorism strategies, international security, international relations theory, and US foreign policy. Dr. Freeman received his PhD in political science from the University of Chicago in 2001.

Anna Gomberg is a graduate student in psychology at the University of Notre Dame (USA). Her interests include moral development and education, and media literacy.

Kathleen S. Hartzel is an associate professor of information technology in the Schools of Business at Duquesne University (USA). She earned her PhD from the Katz Graduate School of Business, University of Pittsburgh. She has professional experience in the development and support of accounting, manufacturing, and insurance systems. Her primary classroom focus is on systems analysis and design. Her current research interests include the management of attitudes and behaviors during system development

and use; the effects of computer-mediated support on decision making and attitudes in both individuals and groups; and the ethical implications of information technology use.

Jimmie L. Joseph is an assistant professor in the Department of Information Systems and Decision Sciences in the College of Business Administration at the University of Texas at El Paso (USA). He graduated from the Joseph M. Katz Graduate School of Business of the University of Pittsburgh with a PhD in information systems. Dr. Joseph has published in such journals as the *Journal of Management Information Systems, Human Systems Management,* and *International Journal of Electronic Business.* His research interests include human-computer interaction, ethical issues in information systems, and social and cross-border diffusion of information technology.

Kai Kristian Kimppa is an assistant professor with the Department of Information Technology at the University of Turku, Finland. He has graduated as Master of Social Sciences, Philosophy, from University of Turku (2000). He currently teaches information technology ethics and information systems development courses. His research interests lie in major ethical theories and their derivations in regard to the justification (or lack of) IPRs in software and other digitally distributable media. He also researches other aspects of information technology ethics, such as gender issues, issues in regard to TeleMedicine, etc. He is also interested in HCI and UI Design. He has worked in the industry as a design engineer for Nokia Mobile Phones.

Kieran Mathieson is associate professor of Information Systems at Oakland University (USA). His research centers on the use of IT in ethical decision making. A confessed "propeller head," he spends time in the depths of technology as well as in the heights of philosophy.

David W. Miller received his PhD in business information systems from Mississippi State University (2003) and is an assistant professor of Information Systems in the College of Business and Economics at California State University, Northridge (USA). David also has an MS in information systems as well as an MBA. His research interests include: social structuration and technology appropriation, issues in technology adoption and use, technology appropriation and social power, and ethical concerns in information collection and distribution.

Darcia Narvaez is an associate professor of psychology at the University of Notre Dame (USA). She has published more than 40 books and articles on moral development including co-authoring, *Postconventional thinking* (1999), co-editing, *Moral Development, Self and Identity* (in press), and *Moral Development in the Professions* (1994).

Abdullah Abdali Rashed is a doctoral student in the Information Systems Department at the Arab Academy for Banking and Financial Sciences, Amman, Jordan. He received his Master of Science in information systems from the Arab Academy for Banking and Financial Sciences (2000), and his Bachelor of Science in computer science from the Applied Science University, Amman, Jordan (1997). Mr. Rashed's research interests include software piracy, cryptography, and computer programming languages. Prior to entering academia, he worked as a programmer and system analyst in Amman, Jordan.

Wm. David Salisbury is an assistant professor with the Department of Management and Information Systems in the School of Business Administration at the University of Dayton (USA). He received his PhD from the

University of Calgary in Management Information Systems (1996). Dave's efforts are mostly focused on technology to support group collaboration, and he is currently working on understanding how information technologies may actually advance the agendas of international criminal and terrorist groups. His work has been published in *Information Systems Research, Small Group Research, Information & Management* and *Decision Support Systems,* among others.

Andrew Urbaczewski is an assistant professor of management information systems at the University of Michigan - Dearborn (USA). He received a PhD in information systems from Indiana University, and holds an MBA from West Virginia University and a BS in finance (Honors) from the University of Tennessee. His research interests include wireless mobile collaboration, electronic commerce, and electronic monitoring of employees. His research has been published in several prestigious journals and conferences, including *Journal of Management Information Systems, Communications of the ACM, Journal of Organizational Computing and Electronic Commerce,* and *Communications of the AIS.*

Index